MW01047890

GO STAMPS GO!

The Story of the Calgary Stampeders

GRAHAM KELLY

PANORAMA PRESS

PUBLISHED BY PANORAMA PRESS
An imprint of Johnson Gorman Publishers
Calgary, Alberta

CREDITS
Cover and text design by Boldface Technologies Inc.
Cover photos courtesy of Glenbow Museum
(bottom), Canadian Press (centre and top).
Printed and bound in Canada for Panorama Press.

National Library of Canada Cataloguing in
Publication
Kelly, Graham, 1942–
Go Stamps go! : a history of the Calgary Stampeders
/ Graham Kelly.
ISBN 978-0-921835-00-4
1. Calgary Stampeders (Football team)—History.
2. Canadian football—Alberta—Calgary—History.
3. Rugby football—Alberta—Calgary—History.
I. Title.
GV948.3.C32K44 2010   796.335′6409712338
C2010-906046-6

5 4 3 2 1

Acknowledgements

Thank you to all those associated with the Calgary
Stampeders who gave so generously of their time in
helping me tell the story of the football team they love.
Special thanks to Ted Hellard, John Forzani, Doug
Mitchell, Bob Viccars, Basil Bark, Stan Schwartz, John
Hufnagel, Tom Higgins, Wally Buono, Jim Daley, Mike
Roach, Dean Griffing, Harry Langford, Pete Thodas,
Rod Pantages, Sugarfoot Anderson, Norm Hill, Earl
Lunsford, Bill Casanova, Rogers Lehew, Jack Gotta, Tom
Forzani, Willie Burden, John Helton, Larry Robinson,
Harvey Wylie, Tony Pajaczkowski, Jerry Keeling, Wayne
Harris, Ron Lancaster, Pete Liske, Herm Harrison, Ed
McEleney, J.T. Hay, Bob Vespaziani, Normie Kwong,
Mark McLoughlin, Dave Sapunjis, Doug Flutie, Jeff
Garcia, Dave Dickenson, Will Johnson, Alondra
Johnson, Tony Anselmo, Bob Ackles, Scott Ackles, Marv
Coleman, Matt Dunigan, Henry Burrls, Joffrey Reynolds,
Demetris Tsoumpas, Jamie Crysdale and Jay McNeil.

I am deeply indebted to Daryl Slade, who provided
me with many photos. His book *Stampeders: The
Year of the Horse* is an invaluable statistical history of
Calgary football prepared by the Number 1 statistician
in the CFL and the country's foremost collector of CFL
memorabilia.

Special thanks to my son, David Kelly, who contributed
to the cover and prepared the photographs.

I am deeply indebted to my publisher Dennis Johnson
for having confidence in me. I also thank a former
editor Don Loney for his invaluable insights and
support, as well as the sports editors of the *Medicine
Hat News*.

Finally, none of this would be possible without the
encouragement of my wife, Lorena, David, Janice,
Kaitlind, Zephran, Zaria, Robert, Stacy, Kassidy and
Russell, and my late daughter-in-law, Pamela.

To Bill Powers and Stan Schwartz,
the heart and soul of the Calgary Stampeders

Contents

CHAPTER 1

1

Home on the Range
Rugby on Canadian Prairie
1875–1940

CHAPTER 2

21

Get Along Little Doggies
The Birth of the Calgary Stampeders
1945–47

CHAPTER 3

27

Wagon Train!
The Birth of the Grey Cup Festival
1948–49

CHAPTER 4

55

All Hat, No Cattle
The Decade of the Damned
1950–59

CHAPTER 5

66

The Long and Winding Road
The Greatest of Them All
1960–71

CHAPTER 6

95

Oh, Bury Me Not on the Lone Prairie
SOS Means "Save Our Stamps!"
1972–89

CHAPTER 7

125

Happy Trails
The Golden Era
1990–2001

CHAPTER 8

185

Varmints
Football Follies
2002–04

CHAPTER 9

195

When It's Springtime in the Rockies
Smilin' Hank and Hufnagel
2005–09

CHAPTER 1

Home on the Range

Rugby on the Canadian Prairie
1875–1940

On a bright day late in August 1875, Inspector A.E. Brisebois and 40 North-West Mounted Police rode across the prairie now bearing the district name of Calgary's Crescent Heights and halted on the high bank of the Bow River near the end of today's 2nd Street NE. There they surveyed the natural beauty on all sides, knowing at once they were close to their destination and an opportunity to relax.

Before them was the place where the Elbow River joined the Bow, a perfect site for the fort they had come to build. It would be named Fort Calgary, after a castle in Scotland, according to one source, or a place on the Isle of Mull, which in Gaelic means "Swift Water," dear to Colonel MacLeod's heart.

Like many towns on the prairies, Calgary's permanent location was determined by the Canadian Pacific Railway, which arrived in 1883. The CPR had been deeded the land around the confluence of the two rivers, and its employees laid out a town site incorporating what had been there for years—wood-frame stores, tarpaper shacks and tents.

In 1884 Calgary was incorporated as the first town in the District of Alberta, which was part of the North-Western Territory encompassing most of vast lands lying west and north of central Canada. Calgary became a city nine years later. The first "Stampeders" were the cowboys who worked the open range south of Calgary, especially between 1880 and 1912. It was then the qualities that would characterize Calgarians were firmly established: self-reliance, determination, an almost religious fervour for free enterprise and the survival of the fittest.

1

In 1882 two brothers raised in the Cabbagetown district of Toronto moved west to seek their fortune. James and Sam Lougheed followed the CPR to Winnipeg and then to Medicine Hat, where they ran a general store from a tent. A year later, the brothers, lawyers by profession, moved to Calgary, where James married Isabella Clarke Hardisty, the niece of R.C. Hardisty, a Hudson Bay Company factor rumoured to be the richest man in Western Canada. Isabella was related to Donald Smith, the majority owner and governor of the Hudson's Bay Company, a key financial backer of the CPR and the principal shareholder of the Bank of Montreal. Smith was the most powerful man in Canada. Soon, through marriage, James Lougheed would occupy a similar position in the up and coming frontier town of Calgary.

With the CPR and Bank of Montreal numbered among his clients, Lougheed's law practice flourished. Among his future partners was Richard Bedford Bennett, who, in 1930, would become the first prime minister from Calgary.

Through good luck and connections, James Lougheed established the family fortune not only by the diligent practice of his profession but also by purchasing land at rock bottom prices across the Elbow River, where the CPR decided to build its station soon after. Sitting on prime real estate, he became the first economic and political force in Calgary. He was also part owner of the *Calgary Herald*.

Although his grandson Peter would play for the Edmonton Eskimos and become a director of the Calgary Stampeders, there is nothing to indicate that James Lougheed and his immediate family had any interest in athletic activities, although certainly politics has always been considered a blood sport. But while the future senator and grandfather of a premier was busy establishing his family and fortune in the little city by the Bow, the game of football began to flourish. Mounties stationed in Regina, Edmonton and Calgary brought with them from the East the relatively new game of rugby football. The game was played as early as 1889

The playing field at the North-West Mounted Police barracks on the banks of the Bow River. Among the recruits who marched west in 1874 were European immigrants who brought the game of rugby with them. COURTESY GLENBOW MUSEUM

with the first Battle of Alberta staged soon after. J. Llewellyn Wilson, a member of the first Calgary team, recalled the game in the *Calgary Herald*, October 14, 1911: "We had a very hard time getting anything of a team together. We started from the station after holding the train for several minutes with only nine men. Another jumped on board as the train was passing what is now known as 2nd St. East, and we picked up two men at Innisfail on the journey up. When we arrived at Edmonton we claimed Randall who had recently moved there and who had been playing for us. We also accepted one man from the Edmonton club but declined to have another, preferring to play without too many strangers. We had a ripping game.

"We decided, taking all things into consideration, it was advisable to play a defensive game as we had some of the best backs to be had—Ewan Moore, Arnold Wallinger, Arthur Winterbottom and Moran. Major A.G. Wooley-Dod was the centre and forefront of the forwards, and did good, yeoman service. During the course of the game, we made some changes in the position of the players but not in our backs. The result was pretty satisfactory. The Edmonton players could scarcely get behind our backs, who, according to orders, went for low-down tackling.

"Arnold Wallinger was particularly good at this. He would dive for a man's ankles like a baseball player diving for the plate. Well, the game ended in a score of one to nothing in favour of Edmonton, which was pretty satisfactory considering we had no opportunity of practising together as a team. The Edmonton boys entertained us right royally afterwards.

"I may say that although we were very good personal friends with all of the Edmonton boys, as teams, we were very jealous and every match between ourselves was 'out for gore.'

"In one match against Edmonton played on the athletic club grounds near the old General Hospital, we had to stop the game, as Tom Critchley had all his clothes torn off. We formed a circle around him to the dressing room to get new clothes. A little while after, Adamson, the heavy man of the Edmonton team was disabled. We stopped the game and agreed to drop a man to even up. I forget what the score was but we won.

"I may add that in those days, the defending team had to furnish the ball, which was to become the property of the winner, and I still have in my possession a ball which we won from the N.W.M.P."

At a meeting August 27, 1908, Canadian football began in the burg by the Bow with the formation of the Calgary Tigers. The game they would play was called rugby football, the emphasis on the word *foot*. The game featured running, punting and dropkicking. The ball was put into play by a lineman kicking it back to the quarterback with his heel. From there it was lateraled or handed-off for a run around the end or up the middle. Often the ball was lateraled out and then punted with the onside wings and backs racing down field to recover the ball on the ground or catch it in the air on the dead run. That's what made the game exciting in the days before the forward pass.

The players wore canvas pants that came to just above the knees, long heavy socks, high-top cleats, woollen sweaters and leather helmets, though many players wore no headgear. No shoulder pads were worn until the late 1920s. The most common injuries were broken bones, sprained ankles and concussions, the latter usually not recognized as such. The players on many teams threw money into a pot that went to the player who first drew blood. The games lasted just over an hour. Practices began around the middle of September, with league play starting the first Saturday in October, concluding five or six weeks later. By Halloween, the fields were devoid of grass and hard as cement.

In those days, backfields consisted of a quarterback, three halves and a fullback. Nine players were up front: two outside wings we would call ends, two middle wings (tackles) two inside wings (guards) and three scrimmagers, the middle of whom we call the centre. The side scrimmagers, called scrims, clasped the centre scrim with an arm to form a three-man linking front. The quarterback could not carry the ball across the line of scrimmage. He directed traffic behind the line. That changed in 1921 when the Thrift Burnside rules were adopted. The number of players was then reduced from 14 to 12, the side scrims being eliminated, a move made several years earlier at Calgary's Central High School by Coach Joe Price. The Calgary

Football gear circa 1908 as illustrated in The Albertan. *Beyond cleats, gear was minimal.* COURTESY DARYL SLADE

Tigers came up with the innovation of snapping the ball rather than heeling it.

Following the creation of the Tigers under the presidency of Dr. E.G. Mason, the YMCA and Hillhurst Athletic Club put teams on the field. Practices were held at Mewata Park Tuesday and Thursdays at 5:00 PM.

The first intercity game was played October 10, 1908, between the Tigers and YMCA, the black and gold clad Tigers winning 10–5 by scoring two rouges, a try (touchdown) and a dropkick. The Y scored a try. Two weeks later, the YMCA avenged their earlier defeat at the claws of the Tigers, winning 24–17 before a large crowd at Mewata. The Tigers and YMCA won their games against Hillhurst to finish 3–1, with the Tigers declared city champions on the basis of their better record.

Rugby football was also alive and well in Edmonton. In 1907, Deacon White, the first great to grace an Edmonton gridiron and become a legend, arrived on the scene from the United States. The next year, he organized a team called the Esquimos and challenged the Tigers to play for the championship of Alberta in a home-and-home series, the first game taking place at Mewata on Thanksgiving, November 14. (The date is not a misprint).

Edmonton won the opener 7–1 when Wilson intercepted a lateral, "plucked it from the air, tucked it under his left arm and with only one man between himself and a touchdown fled down the field as an Eskimo runs when pursued by a polar bear" (*Calgary Herald,* November 16, 1908).

Although the reporter agreed Edmonton was the better team, he nonetheless concluded, "The result of the game played was no cause for Thanksgiving. The scores were flukes but the best team won. The result should have been different, for Calgary made a try that they earned but which was disqualified because the officials were rubbing noses with some horses and the big score of the Edmonton boys was caused by an occurrence that resembled a real fluke so much that very few people would call it anything different" (*Calgary Herald,* November 16, 1908).

It would not be the first time a Calgarian blamed a loss to Edmonton on a fluke or a referee.

The return match took place in Edmonton November 21, the importance of the game underscored by the fact Lieutenant-Governor G.V.H. Bulyea performed the ceremonial kick-off before a crowd of over 1,200. Edmonton won again, 12–2.

But a good time was had by all as the Esquimos treated the Tigers like royalty, putting them up for three nights and giving them a banquet Saturday night at Cronn's restaurant, after which the Calgarians were guests of Esquimo Ray Prandon at the Dominion Theatre. The trip was profitable, too, with the club receiving $100 as their share of the gate.

Edmonton domination was short-lived as the Tigers won the 1909 provincial title, 25–1 and 21–6, and were awarded the Belanger trophy, the first trophy put up for any athletic competition in the province.

The Tigers defeated the Y twice in 1910 to retain the city championship and the right to play the Eskimos, nee Esquimos, for the Belanger Cup, the first game of which took place in Calgary, Monday, October 31, both Halloween and Thanksgiving.

Over 2,500 fans showed up at Mewata Park, the biggest crowd to ever witness an Alberta sporting event. Ticket-takers were

The 1909 Provincial Champion Calgary Tigers.
COURTESY GLENBOW MUSEUM

overwhelmed so a number of patrons got in free. Many of them didn't understand the quarters, so at halftime, fully half of them thought the game was over and went home. The rest witnessed the Tigers' 25–7 victory. They won again up north 14–12. After being presented the Belanger Cup, they gave the game ball to C.H. Belanger, the first such gesture in Alberta football. It was decorated in black and yellow with the scores of the games.

The Tigers continued their winning ways in 1911. On October 21, a meeting took place in Regina to organize the Western Canada Rugby Union with teams from Winnipeg, Regina, Moose Jaw, Saskatoon, Calgary and Edmonton. The WCRU adopted the same constitution as that of the Canadian Rugby Union of Eastern Canada with the hope that the West would be able to play for the Grey Cup. They decided that the Saskatchewan champ would play the Rowing Club in Winnipeg November 11, the winner of which would host the Alberta champions. The winner would be awarded the Hugo Ross Cup, named the following year after a Winnipeg realtor who went down with the Titanic.

The 1911 regular season ended with the Tigers and Eskimos undefeated at 3–0–1 and ready to play for the provincial championship on November 4 at Hillhurst Park (now Riley Park on 10 Street NW).

The Tigers were the bigger, more physical team with the lineman averaging nearly 200 pounds. Led by linemen Tiny Woods and Bull Ritchie, wings Doc Gibson, Paddy Johnson and Steve Beattie, halfback/punter Bill Dobbie and quarterback, Calgary's longtime fire chief, Squib Ross, the hometown

The Calgary Herald's cartoonist depicted the 1911 Battle of Alberta as a heroic a struggle for the lovely girl who has won more than one heart. Bragging rights between the two cities emerged as early as 1883 when the Canadian Pacific Railway favoured the Kicking Horse Pass route through Calgary over the Yellowhead Pass through Edmonton. COURTESY *CALGARY HERALD*

heroes vanquished the visitors 14–0 to win their third straight Alberta crown.

On November 18, the Tigers welcomed the Winnipeg Rowing Club to Hillhurst Park, the first time a Western championship was played in Calgary. The Manitobans arrived by train at 5:00 AM on game day. Over 2,500 fans showed up on a cold, windy Saturday afternoon to watch their boys take on the "invincible" Red River oarsmen.

The visitors opened the scoring with a rouge, followed by two kicks to the deadball line by the Tigers' Bill Dobbie, giving the hometown squad a 2–1 lead at the end of the opening quarter. Squib Ross added a single before the half, giving Calgary a 3–1 lead over Winnipeg.

The Tigers had to go into a stiff breeze during the second quarter. When they came out of their dressing room after halftime, lo and behold, the wind had shifted to the opposite direction, and they were facing it once again. How the Tigers handled the next 15 minutes determined the outcome of the game.

It didn't look good when Winnipeg fell on an errant lateral at the 10, scoring on the next play to lead 6–3. But thanks to the outstanding running of Doc Gibbons, Calgary controlled the ball until the quarter ran out and the teams changed ends. In the final 15 minutes, the Tigers scored a safety, two singles and a converted touchdown to win 13–6 and take home Calgary's first Western Canadian football championship.

On to Toronto!

Calgary Tigers in 1911, Calgary's first Western champions.

COURTESY DARYL SLADE

Early football action at Hillhurst Park circa 1912 when Hillhurst School (left, rear) was under construction. COURTESY GLENBOW MUSEUM

Calgary's hopes for a national championship were about to get a taste of Eastern shenanigans. The Alberta Rugby Football Union had affiliated with the Ontario-dominated Canadian Rugby Union in 1911. They had paid their dues, were fully qualified and, therefore, eligible to challenge for the Grey Cup.

While making their preparations to go east, they received a telegram from CRU President W.J. Slee that to be eligible to challenge for the Grey Cup, a union must enter at the annual meeting of the CRU, which would not take place until December. This wouldn't be the last time the nefarious conduct of the CRU would deny the Western champion an opportunity to compete for Earl Grey's treasured trophy.

In 1912 Calgary played in a league with the YMCA and Edmonton. The Tigers' home field was Hillhurst Park, which for the first time was marked off with chalk lines every 10 yards. In the grandstand and baseball bleachers, seats cost 50 cents. Standing room was two bits. Another 1912 innovation saw the Eskimos wear numbers on their jerseys and provide a program so fans could identify the players.

On October 26, Thanksgiving, Captain Arnold Wark led the Tigers to an 18–8 win over the Eskimos and their fourth straight provincial crown before over 3,000 fans at Hillhurst. Next up was the Western semi-final in Winnipeg on November 2. They would arrive on the Imperial Limited early Saturday morning, play in the afternoon and leave again that same evening at 10:00 PM.

Several stars including Dobbie, Gibson, McHugh and Roberts were unable to get time off work. Captain Wark was unconcerned. "Tremble not," he intoned. "What we have are all Tigers and we will show them how the Tigers can play. If we lose, they will have beaten but part of the Tigers. If we win, we win by playing with the Tiger spirit."

It was a tough, defensive struggle with the home team nursing a 4–1 lead late into the final frame. Wark kicked a single. When the Tigers got the ball back with 25 seconds remaining, Wark tried a dropkick field goal, which veered to the left and rolled to the dead-ball line for a single. Final Score: Winnipeg Rowing Club 4, Tigers 3.

The highlight of the 1913 season was a visit from the Hamilton Tigers on an exhibition swing through the prairies, the first documented East–West game. Hamilton beat Winnipeg 26–1, Regina 26–4 and Moose Jaw 25–1 before arriving in Calgary September 27.

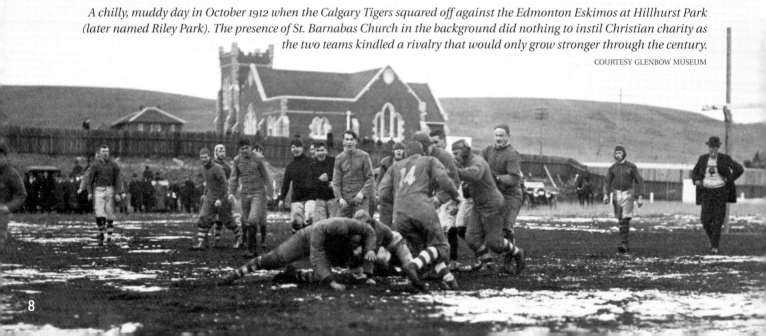

A chilly, muddy day in October 1912 when the Calgary Tigers squared off against the Edmonton Eskimos at Hillhurst Park (later named Riley Park). The presence of St. Barnabas Church in the background did nothing to instil Christian charity as the two teams kindled a rivalry that would only grow stronger through the century.

COURTESY GLENBOW MUSEUM

Over 5,000 fans turned out for the historic occasion. The *Calgary Herald* headline, in part, told the story: SPECTATORS TREATED TO DISGUSTING EXHIBITION.

In addition to taming the Calgary Tigers 19–2, the eastern Tabbies managed to insult just about everyone involved. According to the *Herald* of September 29, "The game, which was interspersed with scraps in many places and a grand finale in the last quarter when police interference was necessary, was the roughest ever seen in Calgary."

That night the visitors were entertained at a dinner and theatre party. Humble pie wasn't on the menu. After Hamilton manager Dave Tope received his financial guarantee and expenses, he rose to speak, saying they had come west to teach the Calgarians the finer points of the game but had been frustrated in that objective by the roughness and unsportsmanlike conduct of the hosts. Only western hospitality allowed him to escape to the train station unscathed.

The Tigers and Eskimos tied for first place that year and played the provincial championship game in Red Deer, which was won by Edmonton 10–7.

The first great era in Calgary football was over.

During the first week of August, 1914, hostilities broke out in Europe. As part of the British Empire, Canada was at war when Britain was at war. That year the Tigers lost the provincial championship to the University of Alberta. With most of their men serving their country, the Tigers disbanded in 1915, replaced by the Canucks, mostly graduates from Central High School along with Bob Priestly and the greatest player of that era, Arnold Wark. After winning the province, the Canucks went to Regina to play for the Western Canadian title. The youngsters from Calgary were no match for the sodbusters, who won their fourth straight championship 17–1.

No senior football was played in Calgary until 1919 when the Alberta Rugby Union resumed with the Canucks and Tigers in Calgary and the University of Alberta and Canucks up north. The Canucks vanquished the Tigers and the U of A at Hillhurst to earn the right to entertain Regina, a team that had not lost a game since 1912. They were at their best on a muddy field before over 2,000 spectators, winning their sixth straight Western championship 13–1.

Arnold Wark's Calgary Tigers in action at Hillhurst Park.
COURTESY GLENBOW MUSEUM

Provincial champions again in 1920, the Tigers headed to Regina. The *Regina Leader* sports editor gave the following account of the carnage: "Those terrible Tigers of Calgary, like young Lochinvar, came out of the west on Saturday and returned to their lair on Sunday morning a badly beaten Bengal with its tail twisted out of shape. The twisting was done by a gentleman named Jeremiah Crapper, aided and abetted by thirteen other jungle hunters and when they finished their operations, the Calgarians were staggering under the load of a 29 to 1 defeat. It was the most crushing defeat ever administered to the Tigers. . . ."

That was the beginning of the end for the first edition of the Calgary Tigers, the last hurrah for Arnold Fraser, Bull Ritchie, Squib Ross and the legendary Arnold Wark.

The following year saw the West challenge for the Grey Cup. First up was Edmonton, who would dominate Alberta football for the next three years. Deacon White's Eskimos slaughtered the Tigers 72–1 and beat the Winnipeg Victorias in the Western Final before losing 23–0 to the Toronto Argonauts.

After being absent for a year, the grid wars resumed in 1923 under the banner of the 50th Battalion with players attached to D Company. Army captains Bob Stephen and Bob Priestly lined up the financing and organized the team. Their uniforms were double blue. Arnold Wark was the coach.

The Eskimos beat the university squad and faced the 50th Battalion for the provincial honours. Few gave the young, inexperienced Calgarians any chance to win. They didn't, falling 13–6. The following year, the Battalion beat the University of Alberta before losing the Western Final 11–9 to Winnipeg. No football was played in either Edmonton or Calgary from 1925 to 1927. But with Dr. E.G. Mason as president, Jack Bannerman, manager, and Tom Williams, coach, the Tigers were reborn in 1928, losing to the Eskimos, who won their sixth provincial championship.

But happy days lay ahead. Led by Les Ferguson and Russ Gideon, the Tigers were soon to win five straight Alberta titles of their own.

In 1929, two groups claimed to represent football in Calgary, the Tigers and Altomahs

A 1927 match pitting the University of Saskatchewan against the Eskimos on the campus of the University of Alberta, Edmonton.
COURTESY GLENBOW MUSEUM

(the name of an aboriginal tribe). The groups settled their differences, and the team was known officially as the Altomah-Tigers. Call them what you will, that year the Calgary team made Canadian football history by completing the first forward pass.

Their star was American Gerry Seiberling. According to *Fall Madness,* published in 1979 by the Stampeders, Seiberling was a half-back who completed the first forward pass to local boy Russ Gideon in a game against the Eskimos on September 21 in Edmonton. However, according to the Canadian Football League, Seiberling was a quarterback who threw the first pass to Ralph Losie. An authority on Canadian football history and the leading collector of Canadian football memorabilia in the country, the *Herald*'s Darryl Slade wrote an article October 10, 2004, in which he concluded it was indeed Losie on the end of the Seiberling pass.

However, the *Herald* reporter covering on the game at the time recorded that the Tigers "came in with the forward pass and made great gains. McKinnon received the ball first for an advance of 30 yards." So according to the reporter covering the game, the first legal pass recorded in Canadian football history was in the fourth quarter at Renfrew Park in Edmonton when the Calgary Tiger's Gerry Seiberling completed a 30-yarder—not to Gideon or Losie, but to Cec McKinnon!

Whoever caught the historic pass, it is only appropriate that a Calgary team was first to use the new weapon considering how the Stampeders have lived and died with the pass that throughout most of their history.

A week later, Eskimo Joe Cook completed the first forward pass for a touchdown to Pal Power against the University of Alberta. That same game saw the first interception for a touchdown when Joe Hess picked off Cook and scored.

The Tigers went undefeated in 1929 and

looked forward to hosting the Western championship. Because Alberta had declined to play in the final the past five years, the WCRU awarded the game to the winner of the Manitoba–Saskatchewan semi-final, Regina.

On Thanksgiving and Remembrance Day, November 11, there was a nip in the air and in many a flask, as well as ice on the gridiron at the Exhibition Grounds. Regina won 15–8 before 2,000 fans. "Dynamite" Eddie James (for whom the Western conference rushing trophy is named) scored two touchdowns for the locals when Fritz Sandstrom was serving a 10-minute penalty. The most spectacular play of the day occurred when Fred Brown intercepted a Seiberling pass and returned it 55 yards for a major.

The headlines in the papers were ominous during the autumn of 1929. STOCKS CRUMBLE UNDER BEAR DRIVE said one on October 29. The next day came ALL TRADING RECORDS SMASHED IN DELUGE OF SELLING. On November 14, the news was worse: STOCK MARKETS CRASH TO NEW LOW LEVELS.

More devastating to Alberta was the searing drought that turned the southern part of the province into a dust bowl. As the Dirty Thirties deepened, so did despair. Sports were a welcome diversion from the hopelessness everywhere.

In 1930 the Altomah-Tigers dominated provincial play, soundly defeating the blue-and-white clad Boosters, who played out of a spanking new stadium, named after Edmonton's mayor Joe Clarke. Next up was the Western semi-final against Regina, who had outscored their opponents 72–6 that season. The Tigers provided the stiffest opposition, but bowed 9–6.

From 1931 through '34, Calgary's team was officially known as the Altomahs, although they were usually called the Indians. Fritz Sandstrom coached the 1931 edition, making generous use of the forward pass that the CRU approved for all rugby unions, although the attendant rules indicated their heart wasn't really wasn't in it. For example, if a team threw two consecutive incomplete passes, they would receive a 10-yard penalty. And if a pass went incomplete within the opponent's 25-yard line, they lost possession. Another rule change that year affected converts. The scrimmage line for extra points was changed from the 35-yard line to the 5. Before 1931, a converted touchdown was a rarity.

In 1931 the Calgary gridders first wore red and white for the first time. The Altomahs won their third straight provincial title and prepared to host both games of the two-game total-point semi-final against the Vancouver Athletic Club.

During the Wednesday afternoon opener (most people had Wednesday afternoon off and worked Saturdays), Calgary fell behind 4–0. In the third quarter, Norman Hides recovered a fumble. Cec Holmes promptly connected with Russ Gideon, who ran 45 yards for the touchdown and a 6–4 victory. They won game two 14–1 with a conservative ground attack. Next up, the western final in Regina.

Because the Altomahs lost six players to injury against Vancouver and two men couldn't get off work on Remembrance Day, GM Rosie Helmer asked the WRFU president, who happened to be from Regina, to postpone the game to November 14. No dice. Battered and bruised, the Altomahs went down 26–2.

The big story of 1931 was the opening of Mewata Stadium. In 1904 Mewata Park was created, *Mewata* meaning "to be happy" in Cree. Located on 10 Street SW, the park was used for a variety of sporting activities, although football was played mostly at Hillhurst.

The new stadium consisted of a grandstand 200 x 34 feet with seating for 2,000, plus a bleacher that held 600. There were dressing rooms and storage space. Mewata Stadium would be home to Calgary senior and professional football for the next 29 years.

The new facility received its baptism September 24, 1932, in a steady rain before 1,500 shivering fans who paid 75 cents each to see the Altomahs beat the Eskimos 1–0 when Alex Mackenzie punted into the end zone, where Al Imrie tackled Ivan Smith for a rouge. (A single point was scored by

Gridiron action between the Calgary Altomahs and Edmonton's University of Alberta squad.

Prime Minister R.B. Bennett performs the ceremonial kickoff, October 14, 1933, at the third game of Alberta Rugby Union schedule. COURTESY *CALGARY HERALD*

no match for the perennially powerful Roughriders, who won handily 30–2.

1932 was the first time a Western all-Star team was chosen. Canadian Press reporters from nine cities made the selections. The sole Calgarian chosen was Alex MacKenzie.

With the Depression deepening, the Eskimos were unable to field a team in 1933. The Altomahs lasted two more years, losing the western final to Winnipeg in 1933 and the provincial title to the University of Alberta in 1934.

A member of that Altomah team was halfback Jim Eagleson, interviewed at age 91 in 2004 by Darryl Slade. "We practised and played hard and we weren't paid," he recalled. "Football was bloody rough and tough in those days, and I liked it very much. For all the good the leather helmet and equipment was then, we might as well not be wearing them. You practically had no protection at all."

kicking the ball through the end zone, a rouge when the player was tackled or conceded a point in the end zone.) Calgary went undefeated during the regular season before splitting the semi-final series with the Meralomas in Vancouver, winning the round 11–10. Back home to face Regina—yet again.

The Queen City squad featured two Americans, halfback Curt Schave and quarterback Austin De Frate, who combined on four completed passes and a touchdown. The era of American imports began in earnest in the early 1930s with Winnipeg and Regina being aggressive recruiters. Calgary didn't follow suit until 1935, putting the club at a disadvantage. That combined that with being worn out from slogging through the West Coast mud made the Altomahs

Jim Eagleson holds a jersey presented by the Stampeders in 2001.

COURTESY *CALGARY HERALD*

In 1935 sportsmen Roy Beavers, J.V. Carmichael, John Thompson, Pete Egan and Larry Price replaced the Altomahs with the Bronks. They organized the Football Booster Club to raise money for the team, a model followed in one form or another until the team was privatized in 1989. They hired Winnipeg great Carl Cronin, who had played for Knute Rockne at Notre Dame. As player-coach in Winnipeg, he temporarily ended Regina's annual trek to the Grey Cup.

The legendary Carl Cronin featured on a Bronks' game program. COURTESY DARYL SLADE

The gridiron Moses was officially welcomed to the city at a Booster Club Luncheon August 1. Later that day, Cronin conducted his first practice before an enthusiastic crowd at Mewata Stadium. That month the city installed lights at the stadium, recognition of the tremendous support for football in the community.

Of interest that year were rule changes allowing forward passes anywhere on the field, with teams no longer penalized for throwing an incompletion in the defending 25-yard zone. Backs would also be allowed to block up to five yards from the line of scrimmage.

With Cronin in charge of a veteran line-up, the Bronks would be a worthy opponent for any challenger. Trouble was, Calgary's only opponent was the University of Alberta. To capitalize on fan interest and give the players a reason to don the red and white, they played a series of exhibition games.

They opened at home on Saturday, September 4, bowing 39–0 to the defending Grey Cup champion Sarnia Imperials. They lost the Labour Day rematch 17–2 before dropping a pair to the Roughriders. The regular season began October 9 with the Bronks bustin' the University of Alberta 26–0 in Calgary and 40–10 ten days later in Edmonton. The Golden Bears defaulted the last two games. Led by their first Americans Chuck McKenna and Oran Dover, Calgary vanquished the Meralomas, 14–0.

Winnipeg upset the Roughriders 13–6 and welcomed the Bronks on November 9. Billed as the greatest Western Canadian football team ever assembled, the Winnipegs (they wouldn't be called Blue Bombers for another year) were undefeated and gunning for their second shot at the Grey Cup in four years. They were led by coach Bob Fritz, who also played quarterback. Other offensive stars were Greg Kabat, Fritz Hanson, Eddie James and Russ Rebholz. Staunch defenders included Bud Marquardt, Jeff Nicklin and Cliff Roseborough. James, Hanson, Kabat and Rebholz are in the CFL Hall of Fame, as are executives of that team, Joe Ryan, G. Sydney Halter and Frank Hannibal.

CFL Hall of Famer Cronin knew the opposition well, having coached them only two years ago. He carefully prepared his boys defensively and tried to lull the Winnipegs into a false sense of security, describing his team as "only mediocre." The game was played at Osborne Stadium in a snowstorm. Despite the home team's firepower, the game was a titanic defensive struggle and settled only by a questionable turnover. That team that was seven points better than the Bronks went on to win the West's first Grey Cup, defeating Hamilton 18–12.

In 1936 the Western Inter-Provincial Football Union (WIFU) was formed among the Bronks, Roughriders and Blue Bombers. Each team could still have a provincial competition, but only Calgary, Regina and Winnipeg were eligible to play for the Grey Cup. Edmonton joined the union in 1949, British Columbia in 1954.

With new imports Jerry Searight and Ed Rorvig, Cronin's Calgarians easily defeated the Lethbridge Bulldogs, Edmonton Hi-Grads and the University of Alberta for their seventh provincial crown in eight years. They opened their WIFU season with two losses in Winnipeg and one in Regina.

The Bronks played their remaining games at Mewata, beginning with the Queen City team on September 26. It would be a match-up between a Rider

team with 10 Americans versus the underdog Calgary squad with three imports. Bad blood existed between the teams with the Reginians claiming that the Bronks were a bunch of "daffodils" that had no business being in the league and that Jerry Searight talked a great game but couldn't deliver. (Searight liked to argue with the referees and carried a rulebook in his pocket. When fans in Regina protested a call the officials got right, Searight stopped the game and admonished the crowd!)

Charlie Harrison booted the locals into the lead with two singles, answered by a Regina field goal. The good guys added a couple of rouges to lead 4–3 with less than two minutes to go when Regina scrimmaged at their 45. On second down, Jimmy Lander threw a pass to Fritz Falgren, who lateraled to Paul Kirk, who seemed in the clear and heading for a winning touchdown. Instead, Searight put his money where his mouth was, tackling Kirk and forcing him to fumble. Harrison picked it up and headed for pay dirt. Final score: Daffodils 9, Roughriders 3.

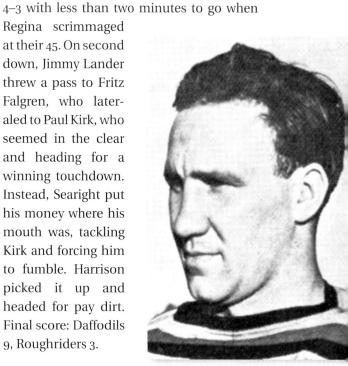

Ed Rorvig.
COURTESY DARYL SLADE

Jerry Searight.
COURTESY DARYL SLADE

Charlie Harrison.
COURTESY DARYL SLADE

*Stavely, Alberta,
star Larry Haynes.*
COURTESY DARYL SLADE

The Bronks lost both ends of a Thanksgiving doubleheader to Winnipeg. When Vancouver defaulted the semi-final and the Bombers lost to the Roughriders, the stage was set for a Calgary–Regina final.

The Riders were given a five-point lead to start the game because they finished ahead of Calgary in the standings. That advantage forced the Bronks to take chances that led to four of six passes being intercepted. They fell 3–1 before 5,000 fans at Mewata Stadium on Remembrance Day.

In 1937 the WIFU set the number of American imports at eight. Most of Calgary's imports came from Gonzaga University in Spokane. They opened the season in Winnipeg, beating the Bombers 13–8. Three days later they handed Regina their first home opener loss since 1910 under the lights at Park De Young.

After losing their season debut at Mewata 11–1 to Fritzie Hanson's Blue Bombers, the Bronks beat Regina 8–7 and 11–0. They finished the schedule by splitting a pair with Winnipeg and losing to the Roughriders. Calgary finished first, the Bombers second. Regina was on the outside looking in for the first time in 27 years.

Grey Cup fever ran rampant in the foothills city, especially after the Bronks went into Winnipeg and

won the first game of the two-game total-point series 13–10. Cronin's crew were given a hero's welcome when they returned home. The Canadians included halfbacks Herb Snowden, Bill Wusyk, Jimmy Gilkes, Joe Turner, Ted Harling and Jack Howard; quarterback Jerry Morrison; centre Homer Anelson, linemen Jack Lawrence, Chet Hagen, Brick Ellis and Bob Harrison; ends Keith Gibson and Gobbo Gilkes and Stavely's Larry Haynes. The imports were halfbacks Ray Olsen, Don Lussier and Johnny Rosano, quarterback Pete Higgins, linemen Russ Hale, Howard Hurd and Johnny Madden, Dick Haughian, Ed Rorvig and Jerry Searight. It was one of the finest aggregations to ever wear the red and white.

With a three-point lead and playing at home, Calgarians were booking berths on the Grey Cup train to Toronto. Someone, though, forgot to tell Hanson he was beat. Running wild, he beat the Bronks 9–1, winning the series 19–14. The loss was a disappointing end to the best football season in Calgary to that point.

1937 marked the first time a league-sanctioned all-star team was picked. Bronks chosen were Rorvig, Hurd and Haynes.

When Carl Cronin began training camp in 1938, a newcomer, Paul Rowe, garnered little attention from the press or yard birds, who watched every practice. That would soon change.

After opening season losses in Winnipeg and Regina, the Bronks welcomed the Eskimos back to the league by running for 381 yards and winning 16–3, followed by a 5–3 victory up north. After losing an exhibition 38–0 to North Dakota

Howard Hurd. COURTESY DARYL SLADE

State Teachers' College, a game in which they lost Ed Rorvig for the season with a torn-up knee, they prepared to host Winnipeg and Regina on the Thanksgiving weekend. The Bronks rolled over the Blue Bombers 14–0, the first time Winnipeg had suffered a shutout at the hands of a Calgary football team. Two days later, Calgary beat the Roughriders 5–3.

A game six days later against Edmonton ended in a Calgary win and controversy. Despite dominating at home, the Bronks were only up 6–3 with two minutes remaining. Starting deep in their own end, the Eskimos passed their way down to the Calgary one, where, on third down Vince Yatchek hit the line. After the pile up was cleared away, Yatchek was six inches

Canadian Football Hall inductee Paul Rowe. COURTESY CANADIAN FOOTBALL HALL OF FAME

from the goal line. He claimed he had crossed over but had been thrown back. Referee Eck Duggan of Edmonton admitted he had lost sight of the ball under the pileup, but he backed up field judge Al McTeer and head linesman Les Ferguson who ruled that while Yatchek's head crossed the line, the ball did not. Coach Bob Fritz lashed out at the two Calgary officials, and when they wouldn't reverse the call, he pulled his team off the field with 33 seconds left.

The following week, Calgary won a ferocious grudge match in Edmonton, 4–0, finishing the season with a mark of 6–2 and a bye into the western final against Winnipeg. The Bombers won both games by a total score of 25–9.

1939 saw many changes for the Bronks. Carl Cronin retired to the insurance business, succeeded by Dick Haughian. Seventeen rookies joined 18 veterans. They would play 11 games, the longest schedule to that point.

Improved lighting made night games at Mewata possible, and the first Calgary game under the lights was played August 25 against Winnipeg, a 12–1 defeat. That was typical of 1937 season when the Bronks finished in third at 4–7.

The semi-final was slated for Regina on November 4. The Riders were on a roll, having won four of their last five.

In four of Calgary's losses that year, they were leading late in the game. They seemed to play better coming from behind. That was the case in Regina. Early in the first quarter, Paul Rowe fumbled at the Rider 5. Harry Guest kicked the ball the length of the field, falling on it in the end zone. Later, Dean Griffing set up a second Regina TD by intercepting a Lynn Warren pass. Regina 11, Calgary 0.

Canadian Football Hall of Famer Carl Cronin during his playing/coaching years with the Winnipegs. Under his leadership, the Broncs became a force to be reckoned with. COURTESY CANADIAN FOOTBALL HALL OF FAME

Bill Wuysik   Chet Hagen   Johnny McKee   Jimmie Gilkes   Wolfie Hughes   Hal Harrison   Stakey Adams   Joe Turner

Bob Cosgrove   Bob Zwank   Charlie Harrison   Biz Bisbing   Bert Border   Jack Lawrence

Fred Irving, Pres.

Al. Hoptauit   Paul Rowe   LARRY Haynes   Bob Harrison   Bud Weaver   Lyn Warren

Dick Haughian

Bob Huson   Gobbo Gilkes   Butch Roberts   Jack Ferguson   Dave Stark   Steve McKinnon

Dr. L.A. Maxwell

M. Newell   Dr. Gibson   R. Helmer   V. Carmichael   W.D. Cheyne   K. Phillips

J. Grogan   J.T. Thompson   Don MacKay   Jap Williams

F. Maxie, Treas.   Pete Egan

Calgary Bronks - Western Canada Finalists - 1939

The Calgary Bronks, Western Canadian finalists, 1939. COURTESY GLENBOW MUSEUM

Dean Giffing.
COURTESY CANADIAN FOOTBALL
HALL OF FAME

The Bronks responded when Hal Harrison picked off Howard Cleveland and lateraled to Wolfie Hughes, who ran 20 yards for the score. On their next possession, league scoring-leader Paul Rowe capped a 72-yard drive with his first of two majors. Calgary won 24–7. They had 21 first downs, the Riders, 2. On to Winnipeg for their fifth straight appearance in the final, the third in a row against the Bombers.

Over 6,000 fans jammed Osbourne Stadium on a brilliant autumn day to watch a tight defensive struggle that went down to the wire. Winnipeg opened with a single. The 6'1", 203-pound Rowe replied with a touchdown. The Bombers completed only one pass the entire game but made it count when, just before the end of the first half, Fritzie Hanson faked an end run, stopped and threw 30 yards to Jeff Nicklin, who caught the ball over his shoulder on the dead run and went the remaining 40 yards for the touchdown. Calgary tied it with a single in the third quarter.

With three minutes left, Johnny McKee picked off Hanson at the Calgary 30. Two passes brought the ball to the one. Expecting a Rowe plunge, the Bronk's completed an easy pass to Harrison in the end zone. Calgary led the round 13–7.

Calgary's six-point lead evaporated on the first play of the second game when Bill Ceretti recovered Jimmy Gilkes' fumble at the Bronks 14-yard line and ran it into the end zone. A few plays later, quarterback Wolfie Hughes was carried from the field with torn knee ligaments. After that it was all Fritzie Hanson, who ran for 182 yards on 18 carries

and 55 yards on punt returns. Winnipeg won the game 28–7, the round 35–20 and the Grey Cup over Ottawa, 8–7.

Larry Haynes coached in 1940, assisted by Carl Cronin at home. The schedule was reduced to eight games when Edmonton dropped out. Paul Rowe would be the star of the Calgary show.

The Bronks opened with decisive wins over Winnipeg and Regina before losing in Bomberville 22–11. Back in Calgary, Rowe rolled over the Riders and into first place with a 17–3 win, but lost a strange game at Mewata. Although the Bronks and Bombers combined for 371 yards offense, Calgary

Souvenir Program

CALGARY RUGBY FOOTBALL CLUB 1940

Calgary BRONKS

Price, Fifteen Cents

Calgary Bronks' souvenir program, 1940. COURTESY DARYL SLADE lost in the last minute 3–1 when Greg Kabat kicked a field goal.

Inspired by Thanksgiving, the Bronks played like turkeys, losing 26–19 in Winnipeg and 17–0 in Regina. Winnipeg clinched first. The Bronks earned the other playoff spot with a 7–1 win at home over Regina.

The best of three final opened in Calgary on November 2. Early in the second quarter, Art Stevenson threw to Bud Marquardt, who lateraled to Lieutenant Jeff Nicklin, who dipsy-doodled down to the 5-yard line. Two plays later, Stevenson hit the end zone. With a rouge and convert, the final was 7–0 for the visitors. A week later in Manitoba, the Bombers took advantage of Calgary miscues to win 23–2 and their fourth straight western championship.

With Europe in flames, most young football players traded in their football moleskin for army khaki, abandoning the gridiron game in Calgary until after the war.

Bronks vs. Blue Bombers, November 2, 1940.
COURTESY *CALGARY HERALD*

CHAPTER 2

Get Along Little Doggies

The Birth of the Calgary Stampeders
1945–47

The headline in the Saturday, October 6, 1945, edition of the *Calgary Herald* proclaimed: THOUSANDS OF CALGARIANS GREET FIRST UNIT HOME FROM OVERSEAS.

The story read: "Cheering crowds that packed downtown Calgary, masses of waving flags and the rousing airs of military bands, combined with the brilliant warmth of a perfect Indian summer day to give a great welcome this morning to the first Calgary unit to return from overseas, the 1st Canadian Infantry Brigade Company, Royal Canadian Army Service Corps.

"Since the first troops began to return from the Second Great War, the city has welcomed many groups, large and small, but today's reception to a gallant unit which was the first to go overseas from Calgary in 1939 achieved a peak of warmth and rejoicing.

"Thousands of citizens packed the concourse in front of the C.P.R. station and along Centre St. and 8th Avenue. On the route to Mewata Armouries there was a cheering mass of humanity. The special train bearing the returning heroes had been scheduled to arrive at 10:30 o'clock and long before this hour, spectators had gathered along the route.

"Delayed on route, the train pulled into the station at 1:00 o'clock. Quickly, the bronzed and battle-hardened soldiers who had served through the toughest fighting of Sicily, Italy and Western Europe detrained and lined up on the station platform to receive a brief welcome from Mayor Andy Davison.

"As the soldiers leaped and jumped from the cars, the band played 'Hail, Hail, The Gang's All Here.'"

Not all the "gang was here." Over 60,000 Canadians lost their lives in the service of their country during the Second World War.

Among those returning from battle were former Calgary Bronks Paul Rowe, Hal Harrison, Jerry Morrison, Herb Snowden, as well as junior stars Al Hammond and Lefty Middleton. Former Altomah junior Major A.E. Langston, Ed Rorvig, Harry Hobbs, Laurie Tarves and Don Hanson also were discharged. Morrison and Rowe had been wounded. Their great sacrifice behind them, their thoughts turned to civilian life and football. One of the all-time greats of the Canadian game, Dean Griffing, was on hand to accommodate them.

Griffing had arrived on the Canadian football scene in 1936 as coach of the Regina Roughriders. A good-humoured, big barrel-chested man with a penchant for cigars and Stetsons, he was once accused of biting an opponent. He pointed to his bridgework and denied the charge, allowing that "I might have gummed him up a little bit." That year Griffing's Roughriders finished second, upset defending Grey Cup champion Winnipeg and then claimed the Western title by edging the Calgary Bronks 3–1. That was his greatest success. He remained with the Riders through 1944 when he headed for Calgary to coach the junior Stampeders.

With so many veteran football players returning from the war, Griffing decided to organize a senior team to compete in the WIFU. "Some of the players are a little old," he said, "but there's a lot of experience there, and experience can win a lot of ball games."

Griffing originated the idea of a football cooperative, whereby after the bills were paid, the players and coach would divvy up what was left.

Griffing called a meeting for September 27th at 9:00 PM at the Renfrew Building on 7 Avenue for all those interested in forming a senior football cooperative. "Everything is up to those who want to play," he said. "It will be up to the players to name their own coach, trainers, and decide on what is to be done with everything connected with the game."

That night the Calgary Stampeders were born. Jack Grogan was appointed president with Archie McGillis as manager. Later, the players elected Griffing coach and Jerry Searight as his playing assistant. The team, according to the *Herald*, "is to be built around gridiron veterans who want 'one more season,' men who are returning to civilian life after serving in navy, army and air force, and players up from junior." They wore purple and gold.

The first practice was held Monday, October 1, at Buffalo Park.

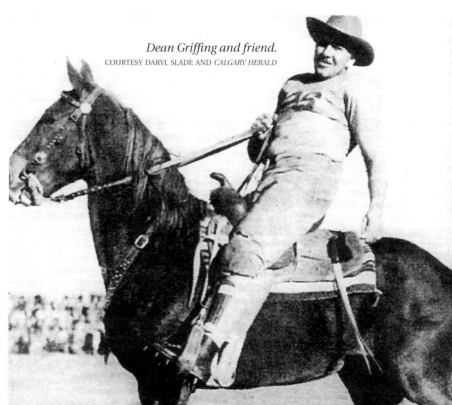

Dean Griffing and friend.
COURTESY DARYL SLADE AND *CALGARY HERALD*

Jerry Searight. COURTESY *CALGARY HERALD*

There would be no regular season. The team would host Regina in an exhibition game October 20 before beginning post-season play.

The original line-up included quarterback Bill Wusyk; halfbacks Ronnie Fish, Neil Cameron, Jack Hobbs, Harry Hobbs, Lou Benini, Lionel Gundry-White, Jimmy Gilkes, Herb Snoden, George Alexander, Dave Tomlinson and Jim Morris; fullbacks Paul Rowe and Bill Miller; ends Terry Tarves, Hal Harrison, Gordon Gilke and Bob Buchanan; and linemen Dean Griffing, Jack Lawrence, Bob Harrison, Jim Stewart, Jerry Searight, Bill Werth, Gerry Woodlock, Bob Buchanan, Harold Buchanan, Harry Anderson, Irvine Kelsey, Ace Bailey, Norm Sanderson, Ron Fish and Bert Shantz. The team trainer was Frank Porteous, the equipment manager Bill (Yunk) Sherriff.

The first Calgary Stampeders Football Club, 1945, at Mewata Stadium. COURTESY DARYL SLADE

Stampeder Gridiron Roster For Senior Football Season

BACKFIELDERS

PAUL ROWE, fullback — 28 years, 190 pounds, played for Oregon University and for Calgary Bronks in Western Conference football. Back after five years' service in the Canadian Army. In England he played for the Canadian team which won and later lost a game to an American Army all-star team.

BILL WUSYK, halfback — 27 years, 187 pounds. Another former Bronk of six years senior gridiron experience who has been coaching North Hill for the past few seasons.

BILL MILLER, quarterback — 23 years, 176 pounds. A former Hilltop junior who helped North Hill through the 1941 season and enlisted with the R.C.A.F. He was overseas for two and a half years and for a time was held as prisoner of war at Leipzig, Germany.

RONNIE FISH, halfback — 25 years, 172 pounds. Back in Calgary after five years in the Canadian Navy. He last played football for North Hill during the 1939 season.

ARNOLD SWEDER, quarterback — 27 years, 165 pounds. Graduate of the Calgary High School leagues who played for the Bronks in their last season, 1940. In school football he performed with St. Mary's.

NEIL CAMERON, halfback — 25 years, 175 pounds, another former Crescent Heights high school gridder back from overseas service. He was with the R.C.A.F. as a wireless air gunner.

JACK HOBBS, halfback — 23 years, 185 pounds, who played most of his football in Windsor although he did play a few games with the West End Tornadoes before enlisting with the Canadian Navy three and a half years ago.

LOU RENINI, halfback — 23 years, 158 pounds, who starred with St. Mary's high school teams. He has served in the Canadian Navy for the past five years and is playing his first season of senior football.

EDDIE FREZELL, halfback — 24 years, 140 pounds. Played his football in the east with Woodstock juniors and has served four years in the Air Force. Now calls Calgary home.

FRED GUNDRY-WHITE, halfback — 24 years, 175 pounds. Another former West End Tornado, who is back after three and a half years Navy service.

HARRY HOBBS, halfback — 20 years, 165 pounds. Starred the last three years with the West End juniors and he has shown he can handle himself in senior company. Spent the last two years on navy duty.

HERB SNOWDON, halfback — 30 years, 185 pounds. Played for the Bronks for four seasons of Western Conference football and established an enviable record as a blocking back. Just back from five years overseas service with the R.C.A.F.

PAT CASSIDY, quarterback — 21 years, 160 pounds. Has spent the last two years in the navy. Was rated the smartest field general to play in the city junior league here.

JIMMY GILKES, half back — 29 years, 160 pounds. Shifty backfielder of the old Bronks who comes back to the gridiron after a spell of Army Service. Jimmy played right half and his jumping jack runs always proved exciting.

GEORGE ALEXANDER, halfback — 27 years, 180 pounds. Played with the Bronks in 1940 and has an educated toe that will help the Stampeders to no end.

ENDS

LAURIE TARVES, end — 25 years, 160 pounds. Played Junior ball with East Calgary in 1940 and has spent the past four years on the high seas with the Canadian Navy.

JIM MORRIS, end — 22 years, 160 pounds. Starred with East and West Calgary junior teams and served three years with the R.C.A.F.

HAL HARRISON, end — 30 years, 210 pounds, played for Washington State from 1934 to '38 and then starred with Calgary Bronks for the next three years. Served with the Canadian Army for more than two years.

GORDON (GOBBO) GILKES, end—31 years, 180 pounds. Another former Bronk who comes back to football after five years with the Air Force. He played for Bronks from 1935 through 1939 and then enlisted.

SID KENDRICK, end — 30 years, 145 pounds, who played junior league ball here as well as for the Bronks before a knee injury forced him to the sidelines. He served more than five years with the Air Force and did a good deal of flying instructing.

TERRY TARVES, end — 24 years, 185 pounds. Played in the Calgary junior league with East End Stampeders and is playing his first senior season because the last four years were spent in the Navy.

LINEMEN

DEAN GRIFFING, centre — 32 years, 195 pounds. The former Regina Roughrider by way of Kansas State, who is coaching the Calgary seniors. Last year he played for Toronto Balmy Beach. Dean moved to Calgary last winter and has been mainly responsible for the organization of this senior club.

KEN FOSS, line — 20 years, 170 pounds. Played junior ball with West End and East Calgary.

ART LEWIS, line — 22 years, 190 pounds. Was with San Diego High School teams five years ago. Has lived in Calgary for the past three years and plays baseball for Calgary Bears.

JACK LAWRENCE, line — 32 years, 200 pounds. Always was a mighty useful performer in the Calgary line for five years of Western Conference football and was frequently nominated for all-star rating. Has been coaching West End Tornadoes in the Calgary junior league.

JIM STEWART, line—26 years, 233 pounds. Just back from four and a half years' service in the Canadian Navy. He played some football with Bronks and Bombers before enlisting.

BOB HARRISON, line — 32 years, 215 pounds. Played a lot of football for senior Bronks after helping Junior Altomans win the Western Canada junior championship in 1933. He has been one of the North Hill coaches for the past few seasons.

CARL GANGCHEFF, line—28 years, 195 pounds. Has spent the last six years in the navy. Was formerly with Regina's Champion College grid team.

JERRY WOODLOCK, line—22 years, 175 pounds. Starred on the 1941 West End junior team and was recently discharged from the navy after four years of service.

BOB BUCHANAN, line—22 years, 175 pounds. Was a pilot officer in the R.C.A.F. for three years. Played with the North Hill juniors for two seasons.

HARRY ANDERSON, line—18 years, 185 pounds. This gridder started playing in the junior loop when only 14 and has starred with the East Calgary squad for the past three years. He's definitely a comer.

HAROLD BUCHANAN, line—22 years, 185 pounds. Was a lieutenant in the navy for three years and formerly played with the North Hill juniors when they won the Alberta championship.

IRVINE KELSEY, line—23 years, 180 pounds. Played with the Bronks in 1940 and was touted as a comer. Has spent the last four years in the R.C.A.F. and is still on active service.

JACK McGILL, line—18 years, 210 pounds. A fine prospect from the junior ranks. He played with the East Calgary Stampeders the last three seasons.

ACE BAILEY, line—31 years, 222 pounds. Is still in the R.C.A.F. Was a former member of the Winnipeg Vics and Deer Lodge and should be a big help to the Stampeders.

ED BUSSI, line—22 years, 175 pounds. Played four seasons with the East Calgary juniors and looks promising.

EARL (DOC) SPENCLEY, line—28 years, 190 pounds. Was with the Peterborough Orphans for three years and has spent the last four years in the army.

RUDY SINGER, line—21 years, 180 pounds. Played with the Regina navy team in 1942 and appears set for a fine season.

NORM SANDERSON, line — 20 years, 165 pounds. A mainstay of the North Hill juniors for the past two years "Sandy's" football future looks bright.

The first Calgary Stampeders Football Club roster, 1945.
COURTESY DARYL SLADE

Over 3,500 fans filed into Mewata Stadium to welcome back senior football. Before the exhibition, the Roughriders presented their old coach, Dean Griffing, with a huge, raw beefsteak, hoping he would chew on that rather than on one of them.

He didn't have to, as his charges easily beat Regina 12–0. The new dog on the western football block looked forward to the playoffs with eager anticipation.

After winning in the Queen City 3–1 on October 27, the Stampeders finished off the Riders 12–0 on touchdowns by Paul Rowe and Jack Hobbs back home. The Roughriders failed to record a single first down or complete a pass. Calgary had 213 yards rushing. There were 15 fumbles, 12 by Calgary, on a wet, wintry day.

To be eligible for the Grey Cup, the Western teams had to play by Eastern rules, which limited blocking to within five yards of the line of scrimmage. (In the west, it was 10 yards.) Given the Stampeders' outstanding offensive line and the running of fullback Paul Rowe, this put them at a considerable disadvantage going into the western final against Winnipeg. To add to their troubles, the WIFU voted for a one-game final in Winnipeg rather than a home-and-home or best-of-three. Jack Grogan was rebuffed when he tried to

Terry Tarves. COURTESY *CALGARY HERALD*

find out who had voted for the single game, considering league Vice-President Vern Carmichael of Calgary hadn't been included in the decision-making.

Calgary's sense that Winnipeg wasn't going to allow them a chance to win was reinforced when the Blue Bomber-appointed timekeeper prevented legal substitution in the fourth Quarter by refusing to allow Stampeder players back on the field.

Nonetheless, the visitors jumped into a first quarter lead when Harry Hobbs completed a 20-yard pass to George Alexander, who was behind the Bomber defenders. He ran 40 yards for the score. The convert went wide. The Bombers turned a Hobbs fumble into a 32 yard field goal. The 5–3 lead held up until late in the final frame when, aided by a suspicious third-down measurement that kept their drive alive, and against a tired Stampeder team denied the right to substitute players, the Bombers marched 28 yards for the winning score. Winnipeg 9, Calgary 5.

Bill Wusyk. COURTESY DARYL SLADE

Stampeders' Souvenir Program, 1946.
COURTESY DARYL SLADE

Fritzie Hanson, the Whirlwind of the West.
COURTESY CANADIAN FOOTBALL HALL OF FAME

A full regular season of eight games was played in 1946 with Calgary's 5–3 record earning them a first-place tie with Winnipeg. Several Blue Bombers had joined the team, including Dave Berry. "I played for Winnipeg," he explained, "but when I came back after the war there was no place for my mother and father to live. My mother was in Lethbridge, where my dad was stationed during the war, and after the war my dad was up in Calgary because he was working for the government. They couldn't get a house anywhere.

"I bumped into Pappy Rowe and Dean Griffing, and I told them the circumstances and they said if I decided to play with them, they'd get me a house. I said, 'You get me the house and I'll play for you.' So they got me a veteran's house, which I was entitled to get.

"So I played for the Stampeders. I made $47.50 for the season. I also worked at the Hudson's Bay. The house was key for me."

Berry enjoyed playing for Griffing. "He was a gentleman. He was as hard as a rock, but he was a good man and a fair man. When you did it wrong, he let you know. When you did it right, he let you know. That's what I liked about him."

There would be no semi-final that year, just a two-game total-point final. Calgary prevailed at home 21–18 but lost 12–0 in a snowstorm in Winnipeg.

Winnipeg's flying wing Bill Wusyk was the first recipient of the Jeff Nicklin Memorial Trophy, awarded to the Most Valuable Player in the Western Conference. It was donated by the First Canadian Paratroop Battalion in memory of its Commanding officer, Lt.-Col. Jeff Nicklin, a Blue Bomber standout killed in action March 24, 1945. Wusyk was the Western Conference scoring leader with 32 points—all kicking.

The 1947 Calgary squad added two imports, halfbacks Del Wardien and Wally Stephens. The great Fritzie Hanson, late of the Blue Bombers, also donned Stampeder livery in 1947. With Paul Rowe, the four ball carriers combined for 698 yards in eight games, big totals for those days. The team finished 4–4 in second place and met Winnipeg in a two-game total-point final.

The Bombers prevailed at home on November 1, 16–4. In Calgary on Remembrance Day, the score was 15–3 for the Stampeders when on the last play of the game, the Bombers boomed a punt into the end zone. Fritzie Hanson raced to the end zone and kicked the ball into play and out of bounds. The series was tied at 19 points. They flipped a coin to see where a third game would be played. Winnipeg won the toss and the match 10–3 four days later. Once again, Calgary football dreams were shattered on the banks of the Red River.

At the end of the season, Tom Brook assumed the club presidency and set about making changes. Dean Griffing was out as coach. Les Lear was in. An incredible ride was about to begin that would include an undefeated season and a Grey Cup.

Playing Coach Les Lear would soon lead the Stampeders to their first Grey Cup victory.
COURTESY DARYL SLADE

CHAPTER 3

Wagon Train!

The Birth of the Grey Cup Festival
1948–49

LES LEAR WAS BORN AUGUST 22, 1918, IN GRAFTON, NORTH DAKOTA, but grew up in Winnipeg. He first played organized football with the Deer Lodge Juniors. He was promoted to the Blue Bombers in 1937 by Coach Reg Threlfall, playing in four Grey Cups with victories in 1939 and '41. (The Bomber water boy at the time was one Norm Hill.) Lear was an All-Canadian four times. In 1944 he became the first Canadian-trained player in the NFL when he signed with the Cleveland Rams. He also starred for the Detroit Lions during his four-year stint south of the border.

Tom Brook was looking for someone with Canadian football experience as well as a pipeline to American imports when, in 1948, he recommended Lear to the board of directors. As soon as they agreed, he opened a door in his hotel suite and proclaimed, "Gentlemen, here is our new coach!" Lear signed a two-year deal at $8,000 per season. August 16, 1949, they ripped it up and signed him for six years at the same remuneration.

Rather than fill his import quota of five with downy cheek collegians, Lear chose gnarly old pros: quarterback and punter Keith Spaith, centre Chuck Anderson, receiver Woody Strode and tackle John Aguirre. Lear kept the fifth spot open for himself.

Although the Americans were important, 31 of the 36 players were Canadian and essential to success. Lear picked up homebrew Winnipeg veterans Bert Iannone and Harry Hood, and a quartet of Canucks from the west coast: running backs Cedric Gyles, Jim Mitchener, Rod Pantages and Pete Thodas. Woody Strode nicknamed them the Deadend Kids.

27

Les Lear. COURTESY CANADIAN FOOTBALL HALL OF FAME

Pete Thodas.
COURTESY DARYL SLADE

"I grew up in Vancouver," Pantages reminisced. "I played at King Edward High School and for the junior Blue bombers. I was approached first by Les Lear and asked if I would like to play for the Stampeders. And, of course, I was excited as hell and said, 'Sure, I'd love to.' When I went out there to spring training, Les asked me if there were any other players that could make the team. And I said, 'Sure, there's Thodas, Ced Gyles and Jim Mitchener,' and they all played for the Stampeders. I was 19 when I joined the Stampeders in '48."

"Rod Pantages went back to Calgary and was asked by Les Lear if he could recommend anybody, so he recommended me," recalled Pete Thodas. "It so happened I was on my way to go to a logging camp, but I went out with the boys the night before so I missed the boat. Then this fellow called me and said they wanted me to come to Calgary to try out. I said, 'Fine.' If I hadn't missed the boat, I would have missed football. Strange, isn't it?"

Thodas went both ways. "Once you were on the field you never left it," he said. "That's the way it was in those days. There wasn't a lot of substitution."

Said Jim Mitchener, "I played for the Vancouver Blue Bombers for several years. Then I went to the University of British Columbia for a few months and wasn't satisfied. I had been accepted at an optometry school in Chicago. In August of '48, I was practicing with the Blue Bombers, and Gyles, Pantages and Thodas were already in Calgary. A fellow who had some connection with the Stampeders came to our practice field and asked for me. I guess the other fellows had mentioned me. He said, 'Would you like to go and try out for the Calgary Stampeders?'

"I said, 'Well, I'll have to go and talk with my mother about it and see what she thinks.'

"He said, 'I'm leaving at five o'clock on the train this afternoon. If you want to come, meet me down at the CPR station.'

Rod Pantages.
COURTESY DARYL SLADE

"So I was down at the station. My mother gave me a brown bag of sandwiches, and away I went to Calgary. I played two ways. I ended up with Calgary playing corner linebacker and flanker. In the Grey Cup, I played 60 minutes."

What about his contract?

He laughed. "Well, we didn't have any contract for a long time. They promised the four of us from Vancouver $500 plus room and board, and $20 a week spending money. The four of us from Vancouver shared a large double room in an old lodge in Calgary—I can't remember the name of it. But we had two double beds. Ced Gyles and I shared a bed and Rod Pantages and Pete Thodas shared a bed. We'd come home after practice and make our own dinner.

"Some fellow gave 5,000 shares in his oil well to the team when we won the Grey Cup. Three of us had decided to go together, and if we won something, we'd share it. Ced decided not to. They divided the stock into 10 lots of 500 shares at $.62 a share. So we got another $600 or something, which the three of us shared."

Norm Hill.
COURTESY DARYL SLADE

Another young Canadian to join he team was Norm Hill, a key figure in the 1948 Grey Cup.

"I grew up in Winnipeg and played on a really good high school team, provincial champions. I played my first two years on the University of Manitoba team, but my family was in Calgary. Late in August, I heard about a practice the Stampeders were having, so I went down there, just to stay in shape until I got back to Winnipeg. But I made the team. I told Les Lear I was thrilled to make the team, but I was going to school. I can't play football in Calgary and go to school in Winnipeg. Lear said, 'We'll fix that up.' So from the very first, once university started in early September, they flew me to all the games, all the time I played for the Stampeders, 1948–50.

"I played for the Bombers from 1951 to '53 so I could do my internship and get my medical degree. In 1954, I quit the Bombers because they wanted to cut my salary, as little as it was, and I went back to Calgary. Gerry James and I were the highest paid Canadians on the Bombers, and they wanted to give him a raise and cut me. I asked for what he was getting, and they said no. Les Lear had made a deal with Winnipeg in 1951 that if ever I was in a dispute with them I would be free to return to the Stampeders. My last year ('54), I made $7,300, my first year, zero."

What did Rod Pantages think of Les Lear?

"I thought he was great," Pantages enthused. "I had no problem with him, other than the fact that we never signed a contract. Pete, Jim, Ced and I drew straws to phone Les up and get him to come down to where we were staying. I phoned Les and said, 'Les, there is something very serious I want to talk to you about.'

"He said, 'Well, what is it about? Can't you tell me over the phone?'

"I said, 'No, it's personal.'

"He came down and found us all sitting there in our room. Damn near three-quarters of the team was younger and hadn't signed a contract. And Lear said, 'That's it. None of you guys will ever play again.' And he walked out.

"We were packing when the president of the club, Tom Brook, phoned and said, 'Don't leave.'

"I said, 'We're going home, to hell with it.'

"He said, 'No, no, come on in and see us.' And that's when we got our contracts signed. That was about two weeks before the Grey Cup.

"Awww! We never lost a game, went to the Grey Cup and won that. I got $500 for the season. When I came home, my dad was so mad he said, 'God, go get a job, do anything. You're getting yourself killed for that kind of money?'

"Of course, I loved it.

"After the '49 season, Pete and I said, 'We're tired of playing for peanuts,' and signed with Montreal.

"My father started looking after my contract when I went to Edmonton in 1952. He looked after all the Pantages Theatre ones here in Vancouver, so he knew what he was talking about. Us guys didn't know anything about it."

Seven thousand fans filled Mewata Stadium August 21 to watch their heroes defeat Ted Reeve's Toronto Balmy Beach 16–7 in a pre-season game. A local sportswriter described Les Lear's Calgary Stampeders as "a football team with a charging line, a clever backfield and a lot of imagination." Newcomers Pantages and Hill scored touchdowns, Bill Wusyk kicked a field goal with Keith Spaith adding a single.

Four days later, they opened at home against the newly christened Saskatchewan Roughriders. Spaith started at quarterback. The halfbacks were Hood, Thodas and Wusyk. Rowe was at fullback. Chuck Anderson was at centre, Bert Iannone and Rudy Singer the guards, John Aguirre and Bill Pullar the tackles. The ends were Norm Hill and Woody Strode. Super subs included Fritzie Hanson, Dave Berry and Rod Pantages. Berry was the only one-way specialist.

"In '46 and '47," Berry explained, "I played receiver. But in '48 a new rule came in allowing unlimited substitution. Because my eyes were going (I had to wear glasses, and at that time you didn't wear glasses and play football), Les Lear said, 'How would you like to play strictly defence?' and I said, 'You've got it,' therefore making me the first player in Canada to play only on defence."

Dave Berry. COURTESY DARYL SLADE

Although the newspaper headline screamed STAMPS DISPLAY POWER, CRUSH REGINANS 12–1, Calgary was only leading 6–1 late in the fourth quarter when Keith Spaith intercepted a Johnny Cook pass and lateraled it to Harry Hood, who raced 75 yards for a touchdown. Wusyk converted making the final score 12–1.

Five days later, perennial powerhouse and Calgary nemesis Winnipeg came calling. The result was even more impressive than the home opener, as the Stampeders crushed the Blue Bombers 30–0. Displaying a balanced attack, Calgary rushed for 203 yards and completed five of ten passes for 115 yards. The Stamps had three interceptions and three fumble recoveries. It was a sign of things to come. Over the regular season, Calgary out-scored Winnipeg 140–22 through six games.

The Bombers were much better four days later in Winnipeg, leading the visitors 5–4 with less than a minute to go. With the ball on his 45, Spaith connected with Strode at the Bomber 20. He went into the end zone standing up. Calgary 10, Winnipeg 5. On to Regina for a Labour Day battle with the Roughriders.

John Aguirre. COURTESY DARYL SLADE

Johnny Bell opened the scoring for the home side with a first quarter TD, converted by Gabe Patterson. After exchanging rouges, Calgary's Gyles ran in for a converted major, leaving the score 7–7 at the half. Each side added rouges.

The climatic moment came late in the final frame. "I was playing left corner linebacker," recalled Jim Mitchener, "and Keith Spaith was behind me. Cook threw to Patterson, and when Keith tackled him, he dropped the ball. I picked it up and ran for a touchdown. They were so angry. They thought it should have been complete. The fans started throwing rocks at us, and we had to put our helmets on and march arm in arm to our bus. Talk about bush league football."

With 12 seconds left, Rider coach Fred Grant pulled his team from the field to protest the officiating of Cliff Roseborough, Les Ferguson, Paul Dojack and Howie Milne. The final score was 14–8, Calgary. The two teams would meet four more times, three of which would be decided by a single point.

On September 13, 7,000 fans watched their beloved Stampeders unleash a balanced attack –171 yards rushing, 120 passing—to shut out the Blue Bombers a second time. Woody Strode, Paul Rowe and Cliff Kliewer each scored majors en route to the 18–0 victory. Next up, back-to-back games against the Roughriders.

The first in Calgary saw the undefeated Stamps fall behind 12–0 in the fourth quarter. Then Harry Hood made a spectacular grab of a Keith Spaith pass for touchdown number one. After kicking a single, Spaith and Strode combined for a major, making the score 13–12.

The rematch in Regina was just as exciting. The Roughriders had 17 first downs to Calgary's 8 and out-passed the visitors 229 yards to 122. They were leading 10–6 late in the fourth quarter when Spaith engineered a brilliant drive climaxed by a handoff to Kliewer, who ran 30 yards to the end zone to pull out a 12–11 win.

That was Saturday, October 2. Two days later, they clinched first place in Winnipeg, downing the Bombers 26–6. Spaith threw touchdown passes to Strode (set up by a 61-yard Thodas run) and Hanson, and scored

one himself. The return game a week later on Thanksgiving was memorable not because of the score (35–3 for the Stampeders), but because Calgarians showered appreciation on Paul Rowe Day, the first time a Calgary gridder had been so honoured. Rowe responded to the adulation and gifts with two touchdowns.

Paul Rowe.
COURTESY *CALGARY HERALD*

With their undefeated streak at nine games, the Stamps headed to Regina for another nail-biter. Tied at seven with just over a minute remaining, Rider quarterback Johnny Cook was sacked. Ken Charlton's punt was blocked, and a play later, Keith Spaith easily kicked it through the end zone for the 8–7 win.

The Stampeders finished their undefeated regular season with a 21–8 win in Winnipeg and a 19–0 romp at home over Saskatchewan. Calgary gave up an average of five points a game, the best record of the modern era. They would do the same in 1949.

Although they preferred to meet the Manitobans in post-season play, it would be the Queen City boys.

At the conclusion of the regular season, the 1948 Western All-Star team was announced and was dominated by the Stampeders. Calgary players honoured were quarterback Keith Spaith, centre Chuck Anderson, guards Dave Tomlinson and Bert Iannone, tackle John Aguirre, end Woody Strode and fullback Paul Rowe. Spaith, Rowe, Strode and Aguirre were unanimous selections.

Game One of the western final went Saturday November 6 before 7,000-plus fans in Regina. For the connoisseur of line play, it was a work of art with each front seven refusing to give an inch. The result was a 4–4 tie, and, although they were still undefeated, the Stampeders took no satisfaction from that fact, considering most of the game was played in Saskatchewan's end.

Calgary led 2–0 at the half on a Keith Spaith single and a Norm Hill rouge. The teams exchanged singles in the third quarter, and Spaith put the Stamps up 4–1 with a kick through the end zone early in the fourth. Later in the quarter, scrimmaging from his nine-yard line, Spaith fired a short pass to Normie Kwong, who earlier in the game snuffed out a Rider scoring drive with an interception. A bone rattling tackle by Ken Charlton shook the ball loose at the Calgary 23. Gabe Patterson kicked the tying field goal.

Back home the next day, a clearly displeased Lear put his charges through a stiff workout. Because they lost five fumbles in Regina on a dry, warm day, he stressed ball-carrying drills.

Said president Tom Brook, "That Regina game was just one of those letdowns after a two-week layoff. I still think we have the best coached team, the best players and they are in the best condition of any club in the west."

Three of the games between the teams had been settled by a point, and the first playoff game was a tie. The other three games resulted in a 36-point differential in favour of Calgary. Which teams would show up for the second playoff game at Mewata on Remembrance Day?

A heavy snowfall hit the night before the game. Hundreds of volunteers cleared the snow from the field and stands, and a record crowd of over 10,000 braved the elements to cheer on their heroes. Tens of thousands more listened to Lloyd Saunders and Gail Egan call the action on CFCN radio.

The huge crowd had barely settled into their seats when the Roughriders' Gabe Patterson raced 78 yards for a touchdown, which he converted. Led by the running of Pantages, Gyles, Thodas and Kliewer, the Stampeders responded in the second quarter. First down at the 20, Thodas hit the hole off right tackle and picked up 34 yards, followed by Kliewer's run of the same distance around left end. Pantages and Thodas got it down to the five, where, on second down, Spaith followed centre Chuck Anderson into the end zone. Fred Wilmot converted, tying the score at six at halftime.

Calgary picked up where they left off with Gyles picking up first downs, and Spaith passing 39 yards to Woody Strode, who made a sensational catch at the one. Paul Rowe punched it in, and the convert was blocked. Calgary 11, Saskatchewan 6. In the final frame, Thodas and Rowe led the way down the field to the one, where Spaith scored the final touchdown. Wilmot converted. That's how it ended, 17–6, Calgary winning its first Western championship since 1911.

Recalled Jim Mitchener, "On the second play of the game, Gabe Patterson runs for a touchdown. We're behind by a touchdown, and we'd never been beaten all year. Coming back and winning that game was the most memorable for me."

After the game, Captain Paul Rowe accepted The N.J. "Piffles" Taylor Memorial Trophy, emblematic of Western supremacy, and Keith Spaith was given the Jeff Nicklin Memorial Trophy as the MVP of the division.

On to Toronto and a Grey Cup date with the Ottawa Rough Riders!

At every Grey Cup since 1948, chuckwagons, country bands, white Stetsons and pancake breakfasts have been a familiar sight. As hosts of the annual Greatest Outdoor Show On Earth, the Stampede, Calgarians inadvertently invented the Grey Cup festival at their first appearance in what previously had been a football game that attracted very little national attention.

Hootin' and hollerin', flipping flapjacks in front of Toronto's City Hall, the wild westerners came east to show support for their beloved Stampeders and the rest of the country a good time. Whistle-stopping through Medicine Hat, Morse, Moose Jaw, Moosomin, Brandon, Bagot and Beausejour, through Buswash, Britt, Barnesdale and Barrie, on to Toronto, the Grey Cup special picked up steam and turned the championship game into the nation's premier sporting event. Stu Adams, Jack Grogan, Ross Henderson, Bill Herron, Harry McConochie and John Thompson formed a committee to organize the train trek to Toronto.

But there was a football game to play. After a day off to celebrate, the team returned to the practice field. "We are taking no chances," declared Lear, "This is going to be the best conditioned team that ever represented Western Canada in a Grey Cup final. We have come a long way, and we aren't going to spoil things by taking it too easy now."

Lear was tough, thorough and innovative. While Dave Berry enjoyed playing for Dean Griffing, he didn't have the same affection for Les Lear. "Let me put it this way," he recalled, "If I passed Les Lear on the street, I wouldn't say hello to him. If I found out he was putting on a coaching clinic a hundred miles away, I'd be the first guy there."

So he was a great coach but not a very good person? "That's a nice way to put it."

Said Mitchener, "Lear was a pretty tough task master, but I personally liked him as a coach. He did a good job for us—always seemed to have us well prepared. I enjoyed life with Lear."

Thodas agreed. "I liked him very much. He was hard-nosed, rough, and tough. I really liked him. What he said, he meant.

He'd always stick by his ballplayers. I thought he was terrific. A lot of people didn't like him, but I sure did."

Norm Hill recalled, "I gave him a wide berth because he was a tough customer. But Lear protected me as far as my career was concerned. He thought my career as a doctor always came first. I appreciated that very much.

"Lear looked after us. We were babes in the woods. He said, 'When we go on the road, girls are going to be around. They are going to be talking to you, and I'm going to want you not to be speaking to them.' Sure enough, in Regina, they were there, wandering around the hotel. They were hired to find out who was going to play and who was injured. They may have been paid for other activities, but that is what they were there for. You wouldn't believe, even at that time, how much money was bet on a football game. Incredible."

Lear transformed the way the game was played, using, for example, a four-man front on defence. "When we pulled it against Ottawa," Berry remembered, "one of their linemen said, 'Where the hell are the rest of your guys?' I said, 'Come on through and you'll find them.'"

Normie Kwong admired his first pro coach. "Les Lear didn't have the assistant help that later people had. He operated largely on heart and was the most inspiring coach I had in my career."

The Stampeders have always been a passing team. Lear began that tradition with Keith Spaith and Woody Strode. While other teams ran twice as much, as Berry explained, "Calgary, in essence, brought in the passing attack. The ratio between running and passing with us was 60–40. The other teams hadn't really seen a passing game like Spaith and Strode put on. It was usually two bucks and a kick or a run, a pass and a kick. We used the pass the way they do today."

The team was comprised of four imports, five when Lear (a guard) suited up. They were Spaith, Strode, centre Chuck Anderson and tackle John Aguirre. There were 11 holdovers from the 1947 squad, including centre Harry Anderson; guards Dave Tomlinson, Rudy Singer and Steaky Adams; tackles Bill Pullar and Rube Ludwig; ends Dave Berry and Bob Leatham; halfback Fritzie Hanson; fullback Paul Rowe; and QB Bill Wusyk.

There were the rookie ex-junior whiz kid halfbacks from the west coast, Gyles, Mitchener, Pantages, and Thodas; six more from Calgary junior ranks, including half-backs Normie Kwong, Fred Wilmot and Jim Dobbin; tackle Jim McGill; guard Norm Carter; QB Harry Irving; and end Norm Hill.

Over from the 1947 Blue Bombers were halfbacks Harry Hood and Cliff Kliewer, end Chick Chickowsky and guard Bert Iannone. Nicknamed the Red Raiders, they were the men who rang up the only undefeated season in modern Canadian football history.

In a conversation at their eastern Grey Cup headquarters with the late, great sports-writer Jim Coleman, Lear, whom the scribe said had the disposition of an arthritic grizzly, described his team: "Take a look at my cowboys. We have Jewish cowboys, Negro cowboys, Chinese cowboys, Greek cowboys, You name it, we got 'em." In order they were Rube Ludwig, Woody Strode and Chuck Anderson, Normie Kwong, Pete Thodas and Rod Pantages.

Said Thodas, "The strength of the team was the quarterback, Keith Spaith. He had a great arm. We had some veterans in Harry Hood, Paul Rowe, Rube Ludwig, Johnny Aguirre, Bert Iannone, Chuck Anderson and Woody Strode. Woody, Chuck, Johnny and Keith had played in the States for different professional teams. Rube, Harry and Bert all played for Winnipeg prior to coming to Calgary. That was the nucleus, and then they added the spice, if you will, in Pantages, Normie Kwong, Teddy Gyles, Jimmy Mitchener, Normie Hill and me."

Mitchener played with or against the great quarterbacks of that era. How did Spaith compare?

"Oh, Keith was wonderful. He was a great quarterback. He was a drop-back passer. Sam Etcheverry, Bernie Faloney and Jackie Parker could run. But Keith could throw the ball anywhere, and he was a great punter. He was certainly one of the best who ever played in Canada. Parker had speed none of the others had. I think Sam was the toughest of them all."

In 1948 Spaith completed 75 of 151 passes for 1,246 yards, 13 TDs and 10 interceptions. His punting average was 42.5 yards.

Fritzie Hanson appeared in five Grey Cups with Winnipeg, winning in 1935, '39 and '41, losing to Toronto in 1937 and '38. Although he almost had a leg blown off by an errant grenade on a military range, Hanson returned to the gridiron with Calgary in 1947. His presence elicited mixed reactions.

"Fritzie Hanson was the greatest ball player this country has ever seen," declared Berry.

Even in 1948? "You're damn right. As a matter of fact, if he hadn't caught Gabe Patterson in the final we wouldn't have gone to the Grey Cup. Hanson was about 35 and Patterson 22. He picked up a fumble and took off, and Fritzie took off after him after giving him a 10-yard head start, and caught him on the 40-yard line. He could run, Old Twinkletoes. Can you imagine what he'd have done in his youth if he had 10-yard blocking in front of him? He would have made records that would never have been broken. The greatest football player Canada ever had!"

Pantages was less impressed. "Hanson was fast, all right, but he sort of lost a lot, and it was the end of his career in 1948. I had a big argument with Lear in Winnipeg. We were playing our second game. Us young guys had run the ball down to about the 20-yard line. And then Lear would take us out and put Fritzie Hanson, Paul Rowe and Harry Hood in, and they'd score. I said to Lear, 'C'mon, Les, us guys are running the ball down there, and then you put the old buggers in and they score. We want to score, too, you know.'"

Shortly after the war, African-American players made their appearance in Canadian football. Always referred to as "negroes" at that time, their experience north of the border varied from dismal in Regina and Winnipeg to welcoming in Edmonton and Montreal. Calgary ranked somewhere in between. Racial prejudice within the teams usually came from the white Americans, not the Canadians who made up the majority. Regina was bad because a good number of Roughrider imports were from the Deep South. Teams that recruited more from the northern and western states provided a less difficult experience for Negroes. Still, it wasn't easy for black players. In addition to prejudice, loneliness in the absence of a black community was a problem. Only Edmonton tended to have more than two black ballplayers at a time.

The first African-Americans to play for the Stampeders were centre Chuck Anderson and receiver Woody Strode, both former teammates of John Aguirre and Les Lear. Woodrow Wilson Woolvine Strode was born in 1914 at Los Angeles, the son of a Blackfoot mother and an African-American father. After serving in the Pacific during the Second World War, Strode attended UCLA, where he made All-American while starring with Jackie Robinson and Kenny Washington.

Woody Strode, the Jackie Robinson of football.
COURTESY DARYL SLADE

He took cinema and theatre classes, and was soon working as a stuntman and actor.

From 1934 on, the NFL had an unwritten rule that allowed no coloured players. Said Sugarfoot Anderson, "Preston Marshall in Washington and George Halas in Chicago didn't want Negroes. They tried to ban Woody, Chuck Anderson, Kenny Washington and me from playing in the NFL."

Dan Reeves, owner of the Cleveland Rams, wanted to move the team to Los Angeles. The management of the LA Coliseum insisted they couldn't play there if they discriminated against Negroes. Reeves also wanted local stars to sell the product in California, and Kenny Washington, a quarterback, fit the bill. Reeves wasn't an idealist like Branch Rickey, who signed Jackie Robinson. He wanted the Coliseum, and he wanted to sell tickets, so despite the outraged objections of fellow NFL owners, he signed Washington, the first African-American to break the colour barrier in American professional sports. On May 7, 1946, Woody Strode was signed, the second black athlete to crack the colour barrier.

The Ram backfield coach was Bob Snyder, a future Calgary coach. "We were worried about how the other players would react to the signings," he recalled, "but there was not one incident. Three weeks before training camp, [quarterback] Bob Waterfield and Kenny worked out together by themselves. That broke the ice."

Later, Snyder observed, "I have no proof of this, but it's always been my feeling that signing Washington and Strode tipped Rickey over to do what he did with Jackie Robinson. Our signings took the pressure off."

Like Robinson, Washington and Strode endured racial baiting and deliberate attempts to injure. After two years of hell in the NFL, Strode was happy to answer Lear's call and head north. He was 34 when he became a Stampeder in 1948. He retired a year later to pursue a movie career that began in 1941 with the movie *Sundown*. He appeared in over 75 movies, including *Spartacus, The Ten Commandments, The Man Who Shot Liberty Valence, The Cotton Club* and *The Quick and the Dead*, which was released in 1995 after his death at 80 and dedicated to him. He shaved his head and played the part of Lothar in the 1949 television show *Mandrake the Magician*.

"Woody and I were the ends," Hill recalled, "and we got to be really good friends. He was a fine man. He had a beautiful build, just extraordinary. He could do 100 pull-ups with one hand.

"He was a great guitar player. Once when we were in Winnipeg, staying at the Royal Alexander, he got together with his friend Nat King Cole, who was playing a bistro in town. Chuck Anderson and I were up in the room with them, and Woody was playing and Nat was singing. The deskman phoned up and told us to quiet down, which we did for all of 30 seconds.

"It was really hot that night, so we took our shirts off. A small hotel detective knocked on our door and Woody and Chuck, two big black men opened it. The dick took one look at them and said, 'Sorry, wrong room!' and dashed off down the hallway."

As a Stampeder, Strode picked up nine TDs and 964 yards on 44 receptions. The two-time all-star was instrumental to both Calgary majors in the 1948 Grey Cup. Strode loved his years in Calgary.

Calgary wasn't free of racism, though it was nothing like the American South. Sugarfoot Anderson, who joined the team in 1949, recalled an encounter with racism.

"Our country club here didn't allow Jewish or black people there, but they said Woody and I could come. . . . I didn't raise no Cain about it, I just never did go. If I hadn't been a Stampeder, they wouldn't have let me in, so I just didn't go. Coming from Arkansas, nothing that happened to me in Calgary was anything to write home about."

Over 1,000 fans jammed into the CPR station Thursday evening November 18 to give a royal send-off to their football heroes. Most of the players wore cowboy outfits, with Woody Strode and Dave Berry looking like they had stepped off a dude ranch. Fifteen minutes was spent singing cowboy songs accompanied by Strode strumming the mandolin and Bill Wusyk playing the harmonica. "Home On The Range" was the favourite.

The Stampede Special carrying fans pulled out of the station at 9:45 PM Tuesday, November 23. Over 1,000 Calgarians came down to take a look at the 15-car train.

The *Albertan* reported: "Heading the special is a baggage car which had been transformed into a barn for 12 horses being shipped east for the parade. Bill Herron, member of the Stampeder football club

Hogtown, Here We Come!
COURTESY *CALGARY HERALD*

executive and well-known Calgary horse fancier, shipped four of his prize pinto ponies. They will be ridden by himself, Mrs. Herron, his son Bill, Jr. and Mrs. Merle Stier. . . .

"Next was the lounge, another baggage car made over into a dance hall and bar. During the journey, Jack Friedenberg and his orchestra will provide music for western dancing and sing songs. . . .

"The remainder of the train was made up of sleeping cars, two compartment cars and two diners. . . .

"Happiest of the 250 passengers were hospitalized war veterans who were chosen by draw among veterans at Col. Belcher Hospital and No. 2 Convalescent Hospital.

"Youngest rooter on the train was four year-old Paulette Price who is making the trip with her parents Mr. and Mr. Larry Price. Outfitted in cowboy garb she said she was going to cheer the Stamps on just like her mother and father.

"INDIANS ABOARD

"Chief David Crowchild and Chief George Ryder of the Sarcee Reserve were on board and will appear in full dress outfit in the parade. Bob Heiberling whose chuckwagon outfit is regularly seen in the Calgary Stampede went along to help J.B. Cross, honorary president of the football club, drive the C.C. Cross Buckhorn ranch wagon at the head of the parade. . . . Reg West, C.P.R. passenger agent in Calgary will handle the railroad angle on the eastern journey. Mrs. West was very definite about one thing as she boarded the special: 'We'll bring the Grey Cup back!'

"During stop-overs at Moose Jaw, Regina and Winnipeg the fans will leave the train for a few minutes and give an impromptu western show for those at the station."

Dave Berry described the trip to Toronto. "Every time we stopped, we got off the train and did calisthenics. I remember we stopped at one town and there must have been four feet of snow—it was snowing like hell—and we'd run from the end of the train to the engine and back and then do exercises until the old guys said, 'All aboard.' And then we got aboard.

"Wives went along (mine didn't because we had a bunch of kids at home), but the guys couldn't even talk to them until coming home. Once the game was over, the rules were out the door, so coming back was a little different. That was wild and woolly. But before that, no fooling around. You bunked with the team, and you stayed with the team. You didn't go running around looking for your wife or anybody else."

While the players arrived a week ahead of time, the Stampede Special pulled into Toronto's Front Street Union Station Friday morning, November 26. Decked out in cowboy outfits, whoopin' and hollerin', the fans immediately made their presence felt. Bob Mamini's article was headlined STAMPEDER FANS PUT ON WESTERN SHOW FOR EAST: Display Amazes Toronto

"The Stampede Special brought a bit of the Old West to staid Toronto today and let the East know that prairie football fans are right back of Calgary's challenge for the historic Grey Cup.

"With cowboy band and 250 travellers off the Special, joined by 70 who made the trip by air, Union Station echoed to the Stampeder victory song, 'Put On Your Red And White Sweater,' as cowboys and cowgirls from the great open spaces put on a Western show for Torontonians.

"For enthusiasm and spirit, those on the Stampeder Special agreed there never has been anything to match this trip.

"Westerners will spend on an average of two to three hundred dollars apiece to see a $2.00 football game, the top price for the Grey Cup final."

Albertan sports editor Tom Moore described the Friday night festivities at the Royal

York Hotel: "The show here tonight really belonged to Viscount Alexander, Governor-General of Canada and the 48th Highlanders of Toronto, but Calgary Stampeder football fans stole it without trying.

"For probably the first time in Eastern Canada social history, toppers and tails, ten-gallon hats and blue jeans, décolleté evening gowns and riding togs were mixed in colourful profusion in the Royal York Hotel and Toronto loved it.

"The occasion was the annual St. Andrew's Ball, top bracket fixture on Toronto's social calendar with the Governor-General the guest of honour, the 48th Highlanders as guard and most of Ontario's top dignitaries and socialites on the guest list.

"There were also the cowboys.

"Still celebrating their jaunt into Toronto for the east-west Earl Grey Cup final Saturday, Stampeder fans Friday evening were staging their square dances in the Royal York lobby when the Highlanders marched in. When the Westerners found out what it was all about they cleared the square dancers off the floor and prepared to offer hearty, if unofficial, support to the welcome planned for Viscount Alexander.

"It was quite a welcome.

"Coming in accompanied by aides and other dignitaries, it must have been quite a jolt for the Governor-General when he found his formal guard of honour backed by whooping Westerners in ten-gallon hats and gaudy shirts.

"They sang 'Home On The Range.' They sang 'For He's A Jolly Good Fellow.' They cheered again and found hundreds of Torontonians carried away by the situation, joining in the wild whoopees like they had been brought up in cattle country.

And the Governor-General?

"There was a wide grin on his face as he marched briskly to the elevators, and you can't convince any Calgarian there he wasn't thinking of days in the past when he wore a ten-gallon hat himself and whooped it up at the Calgary Stampede."

Varsity Stadium could accommodate just over 20,000 spectators. No previous Grey Cup had attracted such widespread interest, which was remarkable considering the Toronto Argonauts, winners of the three previous championships, weren't in it.

The Stampeders were allotted 3,500 tickets; the Ottawa Rough Riders, 4,000.

On Saturday morning, Grey Cup day, the Calgarians saddled their horses, got the chuckwagons ready, and staged the first Grey Cup parade. Leading the parade was Hiram McCallum, a former Calgarian and then Mayor of Toronto, decked out in gabardine, plaid shirt and Stetson, astride a handsome black mustang. Right behind in full dress were the Sarcee chiefs, followed by the rest of the men and women on horseback. It was the first real example of "Can do, Calgary," of showing the rest of the country that Calgary was a great city that would soon be the heartland of the Canadian West. In the process, they created the Grey Cup festival.

The 1948 Grey Cup came three years after the end of the war. It was the first national celebration since the war to bring Canadians together from all regions of the country to have fun around a football game and reminisce about the incredible national sacrifice and undertaking that was WW II.

At city hall, flap jacks were flipped, bacon fried, coffee poured and western songs played and sung.

Legend has it that one of the group rode his horse into the lobby of the Royal York Hotel, prompting management to post a sign, "No Horses Allowed In The Lobby." However, no contemporary accounts mention such an event, and if it actually happened, the rider has never been identified. The game and its accompanying festivities were covered extensively by the *Calgary Herald* and *The Albertan*, but no story makes mention of the horse in the hotel. The coverage reports that celebrations were boisterous but fairly harmless. *Herald* reporter Vern De Geer wrote: "A prominent member of the Royal York Hotel staff told this writer that Calgary folks had created more noise and less damage than any celebrating group in the history of the largest hostelry in the British Empire." According to Frank Dabbs' biography of rancher and oilman Bill Herron, Calgary's cowboys and Indians rode their horses through the great hall of Union Station. Herron planned to ride his horse into the Royal York but was persuaded not to by his friend, the hotel manager.

The Grey Cup was a special time for veteran Calgary fullback Paul Rowe. Born and raised in Victoria, Rowe went to the University of Oregon and upon graduating joined the Calgary Bronks. No. 50 was in his eighth season with Calgary, having missed a few when serving in the army overseas during the war. A perennial all-star, like many of the Stampeders, this was his first crack at the Grey Cup. He was the Western Conference scoring leader in 1948.

Tom "Scotty" Melville of the *Regina Leader-Post* wrote: "The Stampeders moved in the 17 miles from their retreat at the Pig and Whistle Inn Friday night to bed down at the Royal York and were given a tremendous reception. When the fans learned the Dave Dryburgh Memorial Trophy, a new award for the Western Conference high scorer, was in the hotel, they held back Paul Rowe and insisted the trophy be given to him in the rotunda. The sportswriters from the western dailies were rounded up as they unwrapped the beautiful trophy and turned it over to Rowe. 'Save the box,' a gal in breeches shouted, 'We'll use it for the Grey Cup.'"

Named after a long-time *Leader-Post* sports editor who died the year before, Rowe was the first recipient of the award.

If that wasn't enough excitement, Rowe was wakened in his hotel room in the wee hours to be told his wife had given birth at Holy Cross Hospital, 12:30 AM MST, to a baby boy, a brother for two-year-old Barrie.

The team arrived at Oakville's Pig and Whistle Inn on Sunday. They would train at nearby Appleby College.

Jim Coleman described their arrival: "On the grimly dark and dank afternoon of Sunday, November 21, 1948, a motley group of cowpokes boarded a bus at The Pig and Whistle Inn on the shores of Lake Ontario, west of Toronto. The Pig and Whistle consisted of a central dining hall surrounded by tiny cabins with two beds in each cabin.

"They MUST have been cowpokes because, certainly, they didn't resemble the Metropolitan Opera's corps-de-ballet. They came in the wildest assortment of shapes and sizes—tall, short, fat and skinny. The common denominator of this awkward squad was a white ten-gallon hat, which each member of the group was wearing, just a little bit sheepishly.

"A conservative and respected Toronto bookmaker was standing with a group of newspapermen when the white ten-gallon hats began to gather uncertainly around their bus.

"'If those bums are the members of the Calgary football team,' the bookmaker said with a sigh, 'I'll lay 3-to-1 that Ottawa will clean their clocks next Saturday afternoon.' I was making $130 a week, (minus income tax) at the time. Before the bookmaker closed his mouth on his cigar, I bet him a week's salary on Calgary at 3–1."

Calgary coach Les Lear was fairly confident of the outcome because he and quarterback Keith Spaith had scouted the Eastern final. Said Lear, "I don't think they'll be able to change their tactics with only a week between the Eastern and Canadian finals, and we learned plenty scouting the game. We came to win the Grey Cup. The boys are in great mental and physical condition and there will be no alibis if we don't take the Cup."

Said Ottawa coach Wally Masters, "I don't know a thing about Calgary, but I know we're ready. We haven't any injuries worthy of note, and I am more than pleased with the way the boys trained this week. I can't recall one game over the season where the mental attitude has been as good as for this one."

The oddsmakers made Ottawa 8–5 favourites.

For all his confidence, Lear took nothing for granted, and Pete Thodas got a kick out of his coach's paranoia. "God, it was funny. Les Lear wouldn't allow planes to fly over our practice. And he took us down to the basement in this school, and he closed all the doors," he recalled. "The team's down there and he brought film of an Ottawa game, and we watched it. In those days, you either didn't have film or weren't allowed to have film—I don't know which. Anyhow, we watched the film, and in particular we watched how they liked to pull that sleeper play. Of course, we pulled it on them."

The cuisine, however, was no laughing matter, Thodas remembered. "And then eating cheese sandwiches every day. I can recall the guys all getting teed off with their cheese sandwiches. Chuck Anderson just said to hell with it, took off and left camp. They sent Bert Iannone after him and he brought him back. We would have been without a centre. It was funny."

Not that the Stampeders were in Toronto to sample the cuisine. "We were on the field at eight-thirty in the morning," recalled Thodas, "and we worked out until about eleven o'clock. Then we went for lunch, back on the field at one-thirty and off by four. Friday afternoon we bussed in and stayed at the Royal York. There was nothing in the lobby because they cleared all the furniture out after they were riding their horses in there." The urban legend had been quick to take root.

After watching the Rough Riders in action, Les Lear said, "Ottawa has a big, fast, aggressive line. It is knee-deep in reserves. Our team will have to be at its best to win, but we can do it."

Keith Spaith agreed, adding, "The Ottawa line doesn't charge. It drifts and you can beat that with deception. We have the deception."

Grey Cup day, November 27, dawned overcast and cool with the temperature at game time +7°C. Before the game began, recalled Dave Berry, "Les Lear told us to play our game, play our position and don't get too many stupid penalties. That's all. Do it right and you'll win. Do it wrong and you'll lose."

Before the game began, Lear skirmished with the curmudgeonly CRU over the number of men who could suit up. He asked for 29, Ottawa agreed to 26, but the CRU said 24. As it turned out, it didn't matter as the Stampeders got through the game relatively unscathed. Lear did prevail in his request to have more than one football available in case the original got wet. And despite objections from Ottawa, Calgarian and veteran referee Les Ferguson was allowed to work the game as umpire.

At 1:00 PM, Governor-General Viscount Alexander performed the ceremonial kick-off. The Stampeders wore their dark red-and-white striped uniforms; Ottawa, white, black and red.

Wilf Tremblay kicked-off to Jim Mitchener at the 34. The teams battled back and forth through the first quarter, near the end of which Tony Golab punted for a single from the Calgary 45. Ottawa 1, Calgary 0.

Harry Hood in action in the 1948 Grey Cup game. COURTESY DARYL SLADE

One of the most interesting plays in Grey Cup history resulted in the Stampeders taking the lead in the second stanza. With Ottawa at third and 1 on the Calgary 44, Howie Turner faked the punt and took off. Strode nailed him for a two-yard loss. Spaith hit Harry Hood on the Rider 48 and then found Woody Strode at the 13. With everyone regrouping after that big catch, Norm Hill drifted over to the other side of the field and lay down on the enemy 20-yard line. Ottawa fans yelled themselves silly, pointing at the crafty Hill, but to no avail. Everybody in the stadium except the Ottawa Rough Riders knew Hill was there. Time was whistled in, Spaith dropped back to pass and threw to Hill in the end zone. The ball hit Hill's hands and bounced up in the air. A defender knocked him flat on his back, but the ball fell into his lap for a touchdown. Fred Wilmot kicked the convert. Calgary 6, Ottawa 1.

Hill, now a retired Winnipeg neurosurgeon, said he probably got a big assist from Canada's figure-skating star Barbara Ann Scott. "Apparently, right before that play, Barbara Ann Scott was coming into the stands in that area. Everyone, including the Ottawa players, wanted to get a glimpse of her, so they weren't paying any attention to me."

Said Thodas, "Where I was positioned in the huddle, I was left halfback and Normie was left end. He'd be right beside me, and Johnny Aguirre, who was playing

Canada's Sweetheart Barbara Ann Scott may have unwittingly and indirectly helped the Stampeders win the Grey Cup. COURTESY DARYL SLADE AND *CALGARY HERALD*

left tackle, was opposite me. We got back into the huddle and I said, 'Where the hell's Norm Hill?' And Aguirre grabbed me and said, 'Get your ass in the end position.' He pulled me where Normie would normally be standing. I said, 'What's going on?' and he said, 'He's out there sleeping it.' And I said, 'You've got to be joking.'

"Keith threw the ball, and there he was. Aguirre knew it and nobody else. He got back in the huddle and pulled me over and told Keith, 'He's out there, don't look! Get out there and throw the ball.'

"I think there was mud on the ball. It squirted, and he popped it up and it finally fell into his arms and he sat down in the end zone."

Hill confirmed that the sleeper play was his idea. "Lear had decided before the game there would be none of that trick-play stuff,

but he forgot to tell the players. So I just did it. John Aguirre went into the huddle and told them I was out there. [The ball] bobbled up in the air and I had to catch it again."

In the third quarter, Ottawa quarterback Bob Paffrath directed a powerful attack with Tony Golab and Howie Turner. Starting at the Stampeder 46, where the Westerners lost possession because of illegal blocking on a punt, the Riders marched to the 1. Paffrath plunged into the end zone and Eric Chipper converted. Ottawa 7, Calgary 6.

In the fourth quarter, with the ball on their own 37-yard line, Paffrath threw an overhand pass back to Pete Karpuk, thus making it a lateral. The ball went wide and hit the ground. Karpuk thought it was an incomplete pass, but Calgary's Woody Strode picked it up. "I looked up," said Strode, "and there was a referee standing right in front of me. I looked right into his eyes. He didn't nod his head or blow a whistle or even blink. I didn't wait to ask the man any questions. I just thought I'd better take the ball away from there and talk afterwards."

When he was about to be tackled at the 25, he lateraled to Jim Mitchener, who took it to the 10. Thodas recalled, "Woody picked it up and started running and lateralled to Mitchener, and I'm right beside Mitchener and I'm telling him to lateral it to me, but he swallowed it at the 10-yard line.

"Then they just called an off-tackle play, and I went across. I met Karpuk on the goal line with the best straight-arm I ever made. Sportswriter Jim Coleman had me down as the best back of the day. I averaged seven and a half yards a carry and caught five for five. I had a good day."

"I've got a still picture of Thodas running that off-tackle play to the right," Mitchener recalled. "You never saw a play better executed in your whole life. Everybody was blocked.

There was eight feet of space that Thodas ran through. It was the most beautifully run play that I have ever seen."

The touchdown was the first Thodas had scored all season. Rod Pantages laughed at the memory. "In 1948 I had scored, Ced had scored, Jim Mitchner had scored and, you know, afterwards we always used to drink beer and have a good time. Pete said, 'Don't worry, when I score there'll be a half-day holiday.' The little fart scored the winning touchdown in the Grey Cup—and they had a half-day holiday in Calgary when we got back from down east. Unbelievable!"

Ottawa, however, wasn't done. With less than two minutes remaining, Paffrath drove his team deep into enemy territory. He dropped back and threw toward the end zone. Harry Hood leapt in front of the receiver and made the interception. That was it. The Calgary Stampeders had won their first Grey Cup, 12 to 7, and completed a perfect season to boot.

Fullback Paul Rowe, President Tom Brook and Playing Coach Les Lear.
COURTESY DARYL SLADE

After the game, CRU secretary Percy Robinson presented the Grey Cup to Tom Brook. Two hours later, players from both teams took part in a national radio broadcast from the Toronto Men's Press Club, welcomed there by Mayor McCallum. Paul Rowe hurt a knee early in the game and could barely walk, but the smile on his face belied the pain. A reporter noted that "Fritzie Hanson, who announced that this is 'definitely his last football season,' didn't look a day older than the slim galloping ghost who brought the West its first Grey Cup with Winnipeg in 1935."

While the players were doing their duty at the Press Club, the fans were whooping it up in downtown Toronto. In the custom of the day, when the gun sounded to end the game, fans poured onto the field and tore the goal posts down. They set them up in the lobby of the Royal York around which they had

a rousing western hoedown. In the entrepreneurial spirit of the west, one individual sawed slices off the goal posts and sold them for a buck a piece.

The next day, the Stampede Special pulled out of Union Station at 1:45 PM.

The man who would win three more Grey Cups in six tries, setting several records on his way to the Hall of Fame, saw little action that day in 1948. Alberta's future Lieutenant-Governor Normie Kwong was a wide-eyed rookie that year. The Calgary native played junior football with the North Hill Blizzard.

"I knew I wasn't going to start, but it was still an exciting time to be there. You hoped against all odds that you would play a lot. Of course, there were other veterans ahead of me at the time. I went in for about four plays. That was just because Les Lear made sure everybody got into the game so they could say they played in the Grey Cup. The

The 1948 Grey Cup champion Calgary Stampeders celebrate in their dressing room after defeating the Ottawa Rough Riders. COURTESY CANADIAN PRESS, *GLOBE & MAIL* PHOTO

following year, though, I started the game and played most of it."

Kwong was proud to be part of the first Grey Cup festival. "Yes, I was part of the original start-up of Grey Cup week. We went down to Toronto ahead of the fans, of course, but we came back with them on the train.

"It was really a spontaneous time. Everything happened because someone thought of it at the time. Nothing was planned. On the way back, people met us at every little whistle stop along the way, and the coach made sure that one or two players were always there to greet the people no matter what time of night. There were people there right across Canada."

"For winning," Pantages said, "we got a belt like those bronc riders used to get. We never got any money, just a lot of fun."

Mitchener concurred that the Grey Cup wasn't about money. "How lucky can you get? Not many people get to be in a Grey Cup. My one year there was a history-making year for Calgary. It was great fun."

The *Calgary Herald* reported that local radio repair shops were busier during Grey Cup week than they had been in years. Radios

Normie Kwong, the China Clipper, in Edmonton Eskimo livery. Traded by Calgary, Kwong was named the Schenley Most Outstanding Canadian in 1955 and 1956 and Canadian Athlete of the Year in 1955. He was inducted into the Canadian Football Hall of Fame in 1969, Canada's Sports Hall of Fame in 1975, the Edmonton Eskimos' Wall of Honour in 1983 and the Alberta Sports Hall of Fame in 1987.
COURTESY CANADIAN FOOTBALL HALL OF FAME

were installed in offices and stores all over the city so workers and customers could follow the action. Patients at Colonel Belcher hospital all had earphones and radios. Meanwhile, the police court session was one of the shortest in memory as officials rushed through in order to get home and listen to the game.

Alderman P.N.R. Morrison, acting mayor, proclaimed Wednesday, December 1, a civic holiday "in order that all Calgarians may turn out to welcome home the victorious Stampeders team."

The Victory Special pulled into the CPR station at noon, December 1. Before arriving, wives and girlfriends of the Stampeders were given corsages and boarded the train at Shepard, along with the hero of the 36th Grey Cup, Norm Hill. Greeting the conquering

Souvenir literature celebrating the Stamperders' first Grey Cup.
COURTESY DARYL SLADE

A tickertape parade
along Calgary's
8th Avenue greeted the
Grey Cup champions.
COURTESY GLENBOW MUSEUM

heroes were Mayor J.C. Watson, the Calgary Tank Regiment Band and cheerleaders from the city's high schools.

The players were escorted through the station between lines of Boy Scouts to convertibles. The Grey Cup was carried in a jeep specially fitted with a saddle. The procession went up Centre Street to 8th Avenue and wended its way through 4th Street and 7th Avenue before stopping at a platform on the east side of the Palliser Hotel on Centre Street. There the Mayor congratulated the team, and Mewata Stadium PA announcer Danny Spittal introduced all members of the organization. Tom Brook, Les Lear and Paul Rowe responded, much to the delight of the over 30,000 in attendance in a city with a population of 104,000. Among them was a little boy named Murray Gibbs accompanied by his mother. Sixty years later, he was in the crowd welcoming the Stampeders back from Montreal after winning their sixth Grey Cup.

In 1949 the Eskimos returned to the WIFU, and the schedule was expanded to 14 games.

Nineteen members of the Grey Cup champions did not return, including Chuck Anderson, Steaky Adams, Chick Chickowsky, Fritzie Hanson, Ced Gyles, Jim Mitchener,

Calgarians thronged Calgary's downtown to welcome home the Grey Cup champions.
COURTESY GLENBOW MUSEUM

Harry Irving, Rube Ludwig, Dave Tomlinson, Bill Wusyk and Fred Wilmot. Sixteen newcomers joined the team, among them Barney Bjarnason, Vern Graham, Mel Wilson, old Winnipeg star Riley Matheson and Sugarfoot Anderson, who was beginning his 61-plus years career with the club. Ezzertt Anderson, Jr., son of a slave, explained how he became a Stampeder: "Woody Strode and Les Lear came down and got me. They were looking for another end. I had been in the Pacific Coast League with the Los Angeles Dons. I played against Johnny Unitas, Y.A. Tittle and Otto Graham. I had retired after playing 10 years." (The Dons were owned by Bing Crosby, Bob Hope, Louis B. Mayer, Pat O'Brien and Don Ameche, after whom the team was named. Rubbing shoulders with showbiz types got

Anderson bit parts in 32 movies, including *Samson and Delilah* and *The Snows of Kilimanjaro*, starring Gregory Peck, Susan Hayward and Eva Gardener.)

"I played end on both sides of the ball," he continued. "I'm the first guy who made All-Pro both ways. When we started the game, Les Lear would kiss us goodbye and say, 'I'll see you at the end of the game if they don't take you out on crutches.' Lear was one of those top-notch coaches. I call him Canada's Vince Lombardi, a no-nonsense guy."

Led by Keith Spaith, Woody Strode, Sugarfoot Anderson and Normie Kwong, the Stampeders picked up where they left off, winning 10 straight. Through September they outscored Edmonton 61–11 and Winnipeg 52–8. The Roughriders were a horse of a

Sugarfoot Anderson with Shirley Temple and Barry Fitzgerald during the filming of The Story of Seabiscuit.
COURTESY DARYL SLADE

Ezzertt "Sugarfoot" Anderson was inducted into the Canadian Sports Wall of Fame in 1974 and the Calgary Stampeders' Wall of Fame in 1990. In 2010 he was the recipient of Alberta Sports Hall of Fame Pioneer Award. COURTESY CALGARY STAMPEDERS

different colour, succumbing 22–19 and 13–1.

October was a lot tougher. On the first day of the month, they had to come from behind on a Keith-Spaith-to-Harry-Hood touch-down to beat the Eskimos 12–8. A week later, they won in Regina 10–3 before barely getting by the lowly Blue Bombers 3–0 in Winnipeg on Thanksgiving. Back home they returned to form, trouncing Edmonton 31–6. The win-ning streak now stood at 22 games.

The Stampeders then hosted Saskatchewan October 22 in a snowstorm. The Riders out-played them from start to finish with ex-Stam-peder Del Wardien kicking a field goal to win 9–6. It could have been worse. Twice Calgary held the visitors on the 1-yard line. Including postseason play, the Stampeders had gone 25 games without a loss. They would win the rest

of their 1949 regular season games, finishing the two years with a remarkable record of 25–1. The record of 22 straight victories still stands.

Dave Berry downplayed the winning streak. "There was the normal pressure to win. The coach didn't lay it on the line and say you've got to win this one because this is the twenty-seventh game. He said go out and win. We went 25 games before we lost and didn't lose again until the Grey Cup. We lost two games in two years. Regina beat us, then we whipped them in the finals."

Thodas agreed that Coach Lear down-played the streak: "Oh, yeah, Les always used to comment, 'Forget about the last game, you won it, this is a new season starting, this is a new game,'" Thodas recalled. "We kind of conditioned our minds that way—forget we won five or six games. This is the game to concentrate on. That's what we did. If it wasn't for that one tie in the two-game total-point series in the playoffs, we'd have won every game that year.

"Going into the '49 season, the papers started to play it up. Just as soon as we lost one game-we'd lost one game in 25–-we got panned to hell. I thought, *What's this all about? You lose one game in 25 and get panned?* But that's the way they were. What are you going to do? You've got a team that's Grey Cup champions and gone on a winning streak and I guess when you lose the big one they start panning you."

Did keeping the streak alive weigh on the players' minds? "No, not at all," insisted Norm Hill. "You get to the point where you don't expect to lose. You get that spirit on a team. We never thought about losing. You were expected to win and you did."

Pantages had mixed feelings about the 9–6 loss. "It was kind of hard to take. You think, gee, us guys just can't be beat. But it happens. Eventually, you realize you're lucky to be on a team that wins."

On to the playoffs, a two-game total-point affair with the Roughriders opening in Regina November 5.

Before the 8,000-plus capacity crowd could settle into its collective seat, Keith Spaith, scrimmaging at his 37, completed an 18-yard pass to Pantages, who took it all the way to the end zone. After Harry Hood conceded a single, Spaith threw 34 yards to Sugarfoot Anderson, who brought the ball to the 3. Pantages carried it in, giving his team a 10–1 lead after 15 minutes of play. The score at the half was 12–5.

The teams exchanged touchdowns and singles in the second half. Only one convert was good. The final score was 18–12 for the visitors.

For Rod Pantages, the man of the hour, it wasn't a memorable occasion. "I got knocked out in that playoff game. I scored two touchdowns, but I couldn't remember doing it. And I kept asking Thodas, 'Who won today?' He said, 'For cripes sake, we won!' I was running back a punt, and Toar Springstein was going to tackle me. (When you're young you think you can do anything.) I ran right over that son-of-a-bitch—and woke up in the dressing room."

Although happy with the win, Lear was not pleased with the men in stripes. "That is the worst officiating I have ever seen," he complained. "They stole everything but our sweaters out there, and it's a wonder they didn't try to take those, too." His disposition didn't improve when he learned the same crew would handle game two.

Hostilities were resumed in Calgary on Remembrance Day before over 14,500 fans, the biggest crowd in Western football history. The outcome would be decided by who could kick and who couldn't.

Late in the opening quarter, Calgary kicker Vern Graham bounced a field-goal attempt off the crossbar into the end zone.

They closed out their scoring with a rouge in the second quarter. Saskatchewan countered with a 33-yard Buck Rogers field goal in the third quarter and a Doug-Beldon-to-Johnny-Bell touchdown pass in the final frame, but Pat Santucci missed the convert. The Riders led the game 8–4; the Stamps, the round, 22–20. That's when the fun began.

After two and out for the Stampeders, the Riders went to work from deep in their own end. Beldon completed a pass to Matt Anthony, who, breaking for the end zone, was brought down by Pantages at the 37. Beldon to Bell at the 16. Then Paul Rowe nailed Bob Early on an end sweep, and Lear sacked the quarterback. The visitors lined up to kick themselves into the Grey Cup, but the 25-yard Buck Rogers attempt from in front of the goal posts was wide. But wait. Calgary was offside! Del Wardien (cut by Lear the year before) was sent in to do the deed five yards closer. He missed, too. Pete Thodas conceded a harmless single. Calgary lost the battle 9–4, but won the war 21–22.

The Calgary culprit who was offside? Les Lear!

On to Toronto to defend the Cup.

The Stampeders returned to Appleby College to prepare for Montreal, which had finished in second place, six points behind Ottawa. They won the two-game round 36–20. The Alouettes had been founded in 1946 by Argo legend Lew Hayman, Eric Craddock, Leo Dandurand and Joe Ryan. Hayman had four Grey Cup wins on his coaching resume, tying him with Queen's University's Billy Hughes.

His team included future Hall of Famers Eagle Keys, Ches McCance, Virgil Wagner, Herb Trawick and Bruce Coulter. Hayman picked up Stampeder Chuck Anderson and Hamilton quarterback Frank Filchock, who signed a two-year deal worth $20,000 and an off-season job.

After graduating from Indiana in 1938, Filchock was drafted by Pittsburgh but sold to Washington. On October 15, 1939, Filchock threw the first 99-yard touchdown pass in NFL history in a game against Pittsburgh. In 1939 and '44, he led the NFL in touchdown throws.

After the war, New York Giants' coach Steve Owen got the team to trade for Filchock, who was signed to the first multi-year contract in team history at $35,000 over three years. He led the Giants to the league title game against Chicago on December 15, 1946. He was then caught up in a web of misfortune that changed his life forever.

The day before the game, news outlets broke the story that gamblers had tried to fix the game. Implicated were Filchock and halfback Merle Hapes. Sunday morning the district attorney announced the two had been offered $2,500 each plus the winnings from a $1,000 bet to ensure Chicago won by more than 10 points. Filchock denied being approached. Hapes admitted it. He was suspended, but Filchock played, losing 24–14. The next day, Alvin J. Paris was charged with attempting to bribe the two Giants and was convicted January 8, 1947. NFL Commissioner Bert Bell suspended both players even though the judge determined that "Frank Filchock was not an accomplice, and was, in fact, an unfortunate victim of circumstances." He was suspended indefinitely for not reporting the bribe offer to the NFL. The All-American Conference was not affected, but a new league looking for fans didn't want a player with a shady reputation. Filchock signed with the Hamilton Tigers.

Because he had increased the gate in the other three cities during the 1947 season, the Tigers asked their league partners to share his contract. When they refused, the Tigers withdrew from the Big Four. They switched places with the ORFU Hamilton Wildcats.

In 1950, the teams amalgamated as the Hamilton Tiger-Cats.

Although Filchock was a playing coach and had an undefeated season, he signed with Montreal when the Tigers couldn't afford to pay him.

The opposing quarterback in the 1949 Grey Cup, of course, was Keith Spaith, the WIFU MVP two years running. The California native went to Southern Cal. He was drafted by the L.A. Rams but failed to make the team and played for the Hawaiian Warriors of the Pacific Coast League. In 1947 the team was suspended for betting on themselves to win by a certain number of points. They won the game in question but not by enough points to cash in their bet.

Rumours spread through Calgary about the new addition at quarterback. On July 15, 1948, Tom Brook acknowledged that Spaith was one of the Warriors suspended indefinitely from professional football in the U.S.

Brook said, "I find nothing morally wrong with a player who bets on himself and who is always giving his utmost for his club to win. Therefore, myself as well as the players committee not only did not object to Spaith playing for Calgary but unanimously felt that his personal misfortune due to a mistake, which we all make some time or other, could be turned into Calgary's great fortune in being able to obtain the services of a player who so far has justified by his personal conduct, as well as his playing ability, every confidence that we had in him."

Spaith certainly earned his keep as a Calgary Stampeder. In the 1948 Grey Cup, he was on the field all 60 minutes as quarterback and punter, and he made an interception on defence. After the 1954 season, he retired to the construction business in California, where he died at age 52 in 1976. He was inducted onto the Stampeder Wall of Fame on June 28, 2002.

Lear's preparation included having his team run through Alouette plays. Although every club now uses a scout team to prepare for an opponent, Lear originated the practice, once again being light years ahead of his time.

After several days of rigorous workouts, Sugarfoot Anderson proclaimed, "We'll prove we're mighty men!"

Lear declared, "The boys are perfect, both physically and mentally. All that can be done, has been done."

What about the field? "Well," he replied, "I would like a dry field, of course, but even on a snow-covered field, it will be a passer's battle if the footing is good for the receivers."

It wasn't. The grounds crew at Varsity Stadium scraped the snow and ice off the field Friday morning, but the CRU stubbornly refused requests to provide a tarpaulin until they were shamed into it by the infamous Mud Bowl of 1950.

It was snowing and –8°C at 2:00 PM November 26 when Toronto Mayor Hiram McCallum and Calgary Mayor Don MacKay handled the ceremonial kickoff, Mackay holding and McCallum booting the ball into the end zone. The field was charitably described as muddy. Over 21,000 looked on.

It appeared the gridiron gods were favouring Calgary when, on the opening Keith Spaith kickoff, Virgil Wagner bobbled the ball at his 40-yard line and Woody Strode recovered. Paul Rowe got the ball to the Montreal 18. A penalty and an incomplete pass snuffed out the drive. After the teams exchanged punts, the Alouettes got rolling. Starting at his 25, Filchock tossed a 40-yarder to Bob Cunningham and then hit Ralph Toohy for 22. Two plays later, Wagner ran in for the touchdown, converted by Ches McCance.

A few minutes later, Norm Hill fumbled a punt that was recovered by Herb Trawick at his 46. After a penalty, Montreal started at

the 31. Three plays later, Cunningham took it in. The convert was nullified by an offside.

At the end of the first quarter the score stood Montreal 11, Calgary 0.

After picking up a single on a missed field goal, the Stamps forced the Als to punt. Fielding at his 40, Thodas ran 18 yards to the 52. It was Spaith to Strode for five yards and then Hood, Thodas and Pantages took it the rest of the way with Hood doing the honours from two yards out. The convert was good. Montreal 11, Calgary 7.

Just when it seemed Mr. Momentum had signed with the Stampeders, disaster struck. It was two and out for the Als. Spaith dropped back to pass on his 38-yard line, when Herb Trawick beat his block and knocked the ball from his hand. Trawick recovered the ball, cast Norm Hill aside and ran for the touchdown. The convert was good. At halftime, the easterners led 17–7.

In the third quarter, a long drive was snuffed out when Filchock intercepted Spaith at the Lark 25. Keith English and Filchock took off up the field, lateralling the ball back and forth until Filchock dropped it at the Calgary 28. Spaith was sacked for a 10-yard loss, and Pantages quick-kicked. Filchock threw a pass from the 55 to Wagner at the 20. Rod Pantages intercepted but was called for interference. Three plays later, Wagner scored. After three quarters, Montreal led 23–7.

The Als picked up a field goal, a rouge and a single in the final 15 minutes. Calgary tallied a safety touch and a Sugarfoot Anderson touchdown when he picked up a Filchock fumble and took it in. Final score: Montreal 28, Calgary 15.

Sugarfoot recalled his moment of Grey Cup glory. "There was a fumble on a pitch-out coming my way. I knew this guy wanted to take me inside so I just backed out and let him go inside and stepped around him. I read

Sugarfoot Anderson with Rod Pantages and Keith Spaith. COURTESY CALGARY STAMPEDERS

the quarterback's eyes, what he was looking at. He pitched out, and the guy fumbled it. I just picked it up and ran 40-some yards for the touchdown."

The playing field, according to Dave Berry "was a mess. It was muddy, it was really bad—slippin' and slidin' and goodness knows what.

"We were on their 10-yard line, and Harry Hood ran it right down to the 2. Riley Matheson had gone down and blocked a guy about eight yards down the field, and it was so bad they slid another five yards, and the referee called him for blocking over 10 yards," he lamented. "Even in the pictures it shows that he was only about eight yards down the field when he hit

the guy. The referee called it and that was the end of that.

"Starting the second half, they kicked to us. It was a short kick, and Normie Hill went for the ball. One of their players tripped him and another fell on the ball. That's interference. You can't do that. But the referee let it go.

"We argued like hell, so we got a 15-yard unsportsmanlike conduct tacked on us. That was the winning touchdown, by the way. If you look it up, you'll find the same guy made both calls and never umpired again. I'm not saying for one second that we should have won that game. I'm just saying the referee shouldn't have won it. You can't take anything away from them as a team. Virgil Wagner was a great player. So was Herb Trawick."

After the game, Lear had to be restrained from going after line judge Jimmy Simpson.

"The field was nothing but ice, and that affected us," recalled Sugarfoot Anderson. "You could only block 10 yards in those days. Harry Hood took the ball across the goal line, but a guy slid into that no blocking zone. Herb Trawick pulled John Aguirre into that zone. I told the referee what was happening, but nothing was done.

"When you cross the goal line and it's called back and you try again, nine times out of ten you don't make it. Something happens. That's what beat us in that game. We played on ice."

Montreal's Frank Filchock put on one of the greatest performances in Grey Cup history, completing 12 of 20 passes for 210 yards and making three interceptions, two of which ended Calgary scoring drives.

Herb Trawick also impressed. The first African-American to play pro football in Canada, the 5´ 10˝ 230-pound lineman spent his entire 12-year career with the Alouettes after coming north from Kentucky State University and the U.S. Army in 1946. An all-star seven times, He was inducted into the CFL Hall of Fame in 1975. He died in Montreal 10 years later at age 64.

Sugarfoot described the train trip back to Calgary. "We had a bar car and a dance car. On our way back we stopped in Medicine Hat, and some fans let all the horses and cows out. We were delayed three or four hours while they rounded them up and got them back on the train.

"We had a great time. I'll never forget it. There were thousands of people at the station when we got back to Calgary. You'd think we had won the game. It really shook me up. They closed the schools and the town down."

What kind of bonus did he get for playing in the Grey Cup? "Huh?" he snorted. "I'll tell you what kind of bonus we got. Do you remember those old Hudson Bay coats? His and hers? The ones with the red, black and yellow stripes? That's what we got. And we got a little bitty old ring from People's Credit Jewellers. Wasn't nothing to write home and tell nobody about. I think it had a 15 points diamond on it."

After the game, Les Lear said, "We'll be back next season with the greatest team ever to come East."

That promise would not be fulfilled for 19 long years.

CHAPTER 4

All Hat, No Cattle

The Decade of the Damned
1950–59

Wʜᴇɴ ᴛʜᴇ 1950s ᴅᴀᴡɴᴇᴅ, Cᴀʟɢᴀʀɪᴀɴs ʜᴀᴅ ᴇᴠᴇʀʏ ʀɪɢʜᴛ ᴛᴏ ʙᴇʟɪᴇᴠᴇ the gridiron good times would continue to roll. Most of the stars of the 1949 team were back, the notable exceptions being Rod Pantages and Pete Thodas. Recalled Pantages, "After the '49 season, Pete and I said, 'We're tired of playing for peanuts' and signed with Montreal." But new members of the squad included Royal Copeland, considered the best halfback in the country, who abandoned the good ship Argonaut for Calgary and led the team in rushing and scoring. The great Blue Bomber lineman Riley Matheson anchored the defence and served as an assistant coach. Future Wall of Famer guard Harry Langford joined the club as well.

"I was born in Winnipeg. Les Lear recruited me," Langford recalled. "Although I had a year of junior eligibility left, Les invited me to the training camp in 1949. I signed a contract and went back to play another year of junior. Because I had signed a CRU card, I was eligible for the playoffs with the Roughies and the Grey Cup. Les brought me back, but I didn't get to play. I was under contract in '49 and a member of the team."

For all their talent, the 1950s quickly turned into the decade of the damned for the Stampeders. They made the playoffs only twice despite fielding line-ups that included some of the greatest to ever play the game. They had a winning percentage of .346.

The worst decisions of that disastrous decade were trading Normie Kwong to Edmonton in 1951 for Reg Clarkson (who didn't last a season) and Johnny Bright three years later. The China Clipper played 10

55

seasons in Eskimo livery; Bright, 11. Together they gained 18,735 yards, scored 146 touchdowns and won three Grey Cups for the Green and Gold.

Harry Langford.
COURTESY DARYL SLADE

Royal Copeland.
COURTESY CANADIAN FOOTBALL
HALL OF FAME

The tone for the decade was set immediately when—despite the presence of Copeland, Kwong and Spaith—the Stampeders lost 25–12 in Regina August 26 and 7–4 to Winnipeg two days later, followed by consecutive defeats at the hands of the upstart Eskimos. After dropping another one to the Riders, Paul Rowe came out of retirement, inspiring his mates to their first win of the season, 13–6 over Winnipeg. Inspiration soon gave away to desperation as the club lost five of their last eight and missed the playoffs.

The running game was ineffective, and the defence was terrible, giving up 253 points compared to 77 the year before.

Norm Hill blamed the decline on Lear's assistant Riley Matheson. "In 1950 Matheson became the assistant coach and changed Lear's thinking," Hill insisted. "He sat the Grey Cup team on the bench. He put in all these new guys, like Earl Audet at tackle, and changed everything around. We lost our first five games before he put us back on the field. By then, it was too late. Matheson was a tough hombre, but Lear should never have taken his advice. Lear made some mistakes, like sending Kwong to Edmonton."

Riley "Rattler" Matheson was the only Stampeder to make the 1950 all-star team.

When rumours circulated that Matheson had failed to give his best, he left Calgary in disgust.

Although Kwong was gone, the additions of centre Bill Blackburn, ends Bob Shaw, Paul Salata and Ed Champagne from the NFL gave the faithful hope for 1951.

Also signing on was Canadian running back Davey West. West grew up in the east end of Toronto, where he was coached in high school by Hec Crighton. After wartime service in the RCAF, West bounced round Canadian football, playing for eight teams in all. Though a fan favourite, management

Davey West. COURTESY DARYL SLADE

considered him a pain in the butt because he was vocal about being underpaid. West won four Grey Cups: Toronto, 1947; Edmonton, 1954–55; and Ottawa, 1960.

In 1951 West intended to suit up for Saskatchewan. He hired on to deliver a car from Oshawa to Vancouver. When he arrived in Regina, he couldn't get hold of anybody with the Roughriders because it was a holiday. He continued on his journey and, as he later wrote, "Now I am walking down the street in Calgary, and who do I bump into? None other than my idol Royal Copeland, who stops in his tracks and says, 'What the hell are you doing here, West?'"

Copeland took him to meet Les Lear. "Les asked me how much Regina was going to pay me, and after I told him, he said he'd double it. Presto, I became a Stampeder. The first time I touched the football in my first game against Saskatchewan, I took a kickoff for 95 yards against them." (It was actually 112 yards, September 13, 1952, a club record that still stands.) The 5' 8", 170-pound back led the Stamps in returns in 1951 and was third in rushing and receiving.

Despite his efforts and those of their seven imports, the Stamps lost eight of their first 10 games and finished dead last again with a record of 4–10. They took solace in defeating Edmonton 26–25 in the last game of the season, depriving their rivals of first place.

Fort Wayne, Indian, native Johnny Bright arrived in Calgary in 1952. At Drake University, he set 20 football, basketball and track records. The leading rusher in U.S. college football, he was the first draft choice of the 1951 Philadelphia Eagles. He played with the Harlem Globetrotters. He even pitched a no-hitter in the World Professional Fastball Tournament.

Bob Shaw.
COURTESY DARYL SLADE

Bright led the West in rushing four times. He won the Schenley in 1959 and was an all-star six times. Only Mike Pringle and George Reed ran farther, but Bright went both ways. His record of 171 yards rushing set in the 1956 Grey Cup still stands.

Johnny Bright in Edmonton Eskimo livery.
COURTESY CANADIAN FOOTBALL HALL OF FAME

After missing the playoffs two years in a row, the Stampeders opened the vault to sign Johnny Bright. When the Eagles wouldn't even come close to Calgary's offer, Bright came to Canada.

As a rookie, Bright led the division in rushing, while Shaw and Salata were the leaders in yardage and receptions. Prodigal son Pete Thodas and West gave the team a potent return game. At 7–9, Calgary finished third but upset the Eskimos at Mewata 31–12 in the first game of the semi-finals. It was a different story in Edmonton. Led by receiver Rollie Prather, the hometown team took the game 30–7, the round 42–38. Explaining the loss, Langford said,

"There was a lot going on under the surface with different personalities."

Bright, Blackburn and Shaw were all-stars.

Despite making the playoffs, Les Lear was fired after the 1952 campaign. Harry Langford wasn't surprised. "Henry Viney had an axe to grind with Les. Calgary was still a small town, and the media had a lot of influence. Losing the way we did after the success of '48–'49 was the main factor. If a coach is winning, he's great. If he's losing, he's got to be gone. It's tough to get rid of all the players."

Lear was replaced by Bob Snyder, not the sharpest knife in the coaching drawer. Pete Thodas remembered him well. "We were playing Edmonton, and they were using the Split-T. He tried every type of defence he could but nothing worked. Apparently he was on a first-name basis with Frank Leahy of Notre Dame. He kept phoning Frank, who

would tell him to do this or do that. Finally, he phoned Frank and said, 'Nothing's worked. What should I do?' He said, 'The only thing I can tell you is use the Split-T against them and see how they defend it.'"

Calgarians were full of optimism going into 1953 because of the signings of San Francisco 49er quarterback Frankie Albert and Arizona State running back John Henry Johnson. Twice an All-American at Stanford, Albert was named 1948's Pro Football Player of the Year by Sport Magazine. With Calgary, he finished fourth in percentage completions, second in yardage. Disappointed with his performance, he offered to return part of his salary. He returned to 'Frisco as a coach. Langford thought Albert played well. "I don't think Snyder knew what to do with him."

John Henry Johnson fared much better, leading the team in rushing, returns and interceptions. He won the Jeff Nicklin Memorial Trophy. Discouraged by his team's 3–12–1 record, Johnson left for the NFL to embark on a career that led him to the U.S. Pro Football Hall of Fame. The late Eric Bishop, legendary sportswriter and broadcaster, thought Johnson was the greatest running back in Stampeder history. "He probably was," allowed Langford, "when he wanted to be."

Despite having Bright and Johnson in the backfield, Snyder lived and died with the pass, even though he cut Bob Shaw. He suspended Davey West. It was no surprise he was fired at the end of the season. He was replaced by Larry Seimerling, formerly of the Washington Redskins. He did an incredible recruiting job, signing NFLers Gene Brito, Eddies LeBaron, Macon and Henke and Tom Minor, as well as collegiate stars Rupe Andrews and Howard Waugh. Lynn Bottoms joined the backfield from Calgary junior ranks. With Macon and Waugh on board, Johnny Bright was traded to Edmonton.

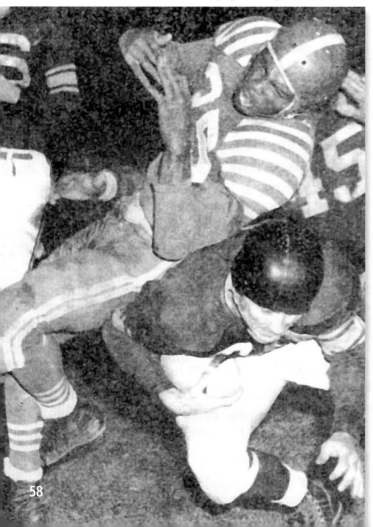

John Henry Johnson in action. COURTESY DARYL SLADE

"When I first went there in 1952," he recalled, "I was Calgary's golden boy, and I could do no wrong. But I went through a series of unfortunate and uncontrollable situations such as receiving a ruptured appendix during a game for which I had to have an emergency operation.

"During the off-season I used to dive quite a bit competitively, and I hit the water at the edge of the pool wrong and I dislocated the caps of my shoulder. I had to play with a chain on my shoulder and consequently I damaged that shoulder quite severely during those 16 games of the CFL season. I had to have an operation.

"Sportswriters claimed those were football injuries. Suddenly I—who had played sandlot, junior high, high school and college and had never been injured except for that Oklahoma situation—became, in their words, injury prone."

At Drake University, Bright was the victim of one of the ugliest racial incidents in the history of American sports. The first black to play in a football game against Oklahoma, the Sooners expressed their resentment by deliberately smashing his jaw. Because no Oklahoma hospital would admit a black man, he had to endure an all-night train ride back to Des Moines, Iowa, before he could receive treatment.

In 1954 the football world was saddened to learn of the death of Harry Hood.

"Harry Hood was 31 when he died," said Dave Berry. "He was an excellent ballplayer. If he had lived, he would have made the Hall of Fame, no doubt about it."

"He had cancer," recalled Thodas. "Very strange. Harry Hood was a nice guy, but he palled around with Keith [Spaith]. They had their own little group. Other than practice and games, we never saw him socially.

"I'm talking now about Pantages and I. Anyhow, he came out to Vancouver, and he was staying at the Georgia Hotel. He phoned us up and asked us to come on down. We said fine. So we went down.

"We wondered why we weren't going out for dinner or a drink, but we just sat in his room. He started talking about the past, the Grey Cups in '48 and '49. Then he started talking about his father, who passed away from stomach cancer. I said, 'Oh, gee, that's too bad.'

"That's all the conversation there was. The next thing I know, he's back in Calgary, and he's in the hospital and he's got cancer of the stomach.

Harry Hood. His No. 5 was the first number the Stampeders retired. COURTESY DARYL SLADE

"I phoned Rod and said, 'Isn't that amazing? I guess he came out here knowing he's going to pass away, knowing he can't beat it, and he's going around saying goodbye to everybody.

"Ten years later, Rod and I are out of town, and Les Lear phones. He's in town and phones Mamie Pantages and my wife, Marjorie, asking for us. He says, 'Well, tell them I came to say hello. I'll be back in a couple of weeks, and I'll get in touch with them.' He never did call back, and he died, too, about two months later."

The 1954 Stampeders would be led by Eddie LeBaron. A graduate of the College of the Pacific, where he had been coached by Seimerling, Lt. LeBaron was awarded the Purple Heart and Bronze Star for bravery in the Korean War, after which the 5'7" pivot was drafted in the tenth round by Washington. A versatile athlete, he also punted and played safety. After his year in Calgary, he returned to the Redskins through 1959. He was the first quarterback of the expansion Dallas Cowboys. He was a lawyer, sportscaster for CBS and the general manager of the Atlanta Falcons.

Despite LeBaron's talents and Howard Waugh becoming the first player in CFL history to rush for over 1,000 yards, the Stampeders missed postseason play again, although at 8–8 they had their best record since 1949, finishing two points out of third.

That year the B.C. Lions joined the WIFU, coached by Annis Stukus, who had revived the Eskimos in 1949. They recorded their first win at the expense of the Stampeders on September 18.

B.C.'s slogan was "The Lions will roar in '54!"

"We roared," grimaced Stukus, "mostly in pain. We won one game but broke every attendance record in the CFL. We beat

Eddie LeBaron. COURTESY DARYL SLADE

Calgary 9–4, a one-sided win, and as a result, they missed the playoffs. They've been mad at us ever since."

Calgarians were mystified at the Stampeders' inability to win even though they were one of the finest collections of talent ever assembled. So was Norm Hill. "That was a marvellous team," he recalled," but we didn't get anywhere. I don't know what the hell happened. Seimerling was a good coach. Probably the best football player I ever played with, along with Dick Huffman, was Gene Brito at defensive end."

Said Harry Langford, "We had some very frustrating years, in particular 1954 when we had such a powerhouse. But there was a lot

Howard Waugh, the CFL's first 1,000-yard man, in action. COURTESY DARYL SLADE

Hall of Famer Dick Huffman.
COURTESY CANADIAN FOOTBALL HALL OF FAME

of infighting going on between different guys. The California guys didn't get along with the Oklahoma guys, and the Oklahoma guys didn't like the Texans. We had everything but cooperation between everybody. You don't score 109 points in three games and then lose to an expansion team."

Considering how talented Edmonton, Saskatchewan and Winnipeg were that year, missing the playoffs was no disgrace. "Well, it was, really," Langford replied, "when you lose to the Lions who hadn't won a game all year. They knocked us out. That was a little devastating to your pride."

The newcomers played well, with Macon, Brito, Henke and Waugh making the all-star team. Bottoms was the Rookie of the Year. But the supporting homebrew cast was suspect. Said local product Harvey Wylie, "A lot of big-name Americans came to Calgary, but they couldn't repeat the success of '48 and '49 because they didn't have as good a Canadian group as those teams did. They went for big names and forgot about the support staff, so they weren't worth a damn. In '56 and '57, that began to change."

Seimerling was fired, and all the NFLers moved on except Henke and Minor. Spaith and Sugarfoot retired. Seimerling was replaced by Jack Hennemeier. But 1955 was a disaster for the Stampeders when they finished 4–12 in fifth place behind second-year B.C. Langford won his first of four All-star team selections. Unnoticed was the arrival of a youngster from Quebec named Tony Pajaczkowski, whose career in Calgary would lead him to the CFL Hall of Fame.

"I played for the Verdun Shamcats, a junior team," Pajaczkowski explained from his home in Naples, Florida. "Bob Robinette was Calgary's general manager. He came to Montreal and said he was interested in me coming out to training camp. So I went out and ended up being there for 11 years. I was 18 when I signed with the Stampeders, and I turned 19 a week or two before training camp."

Why Calgary and not Montreal? "A fellow from Montreal who had played for Calgary said there wasn't enough Canadian talent in western Canada, whereas there was a lot of competition for jobs in Montreal," Pajaczkowski recalled. "I was lucky to get in the right place at the right time."

Was he a starter from day one? "Are you kidding me? God, no! I went to Calgary in 1955. I weighed about 205 pounds. Why did they keep me at 205 pounds? I don't know. I guess they saw some potential. My second year, they tried making me a starter on the offensive line, but I kept screwing up the plays—especially the play where we had two guards pulling one side or the other. I think Harry Langford and I ran into each other a couple of times. It was my fault every time. In one game, I pulled on a toss, the coach said, 'Everyone knows you don't pull on a toss' and took me out of the starting line-up."

But the Stamps stuck with the youngster, one of the few good decisions they made.

In 1956 the league increased the value of a touchdown to six points, the number of imports to twelve. The Stampeders changed their name from Calgary Football Club to Stampeder Football Club. A process was established to elect a Board of Directors. The first president was Red Dutton. The General manager was Bob Masterson.

Eight games into the season, with a record of 2–6, Hennemeier was fired. Assistant Tommy Thompson was on the sideline for

Tony Pajaczkowski.
COURTESY CANADIAN FOOTBALL HALL OF FAME

Game Nine, a 52–0 loss to the Eskimos. Otis Douglas took over, finishing at 2–5.

Recruiting coups that year were end Jack Gotta, defensive back Harvey Wylie and fullback Earl Lunsford. The Oklahoma State graduate explained how he landed in Calgary. "I went to school on ROTC, studied geology. I had to go into the service for two years, but Calgary said the season would be over by the time I had to go. So I signed that first year and played. After I got out of the service, the only job offer I had as a geologist was in Venezuela, and I didn't want to go there. I was going to sign with Philadelphia in 1959, but Jim Finks, who was the GM in Calgary, told me I couldn't sign with the Eagles because 'We have the option on your contract.' Then he offered me more money, and so I went back to Calgary.

"My first salary was $5,000. The second year [1959] it was $7,500. I played both ways. Every once in a while I got off the field."

A sign of things to come, Lunsford had a great year, setting the rookie rushing record with 1,283 yards and finishing second to Normie Kwong. "Yes I did," he allowed. "I

think that was the reason they wanted me back. I didn't think too much of the year. I was just an old geologist who couldn't get a job." He stayed in football the rest of his working life, with the exception of five years in the 1960s when he earned his PhD in education and the '90s when he taught in Texas.

A Calgary problem was their habit of running quarterbacks out of town. One of the few to last more than a season ('55–'56) was the remarkable Don Klosterman. The leading collegiate passer in 1951 playing for Loyola of Los Angeles, Klosterman was drafted by the Cleveland Browns behind Otto Graham. Traded to L.A. he found himself backing up Bob Waterfield and Norm Van Brocklin. All three are in the Hall of Fame. Wanting a chance to play, he signed with the Stampeders.

On St. Patrick's Day 1957, Klosterman hit a tree while trying to avoid a skier in his path at Banff and sustained a spinal cord injury. While in the hospital, he recounted years later, "The doctor came in to see me. I asked him when I would be leaving the hospital, and he said, 'You'd better ask your friends to buy you a wheelchair. You're not going to walk again.' I ordered him out of the room. Then I picked up a vase of flowers and threw it at him. Hit him in the back of the head with it, and I said to myself, 'At least I can still throw.'"

Persevering with his rehabilitation, Klosterman was walking a year later with the help of a cane. When the American Football League started up in 1960, Frank Leahy asked Klosterman to help him recruit players for the Los Angeles Chargers. He signed away some of the NFL's best talent. Later he was the GM of the Houston Oilers, Baltimore Colts (winning Super Bowl V) and L.A. Rams. He ran the Los Angeles Express of the USFL, hiring its first coach, a gentleman named Hugh Campbell. Klosterman died of a heart attack at age 70 in 2000.

The other quarterback on the roster was the bard of UCLA, Ronnie Knox, who came to town with his manager-father. Talented but eccentric, he made his mark for all the wrong reasons. Recalled Harvey Wylie, "He was a dandy, that one. In October it snowed, and we moved over to Buffalo Stadium to practice in the snow and had bonfires going. Ronnie refused to practice because it was too cold."

After being blackballed from the NFL the following year, he signed with Toronto but retired soon after. His parting words: "Football is a game for animals."

Harvey Wylie welcomed the coaching change. "Hennemeier was just too nice a guy, and we needed discipline. You have a losing ball club, a last place ball club, you need someone to run the show."

Don Klosterman. COURTESY DARYL SLADE

With Klosterman gone, quarterbacking duties were assumed by Jim Finks. The Tulsa graduate was a twelfth-round draft pick of the Pittsburgh Steelers in 1949 for whom he played quarterback and defensive back for six years. Finks quarterbacked the Stampeders until he got hurt. President Red Dutton made him Bob Masterson's assistant, and Nobby Wirkowski took over behind centre Chuck Zickefoose. Finks would soon move up.

The legendary Jim Finks.
COURTESY DARYL SLADE

The 1957 season began on a wave of optimism with the arrival of receivers Jack Gotta and Ernie Warlick. The Stampeders won their first four games, but only two thereafter, finishing third. Wirkowski and Gotta teamed up in the first game of the semi-final in Winnipeg and tied the Bombers 13–13. They lost five fumbles and game two in Calgary 15–3.

Earlier, on October 26, the Stamps had lost in Regina 32–6. Before their train pulled out of the station heading for their game two days later in Winnipeg, Masterton slugged Harvey Wylie, who told *Herald* sports editor Gorde Hunter, "I was putting my coat into my berth when Masterson came down the aisle. He shoved me, and I shoved him back. And then he said, 'Don't shove me,' and then hit me on the mouth." When Hunter asked if there was any reason for the attack, Wylie replied, "I guess he was mad at me for dropping that punt," a miscue that led to the first of three Bobby Marlow touchdowns.

The next day Hunter asked Masterson what happened. "I was walking down the aisle with a suitcase in each hand, and when I passed a group of players one of them gave me a hard elbow to the ribs," Masterson said. "Maybe it was horseplay, but I was in no mood for horseplay after the ball game. I dropped one bag and swung around instinctively and hammered out with a backhand and didn't even know it was Wylie."

Red Dutton flew to Winnipeg on the Monday morning to investigate the situation. He talked to Wylie and the players who were in the car. Two days later, the former Washington Redskin great and University of Toronto coach resigned because, he said, "Recent publicity has resulted in a highly embarrassing situation for myself, my family and the club. . . . It appears that any continued association with the club would not serve in its best interests or my own."

Years later Wylie said, "The point of the matter is the man was drunk. That's what started it. He was always drunk. Those railway cars aren't very wide, there's not much room to get past. He was just pushing his way down through there. He started to push me. He shoved me out of the way, and I shoved him back. He threw a punch. The next punch he threw, Lynn Bottoms grabbed

Hall of Fame inductee Don Luzzi in action.
COURTESY CANADIAN FOOTBALL HALL OF FAME

his arm, and the press came in the door just after the first punch. So that was the end of Mr. Masterson."

On Halloween, Finks became general manager. He would lay the groundwork for the great Calgary teams of the 1960s before going on to manage the Minnesota Vikings to the Super Bowl after hiring Bud Grant, rebuilding the Chicago Bears and leading New Orleans to their first winning season. He is enshrined in the NFL Hall of Fame.

Once again the Stampeders opened the season with four straight wins, but once again they only picked up two more victories, finishing fourth in 1958 with a mark of 6–9–1. The good news that year was the arrival of future Hall of Famer defensive lineman Don Luzzi, who not only made the All-Star team, but also won the Schenley Award for Most Outstanding Lineman. He had been recommended to the team by a former colleague of Jim Finks at Tulsa, Rogers Lehew, who was a guest coach at the 1958 training camp.

Departing was All-Star lineman Harry Langford. "I retired earlier than I wanted to," he said, "but they traded me to the Lions. I had just opened up a service station in Calgary, and I was making money pretty fast—a lot more than I was going to make playing ball— so I made a decision and said goodbye."

"I enjoyed every bit of my career," Langford went on. "I was one of the guys pretty dedicated to what I was trying to do. I think the highlight, the best team I played on, was '54. I had a pretty good run. Another highlight was been inducted onto the Wall of Fame. That was a great honour I was extremely pleased with. At the end of the 1958 season, my last professional game was the Shrine All-Star game, the last one they had. Bud Grant asked me to captain the West team. I was pretty honoured with that.

"I was proud to be a Stampeder. I was fortunate that in my whole career, high school, junior and pro, I only missed one game. I was the first guy to play 150 consecutive games."

The game he missed? "In 1950 Doug Brightwell from Edmonton gave me an elbow and knocked me silly, and I had a concussion."

In 1959 Finks invited Lehew to be his assistant. A dedicated family man, Lehew had survived an explosion at his New London School when he was eight. The explosion claimed the life of his sister, whom his dad and he dug out of the rubble and took to the funeral home.

In 1959 Lehew moved north. "I always tell people I invaded Canada," he joked. "When I came up here, it was my wife and I and three kids, my mom and dad and my niece. Eight of us came up here. My dad was ill, and I couldn't leave my mother there to take care of him. They were taking care of my sister's daughter. The boys were two years old, my daughter was in Grade One, my niece in Grade Two.

"Jim Finks was my coach at Tulsa. When he became the GM, I was scouting for him. He invited me up as a guest coach. We made a holiday out of it, getting our room and board. I became the assistant to Finks. My title was Minor Football Coordinator. It was my job to develop Canadian talent." Lehew transformed the Stampeders from having the worst homebrews in the league to fielding the best.

The preseason was marked by the ugliest incident in team history. After an exhibition game in Montreal, Doug Brown cut up rookie quarterback Joe Kapp with a broken beer bottle, coming within an inch of his jugular. It took the team doctor hours to remove the glass and sew him up.

"Doug was a basket case," said Wylie. "He ended up killing a priest in Montreal. He shot the priest when he answered the door."

"We had finished an exhibition game in Montreal," recalled Pajaczkowski, "and all the guys went out here and there. By the time I got back to the hotel, I saw this trail of blood on the floor and thought, *What the hell is this?*

"Doug used to stutter, and he got teased a lot about his stuttering," Pajaczkowski explained, "and I think he just lost it that night. Later he killed a priest. It all was linked to his stuttering."

Despite the play of Kapp, who led the league in passing, and the running of backs Gene Filipski and Earl Lunsford, who were Number 1 in the league, the team finished fourth at 8–8, two points behind the Lions. They were tied with B.C. going into the last game of the regular season on the coast but dropped a heartbreaker 10–8.

Ernie Warlick, Filipski and Wylie made all-star.

Despite a 10-year record of 54–100–2 and missing the playoffs eight times, with the likes of Tony Pajaczkowski, Don Luzzi, Harvey Wylie, Wayne Harris and Ron Allbright on hand, blue skies lay ahead.

CHAPTER 5

The Long and Winding Road

The Greatest of Them All
1960–71

THE DECADE OF THE '60S BEGAN ON A HIGH NOTE WHEN THE STAMPEDERS moved into McMahon Stadium, playing their first game against the Grey Cup Champion Winnipeg Blue Bombers on August 15. The move came none too soon. In an exhibition game against Edmonton at Mewata Stadium on July 20, 25 players had suffered lime burns. Called the "black hole" by visiting teams, Mewata on 10 Street SW had to be replaced. When no action was forthcoming, brothers Frank and George McMahon, at the urging of Red Dutton and Gorde Hunter, said, "We'll build our own."

Estimated to cost $700,000, the final figure was $1,050,000. The McMahons kicked in $300,000 in a debenture, the remainder raised through the University of Calgary. Following the retirement of the debenture issue in 1973 and a land exchange with the city in 1975, the stadium and land were owned outright by the University of Calgary and operated by the McMahon Stadium Society.

George McMahon told Dutton he wanted the stadium open for the first game August 15, 1960. "You're crazy!" said Dutton. They bet $1,500 on it. The 20,000-seat stadium was completed in just 103 days! Come the fifteenth, Dutton paid it off with 1,500 one-dollar bills. George McMahon performed the ceremonial kickoff that evening.

Even though the team didn't seem to be improving between 1955–59, players like Tony Pajaczkowski, Don Luzzie, Joe Kapp, Earl Lunsford, George Hansen, Harvey Wylie, Ron Allbright and Gene Filipski, plus Jim Finks and Rogers Lehew in the front office, gave the team hope for the future. Lovell Coleman and centre Dale Parsons signed on in 1960. The next 12 years would be filled with stunning success and heartbreaking failure.

After opening in Regina with a 15–15 tie and setting a record for penalties in the process, the Stamps christened McMahon Stadium by losing to the Bombers 38–23. Western Canada/Crescent Heights High School, Montana State grad Harvey Wylie remembered it well. "That first game was in a dust storm. It was wide open. They had been scraping the ground away for housing developments. We had a wind come up, and the fans could hardly see the field. It was pretty bad. But it got better and turned out to be a great stadium."

That home opener was followed by a 50–7 defeat in Winnipeg, after which coach Otis Douglas was fired.

"The guys liked Otie," recalled Pajacz-kowski," but he couldn't put a team together that was going to do very well. He lacked a bit as a coach."

Not according to Wylie. "Otis was a good, hard-working, knowledgeable coach and he started forming the basis of the team," he insisted. "We started to develop the Canadian base under Otis."

Otis was succeeded by the NFL Hall of Famer Steve Owen, who had coached the New York Giants from 1930–53, winning league titles in 1934 and '38. Under Stout Steve, the team went 6–6–1 and made the playoffs, but they were hammered by Edmonton 70–28 on the round. When Finks wouldn't commit to Owen for the following season, he signed with Saskatchewan.

Finks continued the Tulsa connection by hiring Bobby Dobbs to succeed Otis. Dobbs enrolled at Tulsa University in 1940, playing football and basketball for two years. In 1943 he went to West Point. After graduating in 1946, he was an assistant coach at Carswell Air Force Base and West Point. He then became head coach at Tulsa. Dobbs was a military man to the core. After playing for courtly gentlemen the previous years, several players walked out of training camp. All-star Clare Exelby demanded to be traded, and Joe Kapp, Ron Morris and Ernie Warlick refused to sign new contracts. Exelby and Morris ended up in Toronto, Warlick played out the season and went to Buffalo, and Joe Kapp was traded to the Lions for defensive end Ed O'Bradovich, quarterback Jim Walden, Bruce Claridge and the rights to Canadian Bill Crawford, who arrived in town two weeks later, a late cut from the NFL. Kapp's successor was Jerry Keeling.

In spite of the defections, Wylie was supportive of Dobbs. "They thought it was too hard a training camp for experienced ballplayers, ones that had been around for a

The miracle of McMahon from the official opening brochure. COURTESY CALGARY STAMPEDERS

Coach Bobby Dobbs.
COURTESY CALGARY STAMPEDERS

while. But that was his approach, and that was what was needed, even though he was a little hard to deal with." Wylie did concede, however, that even he had problems with the new head coach. "He tried to get me to get out of half-cut cleats, and I said, 'As soon as the club starts buying my boots, I'll wear what they buy. As long as I'm buying my own, I'll wear what I want. He was that kind of guy."

To Tony Pajaczkowski, Dobbs "was a real high school Harry. In training camp, guys stayed out one night, and he had us write out 100 times our blocking assignments on kickoffs and punts, and turn that in. That's pretty childish, having pros do something like that."

Earl Lunsford remembered how "Bobby Dobbs was a strange man. He had ideas I didn't necessarily agree with. I used to play linebacker. We were over in Montreal, and Wayne Harris got hurt. I told Dobbs I could play middle linebacker because I used to play it my first time up here. He wouldn't listen to me. He didn't believe me because I hadn't been practicing on defence. In the second half, he finally had to put me in [as linebacker], and we stopped them."

Lehew thought he knew why Dobbs created problems. "Dobbs was an army person," he said. "He was from West Point. He worked under Colonel Blaik, who was his hero."

Joining the team in 1961 along with Keeling were Calgarian

Larry Robinson and Wayne Harris, who became the greatest linebacker in CFL history, making the all-star team 11 straight seasons. New in the backfield was Ed Buchanan.

Although Keeling played well enough to trade Kapp, the Stamps also signed former Blue Bomber pivot Eagle Day, who quarterbacked the club until his release five years later. The Stampeders finished third, even though they only won seven games. In a thrilling semi-final, Calgary advanced to the conference championship against Winnipeg by a single point. The key play in game one was a 70-yard interception return for a touchdown by Wylie.

But in the end, the Stamps bowed to the Bombers 14–1 and 43–14.

Lunsford, Luzzi, Pajaczkowski, Harris and Wylie made the all-star team. Robinson was the Western Rookie of the Year. Pajaczkowski won the Schenley as Outstanding Canadian.

"We were having the windup party in Calgary, and I went to the bathroom. Jim Finks came in and looked at me and said, 'Well, you did it. You won the Schenley Award. But you can't tell anybody.'

"I said, 'You've got to be kidding.' He said, 'No, you can't tell anybody.'

"I said, 'Oh, my gawd! What a rotten thing to do to a guy.' Guys were wishing me luck, and I couldn't tell them.

"A funny thing I never understood was that they put me at defensive end in '61 and I won the Schenley—and next year I went back to offensive guard."

The big story of 1961 was Earl Lunsford becoming the first player in any pro league to rush for over a mile. His record came in the last game of the regular season when he rushed for 209 yards in Calgary's 43–7 win over B.C. That set a new single game

Larry Robinson,
1961 Rookie of the Year.
COURTESY CANADIAN FOOTBALL HALL OF FAME

record, and his 1,794 yards set the new season mark. Despite his amazing mile, Lunsford wasn't the Western Schenley nominee, that honour going to Jackie Parker.

Looking back over his career, Lunsford said, "The thing I did that I felt most good about was that I was the first man to rush for a mile. When I did that, I really felt like I had done something. I didn't think I was going to be able to do it. We had to win the last game of the season in B.C. After we got it won in the first half, Dobbs said, 'Okay, now go out there and rush for the yardage.' That helped me a lot. Even coaches you disagree with, you agree with sometimes. If the coach makes sense and is reasonable you can do anything."

Lehew explained why Lunsford might have been overlooked for the top award. "He didn't have that great speed. He wasn't an elusive back who attracts attention."

Recalled George Hansen, "In a game against Edmonton, he ran 85 yards for a touchdown. The coach afterwards said, 'What the heck were you doing? When we looked at the film, it looked like it was running in slow motion. Your offensive linemen passed you three times going to the goal line!'"

Earl the Earthquake Lunsford became the first running back in professional football to rush for over a mile in a single season. During his career with the Stampeders, he rushed 1,199 times for 6,994 yards and 55 touchdowns. In his best game on September 3, 1962, he scored 5 touchdowns, still a club record. Lunsford was elected to the Canadian Football Hall of Fame in 1983.

COURTESY CANADIAN FOOTBALL HALL OF FAME

"Earl was a bull," said Pajaczkowski, who opened holes for him. "He was a tough guy, playing offense and defence. To play fullback and linebacker back to back was pretty tough. You have to be a pretty good athlete to do that. Our all-Canadian line was very proud to be part of his record."

Jim Dillard arrived in 1962, joining Earl the Earthquake Lunsford, Lovell Coleman and Ed Buchanan in the backfield. Pat Holmes was a talented new lineman, Pete Manning a gifted import receiver. New Canadians were Bill Britton, Jim Furlong, Roy Jokanovich and Hal Krebs.

At 9–6–1, the Stampeders had their best record since 1949, finishing three points behind the Bombers. The highlight of the regular season was Earl Lunsford's Labour Day performance when he scored five touchdowns as Calgary trounced Edmonton 49–17. (The record is six held by Bob McNamara and Eddie James of Winnipeg.) Typically modest, the shy Oklahoman said, "I didn't think anything about it. Somebody else was running the ball down there, and I'd get the ball on the 5- or 3-yard line, and I'd run it in."

Harvey Wylie had a great year leading the conference in kickoff returns. One went 102 yards to the end zone, making the fifth straight season he had run one to the house, a record that still stands.

Tony Pajaczkowski hurt his ankle the last game of the regular season. "The first game of the semi-finals I was in plaster and didn't play. I wanted to play the second game. I was in my hotel room, and I called down to maintenance and asked them for a saw. They came up with a saw for sawing wood, and bit-by-bit I cut the cast off. They gave me an injection to numb me and I played."

After demolishing Saskatchewan in the two-game semi-final 43–7, they beat Winnipeg 20–14 in the opening game of the final, November 17. Led by the pinpoint passing of

Eagle Day and the running of Jim Dillard plus a rock-ribbed defence that held the mighty Bombers to 114 yards total offense, it nevertheless took a little razzle-dazzle to put the defending champions away before 17,230 freezing fans at McMahon. At 6:11 of the final frame, stalled on the enemy nine, Harvey Wylie went in for Ed Buchanan, bringing a play with him. Day handed off to Wylie, who fired a TD strike to Larry Robinson in the end zone. Lunsford scored a major, Robinson added two field goals and a convert; Jim Furlong, a single. Jerry Keeling, who had intercepted Hal Ledyard in the end zone earlier in the game, saved the day late in the fourth quarter by knocking away a sure touchdown pass to Ernie Pitts.

Game Two went four days later in Winnipeg, where below zero temperatures and a gale force wind made for one of the coldest nights anyone could remember for a football game.

Winnipeg punting woes gave the Stamps great field position in the opening quarter, but all they could produce were three singles on missed field-goal attempts. Dillard scored a touchdown in the second quarter, matched by two Bomber field goals. A Calgary single gave the visitors an 11–7 lead at the half. Winnipeg stormed back to score two majors in the final 15 minutes, giving the champs a 19–11 win.

Three days later, the Bombers controlled the first half but managed only five points. After Lovell Coleman ran for 116 yards and a touchdown at 2:57 of the fourth quarter, it looked like it would be all Calgary the rest of the way. Team captain Harvey Wylie was magnificent, filling in on offense for the

Hall of Famer Harvey Wylie.
COURTESY CANADIAN FOOTBALL
HALL OF FAME

injured Pete Manning, as well as handling his safety duties. Leading 7–6 late in the game, the red and white were dominating when the most heartbreaking moment in Calgary Stampeder history unfolded.

Charlie Shepherd boomed a punt from his end zone that ended up on the Calgary 25. Two plays later, punter Jim Furlong was roughed. The ball crossed the line, and Winnipeg's Ron Latourelle recovered on the Stamp 33. After a no-yards penalty was tacked on, the Bombers scrimmaged at the 23-yard line with 32 seconds left. Shepherd got it to the 16. Gerry James prepared to kick a field goal. Furlong deflected the ball, which rolled beneath the goal posts at Harvey Wylie's feet. With three Bombers in front of him, Wylie kicked it rather than picking it up. The ball hit Farrell Funston, who fell on it for the winning touchdown. Winnipeg 12, Calgary 7.

"The worst thing in all my playing days was when we went over and played Winnipeg and got beat when Harvey Wylie tried to kick the ball out of the end zone," recalled Lunsford. "It was laying on the ground. He just kicked it, and it hit a guy coming in about the goal line, and it bounced back into the end zone, and he fell on it for a touchdown. If that thing had gone out, we would have won."

"That was probably one of the worst officiated games I've ever seen," recalled Lehew. "There were about five or six things that happened during that game. Things were called one way that should have been called another way that went their way. That was definitely one of them. It should have been no yards."

Wylie agreed that bad officiating had cost the Stamps the game. "That's right. If he had called what he should have called, there would have been a no-yards penalty. And if I had fallen on it, that would have tied the game."

Why didn't Wylie fall on the ball? "The quickest way of doing it was to soccer-kick it," he said, defending his decision. "If a guy gets away a good, powerful soccer kick, it's out of the end zone, it's the last play of the game, it's all over."

Said Tony Pajaczkowski, "After the game, Winnipeg came into our dressing room happy and smiling. We were still sitting there crying, still in our football gear. I wanted to start a fight right there and then and beat somebody up. I was so frustrated."

Said Jerry Keeling, "Harvey felt so bad about that and the rest of us felt bad for him. Harvey was really a good football player."

In spite of the questionable decision that handed the conference title to the Bombers, Wylie won the Most Outstanding Canadian Award that year.

The Stampeders were even better in 1963, finishing second with a record of 10–4–2, two points behind the B.C. Lions. Lovell Coleman led the league in rushing with 1,343 yards, while Bobby Taylor was the leading receiver with 74 catches. He did not make the Western all-star team, although his teammate Pete Manning, with lesser numbers, was All-Canadian. The Stampeder running attack was formidable, not only with Coleman, but with Dillard, Lunsford and Buchanan, who had 1564 yards between them.

"We had a pretty good group," observed Lunsford. "We should have gone to the Grey Cup, and we never did. I would have traded anything for that."

Bobby Taylor was a prime example of the success of Rogers Lehew's program to develop Canadians. "We didn't really have the Canadian talent we needed at that time," said Lehew. "I got very involved with the high schools. I got [Western grad] Bobby on the Mount Royal junior team, and they lost the championship game to Saskatoon. I convinced Jim Finks to send Larry Robinson to Iowa, but, like Bobby, he wasn't interested in going to college. So we put both of them on our roster. Eagle Day made Bobby a football player, throwing to him a lot in practice." Robinson spent his first two years as a quarterback and receiver before becoming the greatest defensive back in team history.

"I sent six players to the States on scholarship," continued Lehew. "Gerry Shaw went to Washington State, Ron Stewart and Joe Forzani to Utah State."

In 1963 it was Calgary vs. Saskatchewan in the semi-final. The Stamps had beat the Riders 17–16 and tied them twice during the season, so everyone was surprised when the Stamps clobbered the Green and White in the first game of the total point series 35–9. Two nights later in Regina, what was called either the "Miracle at Taylor Field" or the "Massacre at Taylor Field" took place.

Calgary Herald sports editor Gorde Hunter wrote: "The Calgary Stampeders won the Western Conference semi-final in their minds prior to the kickoff here at Taylor Field Monday night. They took 26 big points as licence to underestimate the pluck of the Roughriders and two hours later found themselves on the outside looking in.

"It was 39–12 for the Roughriders on the night. It was 48–47 on the round and never in Canadian playoff memory has a team laughed at such odds and come out on top."

On the first series, Ron Lancaster and Ray Purdin, standing in front of the Calgary bench, executed a sleeper play for 61 yards and a touchdown. Minutes later Ed Buchanan got behind Harvey Wylie in the end zone for a 25-yard TD pass. After the opening quarter, the Rider deficit was cut in half.

The Stamps replied with two singles. They seemed to be stiffening when Wylie was called for interference on Buchanan at the 1. Calgary stopped George Reed, but on the last play of the half, Lancaster found Dick Cohee in the end zone. The deficit was nine.

Early in the third quarter, Lancaster hit Hugh Campbell at the Calgary 44, after which he completed a harmless-looking screen pass to Buchanan who dipsy-doodled to pay dirt. Minutes later Cohee scored his second major, leaping in the end zone and stealing the ball away from Jerry Keeling. The 26-point lead was gone.

The Stamps struck back. It was Eagle Day to Coleman for 66 yards, then to Claridge for 16. On the opening playing of the closing quarter, Lunsford ran four yards for the score. Lancaster answered with a George Reed touchdown with two minutes left, set up by an interference call on Doug Elmore.

Still, Calgary could have—should have—won. On the last play of the game, Robinson missed a 35-yard field goal. Rider return man Gene Wlasiuk kicked it out of the end zone. Robinson picked it up at his 42 and punted it back, but it went out of bounds at the 20.

There was lots of blame to go around. The offense sputtered. On defence, Wylie was responsible for two touchdowns. Larry Robinson missed four field goals on a windless night. Bobby Dobbs stayed with the running game even though the Riders shut it down. They passed only 18 times, six of those in the final quarter. Four times within the red zone, they failed to score a touchdown, including one set up when Ron Payne blocked a kick.

"Regina had a good football team," allowed Keeling. "It was just one of those days when everything went wrong for us. We didn't play well. That was a real tough one because we had such a big lead. We probably went in thinking just protect the lead and not do anything too bad."

What about the sleeper play? "Purdin just came off the bench and stepped onto the field. No one saw him. They changed the rules after that so the player had to come to the hash marks."

Two years in a row Calgary had it in the bag. Two years in a row they came up empty. The word *choke* began to creep into coffee shop talk on 8 Avenue.

It was Earl Lunsford's last game. He retired at the age of 29.

Why? "I retired because the doctor told me to retire because I had taken too many blows to the head," Lunsford said. "I got knocked out a couple of times in those latter years. I didn't get my memory going for about a week."

In 2003 Lunsford looked back on his distinguished career that made him Calgary's third all-time leading rusher behind Kelvin Anderson and Joffrey Reynolds. "The most important thing is, I played with many good players. Even in '56 when I went up there, there were guys who were tough as a boot, really tough. In all the seasons I played, I enjoyed being around players who did what they said they could do. We had some great players."

Hall of Fame inductee Jerry Keeling in action.

After losing two of their first three games in 1964, the Stamps won 11 of the remaining 13 to finish at 12–4, a point behind the 11–2–3 Lions. Jerry Keeling and Wayne Harris were superb on defence, making All-Canadian, as did O-lineman Tony Pajaczakowski and Lovell Coleman, who led the league in rushing with 1,629 yards, and became the first Stampeder to win the Schenley Most Outstanding Player Award. It was vindication for the great running back.

"He spent two years in the shadow of Earl Lunsford," said Dobbs, "and when he took over as our first-string fullback, a lot of people doubted whether he could do the job. There shouldn't be any doubt now."

In a game against Winnipeg in 1960, Coleman pulled a muscle on a kickoff return and fumbled the ball. After the game, Bomber coach Bud Grant said he would have cut Coleman on the spot if he had been playing for

Hall of Famer Wayne Harris was named All-Canadian nine times and received the Most Valuable Player Award at the 59th Grey Cup in 1971, won by the Stampeders. The Stampeders retired his jersey, No. 55, in 1973.
COURTESY CANADIAN FOOTBALL HALL OF FAME

him. Thereafter, Coleman reserved some of his better performances for the Blue Bombers.

The Stampeders lost the first game of the semi-final in Regina 34–25, blowing a 24–8 fourth quarter lead. They atoned for their sins by crushing Saskatchewan 51–6 in Calgary. They lost the final to B.C. in three games.

After a sterling nine-year career marked by incredible highs and lows, Harvey Wylie retired. His all-time team rankings include eighth in punt returns, third in kickoff returns, second longest kickoff return (110 yards), most fumble recoveries in a single season (6), second in career interceptions (35), and tied with Vernon Roberson, Chris Major and Greg Knox for most interceptions in a season (10). He ranks with Larry Robinson and Jerry Keeling as the greatest defensive back in team history.

"I played for a good ball club in a great city," Wylie said. "I was born and raised in Calgary. I never wanted to play for anybody else. I had an opportunity to play in the NFL, but I turned it down because I was making my professional career in engineering, and it was home. It was nice to play for Calgary with a lot of great guys and great friends. I'm just sorry we never made it to the Grey Cup."

On September 10, Jim Finks resigned to become the general manager of the Minnesota Vikings. The day before, he

Schenley Winner Lovell Coleman.
COURTESY DARYL SLADE

told the *Herald*'s Gorde Hunter he had recommended Lehew to succeed him. Director Pat Mahoney took over as acting general manager. Bobby Dobbs wanted both general manager and head coach positions, but the board didn't want them combined.

The team held their season windup party at the Highlander Hotel Monday, November 23. It turned out to be a doozy. President George McMahon announced at the party that Rogers Lehew, Finks' assistant, would be the new GM. Immediately after the announcement, Dobbs made his way to the microphone. "I am proud of the way you performed in the Final. You boys gave it everything you had. I wish we could have won, but we didn't. I have no regrets. With that statement, I resign as head coach of the Calgary Stampeder Football Club."

As Gorde Hunter wrote the next day, "You could say Bobby was the death of the party Monday night. His resignation bombshell hit Stampeder players and executives between the eyes, and what was to become a big night for Rogers Lehew turned flat and sour.

"'I want to get this straight,' Dobbs told Hunter later. 'I love Rogers. But I just can't turn around and work for a man that has worked for me for nine years. Yes, I'm bitter about it. The present coaching staff, not Jim Finks, as has been reported many times, is responsible for this team. They couldn't beat Molly Potts before this staff took over, and I'm very disappointed. No team in Canada has won more games since we took over. I picked all the players on this team.'"

Dobbs said he could have worked with Lehew if he had been given complete control of the team.

Despite Dobbs' protestations to the contrary, Lehew

didn't feel his love. "Dobbs' quote in the paper," said Lehew, "was you don't promote a private over a colonel. The first time I met him was when I played for him in the service one year, and he was a captain and I was a private. That never changed. He was respectful of me professionally, but when all was said and done, he was a captain and I was a private, and he could never get past that."

Lehew explained how it all unfolded. "When the season was over, I was interviewed for about an hour and a half. During the process, it came out that in Bobby's interview he asked if I was interviewed. They said I was. The executive member said, 'Dobbs told us if we hire you as general manager, he would resign.'

"I was asked if I could work with him, and I said I could, even though Pat Mahoney told me the job was mine.

"We played B.C. in the finals. We lost the first one here. We went to Vancouver and beat them. We had to play them again on Saturday. I met with some of the executive in Vancouver, and I told them, 'You've got a helluva decision to make. If Bobby wins the game tomorrow—and I think he will—you're going to have a helluva time denying him the job. They said, 'We told him the job would be divided, and we're not going to change our mind.'

"Bobby called me through a friend after the announcement was made," Lehew continued. "He said, 'If you give up the general managership, I'll become the head coach and general manager, and I'll get you into a good position.' I said I've got the job, and I intend to keep it. Fact is, I worked for a guy (Dobbs) for several years who would never recommend me for a job. Some people thought I

Stampeder GM Rogers Lehew.

had backstabbed him. I didn't backstab him. When they asked me if I wanted the job, I said yes."

How did Pajaczkowski react to Dobbs' announcement? "Surprise, but I was happy. I didn't like the guy because he was too High School Harry. It was the final straw when they gave the job to Lehew when he thought he was going to get it. That was a slap in the face for him. None of the players [was] disappointed that Dobbs quit. Lehew was very well liked."

And Keeling? "Bobby ran the team like the army, and he didn't like someone being put over him that he had been over for a long time. When he announced he was quitting, it shocked everybody. They should have talked to Bobby earlier."

Dobbs returned to coaching at Texas Western (UTEP). In 1972, to motivate his team, he threatened to resign if they lost. They lost. Dobbs quit and went into business until his health started to fail in 1978. He died in an Altus, Oklahoma, nursing home in 1986 from Alzheimer's disease at age 63.

Lehew hired Jerry Williams as Dobbs' successor. "He had head coaching experience. He had done a heckuva job as an assistant coach with the Eagles. In 1964 he was an assistant with us."

Keeling was pleased. "When Jerry Williams came in, he really changed the team. He was really a good coach. He started sending all the receivers out with only one guy in the backfield. And we did a lot of different things on defence."

Herm Harrison also admired Keeling's approach. "He was innovative. He would put four basic defences on the board, and he would call in anybody who had anything to do with the ball and say, 'I want you to design any play you can that would beat these defences. I'll use it in a game.' I respected the man so much for that."

Pajaczkowski was more restrained. "Jerry and I got along well until the second exhibition game in Saskatchewan. Jerry was a Y.A. Tittle look-alike, and so I called him Y.A. He really got cheesed off at me. We were standing on the steps of the Saskatchewan Hotel waiting for a bus to take us to the ballpark, and he told me I had a big mouth and why don't I keep it shut and keep name-calling to myself. He and I never spoke again until the end of

Jerry Williams, head coach.
COURTESY CALGARY STAMPEDERS

the year when, after a playoff game, we kind of shook hands and that was it."

The team flourished under Williams, finishing in first place at 12–4. The Bombers knocked off Saskatchewan in the semi-final. Led by Herm Harrison, the Stamps won the first game of the final 22–9 at home. Although Calgary was dominant on a windy night in Winnipeg, Larry Robinson missed three field goals. Bomber pivot Kenny Ploen got hurt late in the game, but Dick Thornton came in and finished off a five-play touchdown drive with a 38-yard run and a 15–11 victory.

In game three back in Calgary, Lovell Coleman was sensational, picking up 144 yards. But once again, Lady Luck was dressed in blue and gold. On one play when Coleman was tackled near the end zone, the ball bounced over the goal line and was recovered for a safety. But the key play came early in the third quarter. The Stamps had the enemy hemmed in on the 1-yard line. Expecting a run, they had everyone up. Ploen flipped it over the defence to Ken Neilson, who went 109 yards for the score, a still-standing record. The Bombers won 19–12.

The post-season curse continued.

Bomber coach Bud Grant conceded that for most of the season the Stampeders were the better team, but come playoff time, the Bombers were the best. Herm Harrison agreed. "We did that a lot. We'd come out

Herm "Ham Hands" Harrison. COURTESY CALGARY STAMPEDERS

of the chute and play hard all year, and for some reason when the playoffs came [we] would tighten up. I just couldn't believe it."

Harrison, who earned his first all-star selection in 1965 explained how he joined the Stampeders the year before. "I was too small to play in the NFL. I was about 170 pounds. Rogers Lehew who had seen me in my senior year said, 'Herm, you can play in Canada.'

"When I came up here, I came up as a wide receiver and almost didn't make the team.

"They said, 'Herm, we've go to let you go. We've got Pete Manning and Bobby Taylor. We just can't use you.'

"And I said, 'What positions are you looking to replace?'

"They said, 'We need linebackers.'

"I said, 'Look, I've got one week left. Will you try me at linebacker?'

"We had a scrimmage that afternoon. Dobbs was really impressed with me in the scrimmage.

"He said, 'Herm, I want you to really concentrate on learning this.' And that's how I ended up making the team.

"The next year Bruce Claridge, who was the tight end, popped his collarbone and Eagle Day said to Jerry Williams, 'You've got to put Herm in.' (Eagle and I always practiced together when everybody would leave the field.)

"'But he's playing linebacker.'

"'He can do both.'

"I went the last seven games both ways. Then Williams said to me, 'Herm when you come back next year, I'm not sure where I'm going to play you. I'll play you the first half on offense and the second half on defence.

"Opening up the second half in a game in Regina, Ronnie Lancaster did a half-roll away and threw back across the field. I picked it off and went down the sideline and scored. Williams said to me, 'You're really making this difficult, aren't you?' He said, 'Know your line-backing duties, don't forget them, but I've got to play you at tight end. With those hands, you're just too valuable to us.' So they kept me at tight end."

Harrison went on to become a Western All-Star six times, All-Canadian three. He joined the Stampeders' Wall of Fame in 1988 and the CFL Hall of Fame in 1993.

In 1965 linebacker Wayne Harris won his first Schenley for Outstanding Lineman.

"I was drafted by the Boston Patriots and put on Calgary's negotiation list," Harris said. "A friend, Donny Stone, who played here, told me it was a great league to play in.

I didn't really want to go east. I liked the west better, so we packed up our things and came to Calgary."

Harris was nicknamed Thumper in high school in El Dorado, Arkansas. Asked about his strengths as a player, he replied, "I just felt I had good fundamentals coaching when I started playing football in high school. I always had great coaches. A lot of things you do on the field become reaction things. I think that was from the coaching and the techniques I picked up.

"I had great leg strength, but mostly just techniques I picked up in high school—trying to read the triangle as it was referred to back in those days, amongst the running backs. I played the football. I was always looking into the backfield. There are just so many things that a running back and a quarterback can do to confuse the running game, and that becomes a reaction thing more than anything else.

"I was a fairly quiet type of guy—still am. I was never a big rah-rah fan."

Harris led by example. "Yes, we had several guys on our team who pretty well did it like that—Larry Robinson, Jerry Keeling, for example," he recalled.

"Jerry Williams came here in 1964," said Lehew. "I told him, don't coach the middle linebacker. He played his position better than anybody I'd ever seen."

Before the 1966 campaign

began, perennial all-star Tony Pajaczkowski was traded to Montreal. He explained, "When I got back from vacation, several people told me they had heard the Stampeders were trying to trade me. I called Lehew up, and Rogers said, 'There are lots of rumours. If I was going to trade you, I'd tell you.' I said, 'Okay.'

"Then I started thinking about it. Here I was in Calgary, and I didn't really have any kind of a job. I had different jobs when I

Wayne Harris, the greatest to ever wear the red and white.
COURTESY CALGARY STAMPEDERS

77

was there, but nothing that would make me come back to on a permanent basis.

"I thought, *If they're thinking about trading me, I'm getting older, I should think about it.* I had an ambition to open a tavern in Montreal. I could see myself greeting everybody and blah, blah, blah, so I thought maybe I should check with Montreal. So I called the Alouettes, and Ralph Goldston got on the phone. He said, 'What's up?'

"'I hear you're trying to make a trade,' I said. 'If you are, and you're wondering if I would come to Montreal, I would.'

"He said, 'Let me get back to you.' Sure enough, in about two hours or so, I got a call from Rogers that the trade had been made. They got Terry Evanshen for me."

After finishing first in 1965, the Stampeders looked forward to the coming campaign, but because of injuries and player turnover, they finished 6–9–1, in fourth place. Pat Holmes went to the NFL. Pete Manning and Bobby Taylor were traded. Additions included Dick Dupuis, Terry Evanshen Jerry Campbell, Pete Liske and Bob Lueck.

A major overhaul was planned. "We changed half the team from what we had in '64," said Lehew. "We had the basis of a good club, no doubt about it. I signed Jerry Keeling and Herm Harrison and later John Helton. I traded for Evanshen. I traded Pete Manning and Bobby Taylor to Toronto for Pete Liske. I could do that because Gerry Shaw was coming in from university.

"On Labour Day, '66, I watched two players walk down the sideline, and I said to someone, 'There go two of the best defensive backs who are ever going to be.' They were Howard Starks and Frank Andruski. I brought both those players in the day before the Labour Day game. Those two kind of put us over the hump. Offensively, with Liske and Keeling, we became a throwing club rather than a running club."

Age finally caught up with Eagle Day. "Eagle's decline was gradual," said Keeling. "You know, he only had one kidney from when he was a kid. We were worried about him because he played a long time, and it was dangerous for him. He was getting up in years." Day is sixth in all-time playoff completions and passing yards. He died in 2008 at age 75 in Oxford, Mississippi.

Herm Harrison recalled Day fondly. "The quarterback that made me was Eagle Day. He was the one that talked them into putting me at tight end because no one had really seen me in action catching but Day. He said, 'You've got to put Herm on offense.'"

New Calgary pivot Peter Liske graduated from Penn State in 1964. After being cut by the New York Jets as a DB, he signed with Toronto and was traded to Calgary. In 1966 he threw for 2,177 yards, 4,479 in '67 and 4,333 in '68. With superb receivers like Terry Evanshen, Gerry Shaw, Bob McCarthy and Herm Harrison, the Stamps staged a dazzling aerial circus. Keeling and Evanshen set the still-standing team record for a 109-yard pass and run for a touchdown on September 27 against Winnipeg. They are tied with two others for the league mark.

Said Harrison, "Pete was the kind of quarterback who would say, 'Okay, Herm, what would you like to do today?'

"And I used to always say, 'Just throw deep to me once.' Everybody thought I was too slow to go deep.

"He'd say, 'Herm, I can't do it right now. We don't have that much time for you to get deep.'

"But in 1968, on my birthday, we were playing Saskatchewan. He said, 'Herm, today you can do anything you want.' He threw deep to me, I caught it and said, 'I told you I could go deep.'

"And he said, 'I was afraid of that. Now you're going to want to go deep all the time.'

"Each one of my three quarterbacks threw a different ball," recalled Harrison. "Jerry Keeling threw a heavy ball. When it came down, you'd better be ready. Pete threw a floater. It would hit your hands softly. Eagle Day could thread a needle. I enjoyed them all."

Evanshen and Keeling were Western All-Stars in 1966; Harris and Luzzi, All-Canadians. Considering he led the league in receiving with 1,200 yards, Evanshen should have been All-Canadian, too. He was the runner up to Hamilton's Zeno Karcz for Most Outstanding Canadian.

Canada's centennial year was spectacular for the Calgary Stampeders. They tied Saskatchewan for first with a mark of 12–4, finishing first by beating the defending champs two out of three. Retiring were Hal Krebs, George Hansen and Dale Parsons. Parsons was a Regina boy who attended Arizona on

Dale Parsons.
COURTESY DARYL SLADE

a football scholarship and then returned to his hometown Roughriders and sat on the bench most of the time without complaint, always cheerful, always a great teammate. He signed with Calgary in 1960 and soon became the starting centre on an excellent offensive line. Tragically, Dale succumbed to cancer in his thirties.

New arrivals included Art Froese, Ron Stewart and Wayne Conrad.

Liske set a new league record with 40 touchdown passes, six of which came in a game against Winnipeg. Evanshen was chosen Most Outstanding Canadian for leading the league in receiving with 90 catches for 1,662 yards (the record at the time for Canadian receivers) and winning the scoring title with 102 points, the last non–place-kicker to receive the honour. Liske won the Outstanding Player Award. Jerry Williams

George Hansen. COURTESY DARYL SLADE

was Coach of the Year. They approached the Western Final with confidence.

In a tough defensive battle in Calgary, trailing 11–8 late in the fourth quarter, the Stamps lined up for the tying field goal. It was a fake! Lovell Coleman drifted out behind the coverage and took Keeling's pass for a touchdown. Calgary 15, Saskatchewan 11.

Defences continued to dominate in Game Two. It had rained in Regina earlier in the day, and by nightfall the turf resembled Arctic tundra, semi-frozen and wet. Once again the postseason curse raised its ugly head, this time striking down Terry Evanshen in the third quarter with a broken leg. His injury proved to be the turning point. When the Calgary receiver went down, an eerie silence fell over the stadium.

"Without Terry we didn't have that deep threat," said Harrison. "He was so elusive. When he got hurt, it seemed like our morale went down. Up to that point, we were in the game, putting pressure on them. But when the injury occurred, you could see heads dropping."

Wayne Harris took a larger view. "We lost Terry. I wouldn't say that was the key to it," Harris conceded. "They had a good football team. I can't take anything away from them. That was one of the coldest games I can recall playing. It was like a skating rink, but there was still a lot of moisture, so when you got completely wet. With the wind factor, it felt like 40 below."

The Stamps lost 11–9.

Back at Calgary, George Reed carried 35 times for 201 yards and a 17–3 win. Denied again, the Stampeders prepared for 1968.

1967 marked the first of five straight Calgary–Saskatchewan conference finals. Wayne Harris loved those years. "I really enjoyed those games," he enthused. "Saskatchewan probably had the best team in the CFL during that period of time. We always gave them a battle. It seemed like they may win the close ones, but we'd then come back and kick the heck out of them the next game. They had a great offensive line and, of course, George Reed, Ron Lancaster, Hugh Campbell. They were very strong. We had a good team, too, and we always had a lot of good tussles with them."

Jim Furlong seconded the motion. Saskatchewan "had a tremendous football team. They were always hard hitting. We used to go there and try to beat their heads in, but strangely enough, they were always clean games. No cheap shots."

"We enjoyed playing them. You knew it was always going to be a tough game but a fair game," Keeling recalled. "We knew them all, we knew their families. We'd go over to Regina in the winter and play basketball and, of course, we'd go out with them afterwards. They knew our families, too."

The two clubs had a mutual admiration society. "We had some great battles with those guys," said Ron Lancaster. "They always had a heckuva team to compete against. Wayne Harris was in another world. We didn't block him very often. It seemed like everywhere we went, he was there.

Terry Evanshen, 1967 Most Outstanding Canadian; Peter Liske, 1967 Most Outstanding Player.
COURTESY DARYL SLADE

Terry Evanshen in action. COURTESY CANADIAN FOOTBALL HALL OF FAME

He was as good a football player as you were ever going to meet. And playing him so many times, you got to know him as a person. He was an awfully good guy."

Rogers Lehew's counterpart in Saskatchewan was Ken Preston. "He and I were great friends. But what irritated me was there were so many Rider fans in Calgary. You'd think if you lived here 40 years, you could at least be a Stampeder fan."

Before the 1968 campaign, Lovell Coleman was traded to Ottawa for Mike Blum, who didn't report. Twelve-year veteran Ron Allbright retired. Newcomers included All-American lineman Granville Liggins, Rudy Linterman, Terry Wilson, Dave Cranmer and Joe Forzani.

Going into 1968, it had been 19 years since the Stampeders had played in a Grey Cup. After the club lost three of their last four games to finish second at 10–6, the year hardly looked like the one when the drought would end, especially since they led the league in team losses while having the fewest yards rushing. But they peaked at the right time.

Calgary vs. Saskatchewan in 1967. COURTESY CALGARY STAMPEDERS

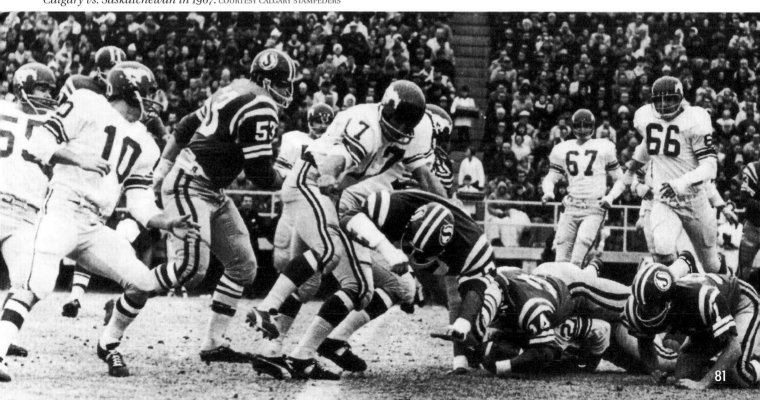

Calgary dispatched Edmonton in the semi-final 29–13 and then went into Regina and walloped the 12–3–1 Roughriders 32–0 and swept them at McMahon in overtime 25–12, forcing nine turnovers. Off to Toronto to face the powerful Ottawa Rough Riders.

Grey Cup day, November 30, was damp and cloudy, +2°C.

The Stampeders out-passed the eastern Riders 258 yards to 185 and enjoyed a big edge in first downs, 24–13. But Ottawa had the edge that counted.

Liske propelled Calgary into a 14–4 lead during the first half by capping off a drive with a one-yard plunge for one touchdown and completing a 21-yarder to Evanshen for the other. The defence came up big. Ottawa had five scoring chances in the first half and came away with four points on a single after Calgary recovered a blocked punt in their end zone and a Don Sutherin field goal.

Early in the third quarter, the Riders smothered punter Ron Stewart at midfield, taking over on downs. Russ Jackson engineered a touchdown drive to close the gap to four, the convert going wide. Soon after, Jackson pitched out to Vic Washington, who dropped it. The ball bounced right back into his hands, and he scampered 80 yards for a touchdown.

Larry Robinson failed to tackle Washington. "They pitched him the ball, he grabbed it, then fumbled it, it hit the ground and bounced up back into his arms—and I cut up too soon," he conceded. "I thought he was done, but he went around me. I got a hand on him, but I didn't get enough. He went down the sideline and scored."

Jackson closed out Ottawa scoring by combining with Margene Adkins on a 70-yard pass and run for a major.

"That one was on me," Keeling remembered ruefully. "They had run this play where

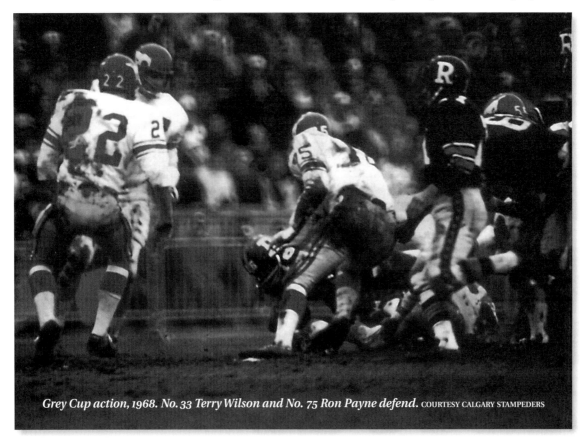

Grey Cup action, 1968. No. 33 Terry Wilson and No. 75 Ron Payne defend. COURTESY CALGARY STAMPEDERS

Adkins was the inside receiver. He would start down the field like he was going up the seam and then break out at about 20 yards. I had to cover him from the safety position. They came out in the second half and ran the same play, except he came down and started like he was going to break out and he broke back into the post all the way across the field. He caught the pass and scored."

In the fourth quarter, Dick Suderman recovered a Bo Scott fumble, setting up a Liske to Evanshen TD. The final score was Ottawa 24, Calgary 21.

In defence of their loss, Calgary was in no shape to play Ottawa. Running back Dave Cranmer broke a leg in the playoffs. His replacement Rudy Linterman went out with torn knee ligaments in the first quarter and Herm Harrison was hurt. If all that wasn't enough, Keeling added, "When we got to Toronto, we all came down with the flu. Our trainer had a big bottle of cough syrup, and just about every time we came off the field, we'd take a big swig of it. I've played with the flu in hot weather, and by the end of the game I'd sweated it out. You can't do that when it's cold. We were lucky we stayed as close as we did in that game."

If it hadn't been for bad luck, Calgary wouldn't have had any luck at all.

"None at all," moaned Harrison, who was the leading receiver in the league that year with 67 catches for 1,306 yards. "It was unbelievable. I broke five ribs in the first five minutes of the game. I still tried to play, but it just wasn't there. I lost 14 pounds before the game because of the flu. I just didn't have the strength." His inability to perform was a severe blow.

Did taking part in the hoopla contribute to Calgary's lack of stamina? "Oh, yeah," Keeling admitted, "and that probably hurt us a little bit, too. It was the first time at a Grey Cup for any of us. There were all kinds

of things going on. The coaches said, 'Go out and have a good time,' and I think we made just about all the things they had going on. We learned to handle that later on. But that was the first time Calgary had been to a Grey Cup in a long time. Everybody was just so happy about it."

Getting to the Grey Cup "was a great feeling," recalled Lehew, "because we hadn't been there in 20 years. Everybody got excited—the whole team got excited. We played a helluva game. If it hadn't been for the play Washington made, we might have won it."

At the end of the season, Peter Liske and coach Jerry Williams signed with the NFL Philadelphia Eagles. Williams was succeeded by Jim Duncan, an assistant of Saskatchewan coach Eagle Keys. As hard-nosed and down to earth as Williams was cerebral, he brought a more balanced attack to the team with Ted Woods and Rudy Linterman rushing for 1,348 yards.

"Williams and Jim Duncan were the two coaches I hired," said Lehew. "Williams was very innovative. Duncan was more basic. They had quite different personalities. The players loved Williams and didn't like Duncan, but sometimes Duncan did more for them."

In his first year at the helm, Duncan had to replace Art Froese and Chuck Zikafoose. He welcomed John Helton, Jim Silye and Howard Starks, who returned after serving two years in Vietnam. During the season, they had to cope with injuries to Don Luzzi, who missed 13 games, and Keeling, who missed four games. Keeling led the conference in

Jim Duncan. COURTESY DARYL SLADE

passing with 3,179 yards and 20 touchdowns. Harrison had 1,043 yards.

The Roughriders were the class of the CFL in 1969 at 13–3. Calgary was second, eight points behind. They beat B.C. 35–21 but suffered injuries to Luzzi, Harris, Keeling, Harrison, Woods and Wilson. They were easy prey, losing the final to Saskatchewan 17–11 and 36–13.

Before the 1970 season began, Don Luzzie, Ted Woods, Gerry Watson and Ron Payne retired. Luzzi won the Outstanding Lineman Award in 1958, and was All-Western six times and All-Canadian on three occasions. He lived the rest of his life in Calgary, devoted to his community.

Terry Evanshen was traded to Montreal for centre Basil Bark, who would later become an owner of the team. Unheralded halfback Hugh McKinnis came in from Arizona and led the division in rushing with 1,135 yards.

"I needed a running back," explained Lehew. "One of the places I often recruited was Arizona State. One of their coaches called and told me McKinnis was going to flunk out. So I signed him."

The team finished in third place at 9–7. After knocking off Edmonton in the semi-final 16–9, they prepared to face the Roughriders, who at 14–2, had the best regular season in their history. The Stampeders were prohibitive underdogs to all except those who remembered that one of the Riders' losses came at the hands of the Stampeders, 30–0, at Taylor Field on August 17. And while the Stamps were a mediocre 9–7, they were 8–2 on the road, including the semi-final.

Make that 9–2 in the first game of the finals as they thumped the favourites 28–11 at Taylor Field. The big play was a 94-yard pass and run for a touchdown, Keeling to Dave Cranmer.

Five days later at McMahon, Calgary was closing in for the kill when disaster struck.

With 39 seconds left, trailing 4–3, Calgary had the ball at the Rider 23. Keeling went back to pass and was hit by Ken Frith. The ball fell to the turf, where Ed McQuarters scooped it up and ran 80 yards for an 11–3 Saskatchewan victory.

Why pass when down by a single point and within field goal range? "I was throwing on second down because we wanted to get a little bit closer to make sure of it," Keeling explained. "I was trying to throw a quick flat pass to one of our inside receivers. They jumped on him on the inside and I had to hold the ball, and by that time Frith came in and hit me." Another key play came earlier when Dick Suderman kneed Lancaster in the ribs and cracked a couple. Gary Lane replaced Lancaster at quarterback for the finale back in Regina.

The weather in Regina was frightful with snow blowing in a 60kph wind. "That was the worst I'd ever seen," recalled Keeling. "In the dressing room before the game, we weren't sure we were going to play or not. Just before the game, Rogers came in and said the commissioner wanted to postpone it until the next day, but the weather forecast for then was the same, and the Grey Cup was the following weekend, so we played." In a great display of courage, the two teams battled in the blizzard.

Calgary took full advantage of the breeze in the first quarter, jumping into a 9–0 lead, the big play a 63-yard punt return by Jim Silye. "I had broom ball shoes on that day," he recalled. "I caught the ball and took one step to the right and that was just enough to get the guys coming at me to commit to their left. I cut back and knifed through a couple of guys, and all of a sudden there didn't seem to be anyone there except the punter, Allan Ford. I gave him a head fake and took off. That was nice, especially since I fumbled a punt in the 1971 Grey Cup."

The Riders answered with 11 points in the second quarter and were up 11–9 at the half.

The teams traded field goals in the second half, and with less than two minutes to go, Calgary's McKinnis fumbled on the Rider 4. Three plays later, Al Ford punted from his end zone, and Calgary took over at the Rider 42. Keeling threw a screen pass to McKinnis, who was knocked out of bounds on the 26 with three seconds left. (If the Riders had let him run, time would have expired!) Larry Robinson came on to try what would be a routine 32-yard field goal, but he was kicking into the gale.

"I didn't think I could make it, but it did go through," Robinson remembered. "I was practicing before the game from the same point, and I didn't get any of them to the goal line. I aimed it about 10 feet right of the goal posts and the wind just carried it in."

Calgary 15, Saskatchewan 14.

Was Robinson lucky? Eagle Keys replied, "I don't know, but I'd like to bet a $1,000 even money every time he tried one under similar circumstances. I'm not taking anything away from the Stampeders. They never gave up, but when Ron Lancaster couldn't play, we had to throw out our game plan today and make changes from the bench."

The Riders fervently believed both George Reed and Gary Lane had scored touchdowns, but the officials disagreed. "Both Gary Lane and I were in the end zone," Reed stated emphatically. "When you're in the end zone from the waist up, it's a touchdown. That was probably our best team. That was the one game that hurt most in my whole career."

A review of game film showed both men made it to pay dirt. Calgary's great John Helton didn't need film. "If George Reed said it, it's true. He's an honourable man," he commented later.

Wayne Harris with 17 unassisted tackles was magnificent.

It had been Jim Duncan's goal to transform the Stampeders from a finesse passing team to a down and dirty one, a reflection of his personality. "I always wanted a bunch of alley cats who would fight and scratch and carry the fight to the other guy," he declared. "We're going to fight our way to a Grey Cup win."

Unfortunately, no. The terrible weather had taken its toll. "Everybody was frost bitten badly at the end of that playoff game,"

Down and dirty Grey Cup action, 1970. Jerry Keeling looks for his receiver while No. 65 Roger Kramer, No. 31 Hugh McKinnis, No. 57 John Atamian and No. 45 Basil Bark keep the Als at bay. COURTESY CALGARY STAMPEDERS

Helton explained. "My wife went with me to the hospital to have the blisters cut. Before that game, whatever I grabbed, I would hold on to. I had strength in my hands, but it wasn't the kind of strength I had before that frostbite. One of the assistant coaches said, 'Take those gloves off, you're not going to be able to feel anything out there.' He's standing on the sidelines dressed up like an Eskimo. The frostbite resulted in permanent injury."

For the first time, both Grey Cup contestants were third-place teams.

Montreal hadn't won a playoff game since 1962. New owner Sam Berger hired former great Alouette receiver Red O'Quinn as his general manager, and O'Quinn hired his former battery mate, the legendary Sam "The Rifle" Etcheverry as his coach.

The rookie coach was severely challenged just before the Eastern semi-final when receiver Bob McCarthy and fullback Dennis Duncan were involved in a barroom brawl. When the *Montreal Gazette* got hold of the story, Etcheverry was forced to cut them both, but his action galvanized his team, propelling them into the Grey Cup.

Calgary got on the scoreboard first after recovering a fumbled punt at the Montreal 15-yard line early in the first quarter. Keeling completed a 10-yard strike to McKinnis, who then took it in from the 5. The Als responded with a TD on a broken play.

Gambling on third and one deep in the Calgary end, Terry Wilson broke through and grabbed halfback Moses Denson around the legs. Denson saw Ted Alfen in the end zone and threw him the ball. The Als added a field goal, going to the dressing room with a 9–7 lead at the half.

In the second half, the Stampeders could muster only a Robinson field goal. Montreal scored two more TDs to win 23–10.

In addition to the frostbite problem, the Stamps had to cope with terrible turf. "It had

A decade before his National Energy Program touched off a firestorm of controversy, Prime Minister Pierre Trudeau could sport his version of a ten-gallon hat at the 1970 Grey Cup.
COURTESY DARYL SLADE

been raining in Toronto," explained Keeling, "and they had just re-sodded the field about a week before. You'd try and cut, and that sod would just roll up."

But it's the same for both teams, right? Not so, said defensive end John Helton. "My feet would slip out from under me. I think I could have beaten Goliath on a fast track, but if the field was muddy or slippery, I was done. My greatest playing weight was 247 pounds. By November it was 238. Without speed and strength, I wouldn't have been able to play. All the linemen I played against were bigger than me. On a bad field, I was nullified."

Two nights before the game, Wayne Harris won his third Schenley award. Runner-up Ti-Cat Angelo Mosca said, "I find nothing to be ashamed of in being second to a guy who is not only the greatest lineman in Canada, but the greatest football player, too."

The Stamps prepared for 1971 more determined than ever to capture the elusive prize. Many of their great veterans were long in tooth, and outstanding linemen Roger Kramer, Bob Lueck and Billy Roy retired. Dave Cranmer was traded to Toronto, but the presence of newcomers John Forzani to go with brother Joe and an unknown running back named Jesse Mims would make a difference.

The year was a tale of two seasons. Calgary started off at 8–1, but finished up 1–5–1, tied with Saskatchewan but awarded first place because of their record. The Roughriders knocked off Winnipeg 34–23 before heading to Calgary for yet another final against the Stampeders.

Trailing 21–10 at the half, Reggie Holmes intercepted for a TD and Jerry Keeling and Shaw combined for two more to win 30–21. They unleashed the running game to the tune of 251 yards to close out the playoffs in Regina 23–21.

For the first time, Calgary would play a Grey Cup in the west, in Vancouver, against the favoured Argonauts. Again they faced poor playing conditions. "It rained all week," said Keeling. "That was Tartan-Turf, the first one in Canada. It didn't drain at all. Water came up every time you took a step. It was that way the whole game."

Defence dominated the 1971 Grey Cup, not surprising since the Stampeders only yielded an average of 13.6 points per game to Toronto's 17.7. The final score was only 14–11.

The 10–4 Argos were coached by the colourful Leo Cahill and quarterbacked by Notre Dame star Joe Theismann. Bill Symons and Leon McQuay gave them a potent running attack.

Labour Day Classic action, 1971. COURTESY CALGARY STAMPEDERS

The offensive star of the game for Calgary was Rudy Linterman, who set up both Calgary touchdowns with his running and receiving. In the first quarter, after a 40-yard Linterman reception, Keeling hit Harrison in the end zone for a 13-yard touchdown. Harrison described the play: "The wide receiver and slot ran deep, creating an alley. I would come right down between them in that alley and then I would cut across the middle because they were clearing out all those guys. Because Dick Thornton was cheating on the speed side, Keeling said, 'Herm, it's there.' He said he would hit me just before I got to Dick and that's exactly what happened. As soon as I caught it, Dick bumped me."

Said Keeling, "Herm didn't have much trouble getting in for the touchdown. Of course, it was also the type of game where, because it was so wet, defensive backs had a lot harder time changing direction than receivers did." After 7:17 of play, Calgary led 7–0.

Early in the second quarter, Toronto drove down to the Calgary 4-yard line where John Helton, Fred James, Dick Suderman and Craig Koinzan forced them to kick an Ivan MacMillan field goal. Seven minutes later, recalled Keeling, "I threw a pass out in the flat to Rudy Linterman. He was splashing around. Someone came in to tackle him, and dove to cut his legs out from under him. He went up and over him and ran down to the 6-yard line." Jesse Mims scored on the next play.

A determined Dick Suderman looms over Argonaut quarterback Joe Theismann during 1971 Grey Cup action.
COURTESY CANADIAN PRESS, *VANCOUVER PROVINCE* PHOTO

At the half, Calgary led 14–3.

Special teams accounted for the only Argo touchdown that came in the third quarter when Jim Silye fumbled Zenon Andrusyshyn's punt. Joe Vijuk picked it up and lateraled to lineman Roger Scales, who ran 36 yards for the only major of his career. "I let the ball hit my chest rather than catching it with my hands," Silye confessed. "If I had caught it, I was gone because the sideline was wide open. In the first half, we controlled the game. Until I fumbled, it was not an issue that we were going to win. We had 'em. Theismann couldn't do anything. We knew we had 'em. And then I fumbled and made it close."

Near the end of the third quarter, Calgary conceded a single, but led still led 14–11.

Near the end of the game, deep in his own end, Keeling threw his third interception of the game, picked off by Dick Thornton. "We got stuck down deep in our own end, and it was hard to run the ball because it was so wet," explained Keeling. "It was getting close to the end of the game, and we had to move the ball or they were going to kick a field goal and tie it up. So I tried a deep pass down the sideline, and I didn't throw it very well. The ball was wet, and I kind of lost control of it." Keeling himself made the tackle at the 14. Bill Symons swept right and lost three yards.

John Helton was inducted into the Canadian Football Hall of Fame in 1985. COURTESY CANADIAN FOOTBALL HALL OF FAME

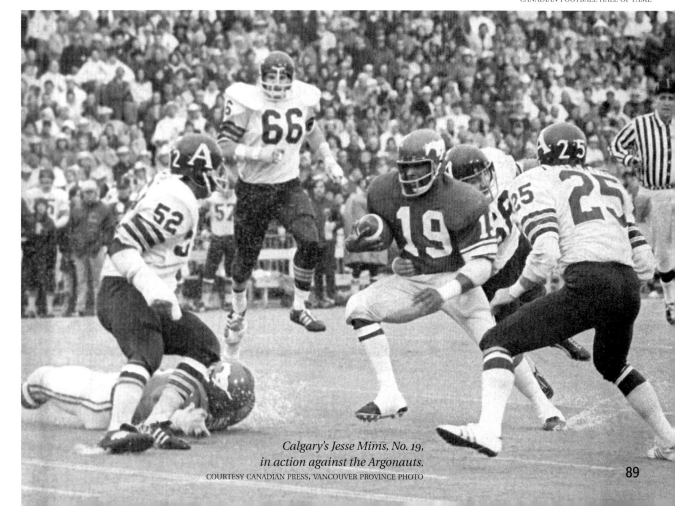

Calgary's Jesse Mims, No. 19, in action against the Argonauts.
COURTESY CANADIAN PRESS, VANCOUVER PROVINCE PHOTO

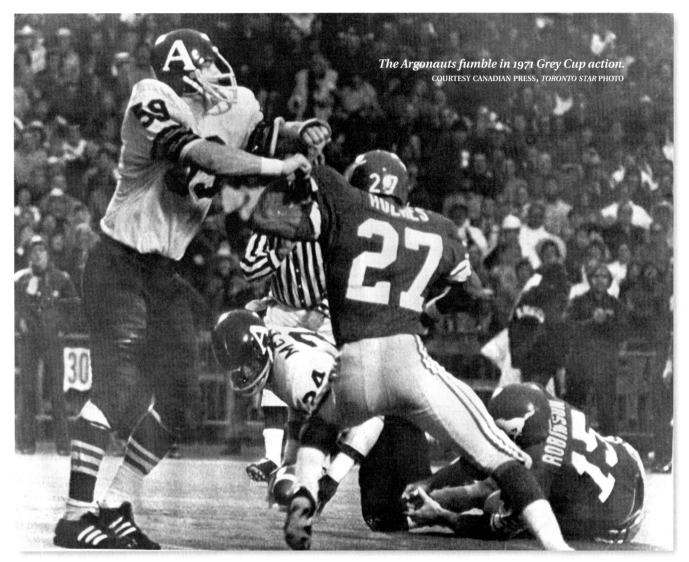

The Argonauts fumble in 1971 Grey Cup action.
COURTESY CANADIAN PRESS, *TORONTO STAR* PHOTO

John Helton described what happened on Toronto's second down: "McQuay was running to the left, and when he was getting ready to turn up field, he slipped, his elbow hit the ground, the ball popped out, and Reggie Holmes recovered it and snuffed out their opportunity."

While Leo Cahill argued the ball came loose when McQuay hit the ground and therefore should not have been ruled a fumble, Argo end Mike Eben saw it differently. "Poor Leon didn't fumble the ball. That ball was gang-tackled. I had a good view of the play, and I saw how it unfolded. He just didn't let the ball drop out of his hands. It was Larry Robinson's helmet on the ball that popped it free. It was a very strong, aggressive play on their part."

The always-modest Robinson described the play: "I was the one who actually hit him. I was forcing the sweep, we both slipped at the same time and bumped together. His elbow hit the ground, and the ball popped out."

But Toronto wasn't done. Calgary couldn't pick up a first down and had to punt, giving the Argos a last opportunity to move into field-goal range. But Harry Abofs mishandled it, and kicked it out of bounds, thinking that the last team to touch it had possession. Not so. In that situation, the kicking team took over. The Stamps ran out the clock.

Calgary 14, Toronto 11. The 23-year Grey Cup drought ended in the rain in Vancouver.

The myth persists that McQuay's fumble cost Toronto the Grey Cup. Not so, said

Wayne Harris. "He definitely wasn't going to get back to the line of scrimmage. Everybody still refers to it as Leon McQuay gave it to us. It wasn't him. Toronto had only crossed the 55-yard line three times the whole day. We had a super defensive unit. They may have kicked a field goal to tie it, but they definitely weren't going to score a touchdown on the run. We dropped a punt that led to the one touchdown they got. So they only kicked a field goal and a single against us. We held them in check all day."

The defence had to hold Toronto because Calgary picked up only one first down in the entire second half. The defensive effort was recognized. Harris was named the Grey Cup MVP, Dick Suderman, the Outstanding Canadian.

While the receivers complained about the hydroplaning effect of the soaked field, Calgary's legendary No. 55, Wayne Harris, wasn't bothered. "I wore the longest cleats I could get. I always did throughout my career. I didn't find the traction that bad. It didn't affect our defence."

Jubilant Calgary fans cheer their Stampeders on to a 14–11 victory over Toronto in the 1971 Grey Cup game.
COURTESY CANADIAN PRESS, *VANCOUVER SUN* PHOTO

Larry Robinson (second from left), Wayne Harris (centre) and Jerry Keeling (right) celebrate their Grey Cup win over the Argonauts.
COURTESY CANADIAN PRESS, *VANCOUVER PROVINCE* PHOTO

A rookie on that team and a future owner of the Calgary Stampeders was offensive guard John Forzani. "Although that was the game Leon fumbled," he reminisced, "maybe the biggest play was Harry Abofs kicking the ball out of bounds. I was five yards from him. He didn't bother trying to field it. It was two feet from the sideline. Out of frustration, he kicked it out of bounds. They throw the flags, and it's still our ball, because you can't cause the ball to go out of bounds like that. We ran out the clock."

Was Grey Cup experience a factor in Calgary's win? "It probably had a lot to do with it," replied Harris. "A whole bunch of us

were getting very long in the tooth. Certainly there wasn't going to be another chance to play in many more, if any. In my case, that was my eleventh year, Keeling and Robinson the same. Some of our defensive backs had been around 10 years or so. We were really an old, veteran football team."

Vital in assembling the 1971 championship team was Player Personnel Director George Hansen, a graduate of Western Canada High School who played junior football with the Bronks and then went to Sunflower Junior College in Mississippi on a football scholarship, transferring two years later to the University of Georgia. He played offensive line for the Stampeders from 1959–66 when Rogers Lehew appointed him minor football coordinator and then director of player personnel. Winning it all gave him a great sense of personal satisfaction. "Oh, it really did. I mean, I almost lost my life at that game," Hansen joked. "Rogers and I were in a spotters' booth in the stadium. I jumped up and down and almost fell out the window. I couldn't have been happier for the guys. We had better teams that didn't go to the Grey Cup, but things went right for us. We played well."

In spite of the low score, veteran Harrison argued that "Our best team was 1971. I thought that team could have beaten an NFL team. The defence was just awesome. Everybody was playing as a unit. Everyone was dedicated to the game. Nobody put themselves forward as a standout. The team effort was so strong. We always won as a team."

The rookie John Forzani loved every minute of it. "That Grey Cup came out of nowhere. It happened in my rookie year, and when you're 24 years old, you're of the opinion that's the way it should be. That was just a great week. You know you're the Western Champions, and you're treated extra special by the hotel staff and everyone else."

What was the victory celebration like? Forzani chuckled, "We were staying in a hotel on the north shore. The coaches and management put us in a big room and left. We went

heavy, hard until the next morning and then, bleary-eyed, we got on the plane to Calgary."

Strangely, winning the Grey Cup was a bit of a letdown for the great John Helton. "This is a terrible thing to say. I loved the Grey Cup because we won a championship and the city was rewarded for being such great fans.

Battery mates Herm Harrison (left) and Jerry Keeling share the Cup.
COURTESY CALGARY STAMPEDERS

93

Howard Starks and I were sitting in the dressing room afterward, and there was a sense of, 'Thank God, we won.' I said, 'Howard, is this all there is'? It was like Cinderella getting home at five minutes after twelve. It's all over, and it's like it never happened. It was wonderful in that you could remember the rest of your life you were a champion once."

Never again would Helton experience that Grey Cup feeling.

1971 Grey Cup Champions.
Left to right: Rogers Lehew, Wayne Harris, and George Hansen.
COURTESY CALGARY STAMPEDERS

Oh, Bury Me Not on the Lone Prairie

SOS Means "Save Our Stamps!"
1972–89

It was 23 years from the Stampeders' first Grey Cup in 1948 to Number 2 in 1971. Twenty-one years would pass before they drank champagne from the venerable mug again. During that time, the Calgary Stampeders fell on times so desperate that the team almost ceased to exist.

After winning the Cup in 1971, their third appearance in the national classic in four years, the word *dynasty* crept into the media who ignored the inevitable aging process that had set in. Rogers Lehew admitted as much. "We should have started making changes. Jim Duncan should have made changes, but he didn't feel like he could cut players who had been with us a long time. It's tough to do."

Nevertheless, the 1972 season opened on a high note with a 31–7 win over Winnipeg. Hugh McKinnis had 148 yards rushing. The defending champs would win only five more games, finishing 6–10 in fourth place. John Helton won the Schenley Award for Most Outstanding Lineman and was All-Canadian for a second time. Western all-Star Gerry Shaw led the offense with 65 receptions for 1,002 yards and 12 touchdowns.

Wayne Harris retired at the end of the season, one spent mostly on the sideline due to an injury sustained when a teammate fell on him in Regina. He left pretty much unscathed. "I never had my knees cut or anything," the relieved veteran said. "My neck hasn't bothered me since I retired. No operations. You take a few bumps and get a few crooked fingers. I was very lucky."

Was it great being a Stampeder? "Yes, it sure was. It was the best part of my life."

The opponent Harris admired most was Ron Lancaster. The feeling was mutual. "You could never fool him twice," said No. 23. "You'd get him early in the game and try to come back and do it later and it didn't work. He just had that sixth sense that enabled him to play the game better. He wasn't the biggest, strongest or fastest—he was just the best."

Harris went to work for an oil company. Herm Harrison also called it quits. He, too, settled in Calgary, where he became an active member of the team's board of directors. Harrison retired as the leading receiver in Stampeder history. He ranks sixth in receptions and fourth in yardage. He is also sixth all-time in receptions and fourth in receiving yards in CFL playoff history. Jim Duncan also faced the '73 season without Hugh McKinnis, Terry Wilson and Dick Suderman, who was traded to Edmonton. Newcomers included Tom Forzani, Rick Galbos and Roger Goree.

Quarterback Peter Liske returned, agreeing with W.C. Fields that he'd rather be here (Calgary) than in Philadelphia. While hoping for a stellar NFL career, he took his release from the Eagles in stride. "It doesn't matter where you play as long as you get a chance to play. You learn to put that sort of thing in perspective. When you play football, you want to win wherever you are. I've been in the NFL and won games there, I've proved to myself that I can do it. After that I don't care where I play and win football games."

Brave words. In Calgary Liske compiled back-to-back 6–10 seasons and missed the playoffs both years. The Stamps compounded the error of bringing him back by cutting Jerry Keeling.

"That was the biggest mistake I ever made in my life—letting Jim Duncan talk me into cutting Keeling," lamented Lehew. "I called Jack Gotta, who was the coach and general manager in Ottawa, and I said, 'I saw your game last night. You need a quarterback. Take him. And he did."

Said Keeling, "We didn't have a good year in 1972. Wayne Harris was injured, we lost some players and a lot of us were getting older. Then Pete Liske came back. I guess they felt they had to make a change at quarterback. For me it was the best thing that could have happened because we won the Grey Cup. Jack Gotta was a great guy to play for. I had a lot of fun that year."

Throughout his career in Calgary, Keeling always seemed to be considered a stop-gap quarterback who would do until the real thing came along. He was replaced by Eagle Day and Liske twice. Did he feel unappreciated? "No, I enjoyed playing defence," Keeling insisted. "It didn't bother me not being the starting quarterback those other years. I was pretty young when Joe Kapp got traded to Vancouver. I'm not sure I was ready to play professional quarterback anyway. And Eagle Day had a lot of experience in the NFL. Nah, that never bothered me."

Keeling was only Stampeder quarterback of his era to win the Grey Cup. He made All-Canadian three times and the Western Dream Team on five occasions—but all as a defensive back. He ranks fifth in team passing. He was inducted into the CFL Hall of Fame in 1989 and onto the Stampeder Wall of Fame a year later.

Jim Silye analyzed the decline of the team after their Grey Cup victory. "Quarterback," he said without hesitation. "Peter didn't quite have what he had before. The coaching was poor. People losing a step. Robbie lost it. I stepped into his shoes. I wasn't as good as Larry Robinson."

The 1973 team scored the fewest points and gave up the most in the league. Their leading receiver was rookie Tom Forzani with 62 catches for 731 yards and four touchdowns; the leading rusher, Bob Wyatt with

325 yards. Leon McQuay, obtained in a trade with Toronto for all-star lineman Granny Liggins, had 49 yards on 19 carries before leaving the team's employ.

Lehew explained. "You can always find a 215-pound defensive lineman. We needed a running back, so I made the trade. Duncan didn't like McQuay because in one game in B.C. he got hurt and could have gone back in, but wouldn't. McQuay got into a big argument with Duncan the Sunday before the Labour Day game. When Duncan told me he wanted him gone, I called him in and said, 'You're gone.' He said, 'You can't cut me.' I said, 'You're out of here.'"

Tom Forzani, aka Screech. COURTESY DARYL SLADE

Calgary's most impressive win was a 25–8 shellacking at Taylor Field, engineered by defensive halfback Frank Andruski, who snuffed out Ron Lancaster's fourth-quarter heroics with an interception and 105 yard return for a touchdown. Few Rider veterans were surprised it was Andruski who did them in.

In 1968 Andruski almost single-handedly swept the Green and White from the playoffs. During game two, he sacked Lancaster twice on consecutive fourth-quarter plays for 10-yard losses. By that time, the Saskatchewan crew, shell-shocked and dazed, were almost backed onto 16 Avenue. With third and 20, they decided to kick and run. Andruski streaked into the end zone, blocking Al Ford's punt. Touchdown Calgary. Grey Cup here we come!

Andruski blocked two kicks in 1967 and one per season from 1968–71, the most in team history and tied for seventh all-time in the CFL. He ranks fourth all-time in Stampeder interceptions with 30 and second in interception return yardage with 676. In 1973, after setting the record for most interception return yards in a season (204), he retired.

The highlight of the season was Wayne Harris Night on September 23. He was presented with a Holidaire Trailer, paid for by donations from the fans in sums involving the number 12, symbolic of the 12 years he played in the CFL. The team beat B.C. that night 13–12, improving to 5–4. They were 1–6 the rest of the way. The five-game losing streak began on home turf on September 30 when Jim Duncan inexplicably let the clock run out in the shadow of Hamilton's goalposts instead of letting Larry Robinson kick a field goal. The Ti-Cats won 31–29 before 21,000 infuriated frozen fans.

Their next three games were also against the East. The Stamps lost them all and were outscored 114–18. Rogers Lehew had seen enough. He fired Duncan, replacing him with offensive coach Jim Wood.

Did the Board of Director's call for Duncan's head? "No, I did," stated Lehew. "I called the president (Tony Anselmo) that morning about six o'clock. We played the night before. I went over to the house of one of our director's and listened to him and others. I told the president as of eight o'clock, he's gone, so if you want me to keep him, you'd better call me before eight o'clock. I called [Duncan] in. 'Jim, we've got to make a change.' And he said, 'Yeah, we do.' I'm sorry it had to happen. We were good friends."

Not everybody was sorry. "The respect I had for Duncan," said Silye, "came from the fact he devised an offensive line blocking scheme that is still used. But the way he treated people? He was condescending. He was rude. I vowed never to be like him."

Larry Robinson was more forgiving. "I wasn't a Duncan fan at first, but the last couple of years he changed his ways and started coaching better. Gerry Shaw had a meeting with him to get him to settle down a little bit. Duncan was pretty uptight. Jerry Williams was the best coach I played under."

When management makes a coaching change, it is usually hoped a new spirit of determination will set in. Even with only five wins, Calgary still had a chance to make the playoffs. However, the team played no favourites. They were quite capable of losing for one Jim as another. Saskatchewan initiated Wood into the head coaching ranks by licking the Stamps 34–7.

Lehew hadn't expected a sudden reversal of form. The Stampeders switched horses in the middle of the stream to pacify the fans that were staying away in droves. Duncan had worn out his welcome and was going the way of all coaches. By firing him, Lehew was hoping to fill those 8,000 empty seats. Attendance picked up for their final home

Centre Basil Bark. COURTESY DARYL SLADE

game, a 14–10 win over Edmonton. They could have made the playoffs by beating B.C. the last game of the season. They lost 15–7.

Frank Andruski, Basil Bark, Tom Forzani, Roger Goree and John Helton were all-stars, Helton All-Canadian.

Two more familiar faces left the Stampeder scene before the start of the 1974 campaign: Rogers Lehew and Jim Furlong. A 12-year veteran, an all-star linebacker in 1965, Furlong contributed to the club in many ways, including punting.

Furlong was a Lethbridge boy, one of the many quality athletes turned out by Jim Whitelaw at Lethbridge Collegiate. After graduating from LCI, he went to Tulsa, where he came under the tutelage of the Dobbs brothers.

Looking back on his years in Calgary, Furlong said, "Winning the Grey Cup had to be my biggest thrill, although getting there in 1968 was just about as big. That year we beat Saskatchewan in overtime in the final. That was a tremendous night."

The low point in his career was the 1962 loss in Winnipeg with the Wylie play. "I was really disappointed after that one because I was sure we were going to win. Losing in the Grey Cup hurts, and it was disappointing to me that we didn't win more. We had good teams since 1962, and we should have won more, but so many times, just like in the 1965 finals against Winnipeg, we blew it. We just blew it."

Canadians like Furlong, Robinson, Shaw, the Forzanis, Pajaczkowski, Bark, James, Silye, Linterman, Hanson and Wylie, to name a few, were the backbone of the Stampeders. You can't win in the CFL without good Canadians, a point coaches and general managers repeatedly made. But when it came to contract time, they sang another song. Furlong felt like a second-class citizen. "I had that feeling a lot. The general manager always gave you the same old story: 'You're a Canadian, you know we can't pay you as much as an American. We're operating the club on a shoestring. We have to save our money for imports.'

"It's hard to generalize, but I'd say that Canadians got paid 25 to 30 percent less than an import of equal ability. But, you know, we were our own worst enemies. When you signed a contract, the GM told you not to tell anyone what you were making. That really worked to the advantage of the clubs."

Furlong didn't think a Canadian general manager would make a difference. "They're brainwashed in the system of getting Canadians cheap. This really bothered guys like Robinson and me when we were playing just as well or better than Americans but the GM wouldn't give us their kind of money."

Still, Furlong wasn't bitter. "I made a lot of friends, I experienced something that few other Canadians have experienced. If I had to do it all over again I certainly would. It was a good life."

Lehew left to become the assistant general manager of the Detroit Lions. "It was a good opportunity, and I just thought it was time," he explained. "The directors were changing. They had made the policy decisions, and I made the day-to-day and football decisions. Some of them wanted to make the football decisions."

Lehew returned to Calgary in 1978. In 2009 he said, "There are three things I started that they still do that I'm very proud of. One, they still have the horse logo, which is one of the most recognizable in sports. The horse going down the sideline I got started in 1967. The President's Ring began in 1967." Lehew was inducted onto the Wall of Fame in 2004.

Lehew was replaced by Gary Hobson, who had been Earl Lunsford's assistant in Winnipeg. The feisty little Hobson was determined to clean house. "Some of our veterans have to go," he averred. "That's pretty tough on Jim Wood, but I'm behind him all the way. We're going to rebuild from the ground up."

Three veterans Hobson depended on were the Forzani brothers—Joe, John and Tom. For three seasons, 1973–75, the three brothers started for the Stampeders. There is no record of this happening in any other professional sport. In 2009, as an owner of the team, John described their relationship. "We were and still are very close, and one of the things that really helped out was that we didn't have to compete for a position. I was a guard, my older brother Joe was a linebacker and Tommy was a receiver. It was one of my great experiences to play with my brothers, and yet I never felt I was competing with them."

John idolized his older brother Joe. "Joe was a tremendous high school athlete and a great influence on my career and life because of the goals he achieved. He represented the city in hockey. I caddied for him when he almost won the Calgary junior golf tournament. The only reason he lost was he cut his hand the day before in football and couldn't grip the club properly. He was a star in St. Mary's basketball and football. For a younger brother, he was a pretty good role model."

John, Tom and Joe Forzani, the only triple-brother act in the history of pro football.
COURTESY *CALGARY HERALD*

All three brothers attended Utah State. "Tommy had a phenomenal college career," John stated. "He was the No. 1 receiver in U.S. major college football with 101 catches. But Tommy didn't really play football in high school at St. Francis. In Grade 10, he tore his knee trying to run a pass pattern, and so he focused on basketball. He became the premier high school basketball player in the city.

"Joe and I told the coaches at Utah about Tommy, so he came down. He barely knew how to put the equipment on, but they gave him a chance, and by the second year he was a starter. He was in the Blue–Grey game and East–West Shrine game. In one of them, he caught 10 passes and was voted MVP."

The Stampeders started the 1974 season with the veteran Liske and rookie Joe Pisarcik at quarterback. The team was still a one trick pony, living and dying with the pass. Coach Wood said, "We have failed to establish a running game. We know we cannot win without one, and we failed to get one. One guy quit camp, Jesse Mims was suspended, others didn't work out."

Despite having the weakest offensive line in the West, new GM Hobson traded nine-year veteran Lanny Boleski to B.C. for rookie Lorne Sherbina, "a top-notch Canadian who will give us 10 years of service." Try three as a backup, typical of the decisions made by management in the mid-seventies. It got so bad that long-time executive George Hansen resigned.

Why did Hansen leave? "Gary Hobson," he stated flatly. "I left under circumstances that made me decide I wasn't going to stay with that group. It wasn't a very good situation with him there, it really wasn't. Certain things had gone on, and when I confronted him, he denied it. I said, 'You can't deny things. This is my town, and I know too many people here.' I didn't go into details because that just hurts the team. I'm red and white all the time."

The Stamps went 1–7 over the first half of the season. After losing 27–0 to the Ti-Cats, Wood decided to change quarterbacks. Liske had no faith in the running game or his head coach. Matters came to a head in the Hamilton loss when he waved the short-yardage team off the field and threw three incompletions from the 5-yard line. That act of insubordination got Liske traded to B.C. for quarterback Karl Douglas and back Henry Sovio, even though Liske was the league's leading passer that year. Joe Pisarcik won five of the last eight games.

The only breaks the 1974 Stampeders got were bones. Typical was a 10–8 loss in Regina. The defence held the Riders to one touchdown, a 44-yard pass and run, Lancaster to Steve Mazurak. Defensive Coach Dick Monroe exclaimed, "I knew what Ronnie was going to do on that play. I just knew it! So I shifted out of zone into man on that side. Rob Pyne was on him, but Mazurak turned the wrong way. If the kid had turned the right way, Pyne would have knocked it down." Said Lancaster, "I threw the ball to the wrong side. I made a mistake on the play, but we got a touchdown."

Tom Forzani, Roger Goree, Rudy Linterman and Howard Starks were 1974 Western all-stars, John Helton All-Canadian. Linterman and Forzani led the league in receptions. Helton won his second Schenley Award for Outstanding Defensive Player.

Gerry Shaw and Larry Robinson retired at season's end. All-star linebacker Roger Goree was released. Two years later, he was All-Canadian with Saskatchewan.

Robinson became the first CFL player to score 1,000 points. At retirement he held the league iron-man record at 234 games. He remains the team's all-time interception leader with 50 and third in points behind Mark McLaughlin and J.T. Hay. He was inducted onto the Wall of Fame in 1986 and the CFL Hall of Fame in 1998.

The good news in 1974 was the arrival half-way through the season of an unheralded running back named Willie Burden. In six games, he ran for 541 yards. The Stamps won three of them.

During the 1975 preseason, Burden looked magnificent, prompting this writer to predict he would win the Schenley that year. Yet he almost didn't play football at all. "I started playing when I was a sophomore in high school," he explained. "I didn't play when I was in junior high, although I did go out for the team. A funny thing happened. I went out on the field for a couple of days, and the coach was giving out uniforms. I didn't get one because I hadn't played the year before. I thought my football career was ending right there."

Dr. Willie Burden, whose university studies led to a professorship in sports management at Georgia Southern University. Burden became a member of the Calgary Stampeders' Wall of Fame in 1992 and the Canadian Football Hall of Fame in 2001.
COURTESY CANADIAN FOOTBALL HALL OF FAME

At North Carolina State, the 5´11˝, 200-pound Burden ran for 2,529 yards, being acclaimed the 1973 Atlantic Coast Conference Player of the Year. He was the first Wolfpack player to rush for over 1,000 yards as he led his team to wins in the Peach and Liberty bowls.

Drafted by Detroit in the sixth round, Burden found things didn't go well in Motown. "I stayed during their entire preseason camp. About five days before the first league game, I was cut. I had injured my knee in my last year of college. I didn't get it operated on until the following spring, kind of late considering training camp opened in July. Although I made a lot of progress, my knee had not come along as well as I thought it should."

Detroit's assistant GM sent him Calgary's way. "Rogers made it happen," Burden recalled. Although disappointed at not sticking with the Lions, Burden said early in 1975, "I just want to play football. Since I've been exposed to the type of game up here, I really like it. Who is to say where the best place to play is? It's what I want as an individual to get out of the game. I have a chance to play here. I'm appreciative just because I enjoy playing the game so much."

Burden felt the dimensions of the Canadian game helped him. "I think probably more than anything else, the wider field helps me. You can run a sweep. In the NFL, you can run only so far before you get to the sidelines. Here you've got farther to go. You can outrun the pursuit and turn the corner. Overall, the Canadian game is much more exciting than the NFL. The three downs make it more exciting, too, because you have to open up and go for longer gains."

Burden proved an elusive runner. He possessed unnatural balance and an uncanny ability to find his opening. He didn't overpower people, but instead slipped along, picking up yards where a lesser back would not. Burden had a great sense of timing.

Jack Gotta said, "He was so great. He made my job so much easier. We're going to Regina to play a preseason game. A rookie comes up to me. 'Coach, how are we supposed to dress? Do you have a dress code?'

"I talked to the whole team and said, 'If you've got a problem with anything, check with Willie, just check with Willie.' So our guys are coming on the plane, and they're dressed well. They're not sneaking mickeys in their bag. When we get back, there's practice the next day at a bad hour. You want to get things done. The first thing you do is give the ball to Willie. First running play, whop! Away he goes. The night before, he carried 22 times and they pounded the crap out of him. Here's the best guy last night going like hell the next day. The others follow his example. Give me a team of Willie Burdens."

Willie talked about his craft. "You've got to hit the hole first of all. You should not miss any holes because that can ruin the confidence your teammates have in you. You've got to be there when you're supposed to. You've got to time the thing out. You work on this with the people up front. Timing just doesn't happen. It's not instinctive.

"No one can do it alone. You work together as a unit. If one part of the team breaks down, the whole play breaks down. You've got to have confidence in each other. If the guys up front feel you're going to run through the holes they make, they're going to make more holes. If you know a hole is waiting for you, you're going to run with more authority. I have a lot of confidence in my offensive line." That would be Centre Basil Bark, guards John Forzani and Lloyd Fairbanks, tackles James Bond and Max Huber and tight end Bob Viccars.

Because of the presence of Burden, the Stamps approached the 1975 season with optimism. They won three of their first five games before singing their familiar losing song. Typical of their season was the Labour Day game, where they blew a 30-point lead. When their record fell to 3–7, Wood was fired, replaced by his assistant, Bob Baker.

Another casualty of the poor start was Jim Silye. "I was cut after the Labour Day game," he recalled. "We were ahead 33–3 at halftime, and Edmonton came back to win. We had a stupid defensive scheme: a linebacker is supposed to come back and cover the slot area, just a quick look in to cover the hook pass to the tight end or slot back. I had the deep outside or deep middle depending on motion. If the motion goes, the linebacker is supposed to drop back. Instead, Blaine Lamoureux took off, and I got beat for the touchdown that won it for Edmonton on the last play of the game. It looked like I got beat but he wasn't my man.

"I got beat in the first half cleanly on a fly pattern, a beautiful catch by the receiver," Silye continued. "I was there, but he caught it. So I got beat for two touchdowns, and Dick Monroe said, 'Jim, we're going to go with four Americans instead of two. We're going to have to let you go.'

"I said, 'Okay, goodbye.' Edmonton, Regina and Hamilton called, but I said no. I stayed in Calgary. I was making more money in business."

Under Baker the Stamps were 3–3 the rest of the way, finishing at 6–10 for the fifth straight time and out of the playoffs, a very disappointing result in the year Calgary was hosting the Grey Cup for the first time.

The offense led by Joe Pisarcik at quarterback ranked second in points scored, carried by Tom Forzani, Linterman, rookie Bob Viccars and Burden. Rookie Vernon Roberson led the league with 10 interceptions, earning All-Canadian honours. Larry Carr was first in fumble recoveries with five. Calgary lost five games by a total of 13 points with Cyril McFall missing 21 of 41 field-goal attempts.

But the big story was Willie Burden, who set a new rushing record with 1,896 yards. Although out of the playoffs, the McMahon stands were packed for the last game of the season against Winnipeg, whose GM was Earl Lunsford. Also there, unbeknownst to Willie, were his mother and brother, brought in by CFCN. They were reunited just before game time.

Needing 137 yards to break Lunsford's record, Burden finished the day with 238. Lunsford presented him with the game ball.

Burden was the Western nominee for the Schenley Most Outstanding Player Award. He was up against Montreal's "Ordinary Superstar" Johnny Rodgers, who had 2,434 total yards. Burden had 53 more.

Although Grey Cup 1975 will best be remembered for the bitter cold and the pre-game streaker, for Calgarians the highlight was the awards presentation featuring Burden resplendent in a baby-blue tux. Not to be outdone, Rodgers donned a plush red velvet tuxedo with matching cape and a three musketeers hat. Willie won the award.

Although some Stampeders have posted more impressive numbers over their careers than Burden, who is ranked fourth all-time in team rushing, his is only one of five uniforms the team has seen fit to retire. He is also on the Wall of Fame and was inducted into the CFL Hall of Fame in 2001. Dr. Burden is now a professor at Georgia Southern University.

The success of Willie Burden convinced the faithful that the team was on the brink of something special. Instead, 1976 turned out to be the worst season in Stampeder history. After losing their first game in Edmonton 24–22, they tied Montreal in the home opener 20–20, not bad against the 1975 Grey Cup finalists. But after that, they didn't win a game until October 9. During that nine-game losing streak, they gave up 259 points while scoring 118. All the troubles on the field seemed insignificant when it was learned GM Gary Hobson had died September 13 of a heart attack at age 49.

Gary Hobson displayed a boundless enthusiasm for Canadian football. A native of Winnipeg, Hobson graduated from Kelvin High School and played junior football with the Westons and Rods. No bigger than a leprechaun, Hobson had to possess a tenacious spirit just to play the game. He also coached, leading the Fort Garry Lions to six provincial and three national championships. He got into the professional game when Earl Lunsford hired him to coordinate amateur football for the Bombers. He became Assistant General Manager in 1970.

During Hobson's tenure, Calgary was a dismal 12–28–1. After making progress his first two years, 1976 was a terrible disappointment for Hobson. He wanted desperately to win. He literally died trying. The day before his death, he told British Columbia's GM Bob Ackles he had received a clean bill of health earlier that week.

President Roy Jennings assumed Hobson's duties. After losing the next game 28–20 to Toronto, they fired Bob Baker. Joe Tiller took over. With a new quarterback in town, former Penn State All-American and Denver Bronco John Hufnagel, the Stamps ended their longest losing streak ever, beating Winnipeg 22–10. Then they tied the Lions at 31 and knocked off the Eskimos 36–28. The final game of the season they were home to the Roughriders. Ron Lancaster engineered a brilliant last-minute comeback, hitting Rhett Dawson in the end zone to win 33–31 and clinch first place. Calgary was fifth at 2–12–2. They had been mathematically eliminated from playoff contention in September!

In addition to Hufnagel, who took Calgary by storm late that year, other newcomers who bode well for the future included receiver Willie Armstead, defensive backs

Terry Irvin and Al Burleson, defensive end Andy Jonassen, and linebackers Jim Baker, Ollie Bakken and Tom Higgins. Defensive linemen Reggie Lewis and Ed McEleney along with DB Ray Odums, RB John Palazeti and guard Willie Thomas came in 1977.

John Helton was the only 1976 all-star, once again All-Canadian.

Joe Forzani had retired after the 1975 campaign, and brother John hung 'em up a year later. Losing hastened his departure. "Yes, but in 1974, I opened the sporting goods business," John explained. "In 1976 we had four stores. My single biggest reason was that outside interest, and I simply couldn't take the time away from it anymore. Now (2009) we are a public company, and we have 600 stores in Canada. I waited until the spring of '77 and said, 'I can't do this anymore.' It was very much the right decision, but it was a tough one." He would be back.

The new coach was Jack Gotta. Raised in Ironwood, Michigan, across Lake Superior from Thunder Bay, Gotta didn't play high school football because he was too small. When he got up to 180 pounds, he played for a semipro team and then attended Oregon State because two local stars were coaching there. He got his degree and an air force commission. When an inner ear problem grounded the aspiring fighter pilot, Lt. Gotta served his time and then tried out for the Cleveland Browns. When the Browns released him, Gotta turned down a chance to sign with Green Bay and headed for Calgary, playing the last seven games of the '56 campaign.

Beginning his pro career at the late age of 26, Gotta made the all-star team on both sides of the ball in his first full season. He made the dream team again in 1958 as a defensive back. The following year, he was traded to Saskatchewan.

"I got hurt," Gotta explained. "I dislocated my shoulder, and they didn't want to pay me, even though I had been a good performer. I came back at the tail end of the year after getting the proper treatment and staying out of the games.

"The night I came back, I played well both ways. In fact, I was given one of those Hudson Bay coats for being the player of the game. The next day, they had to name the 11 imports they were going to play in the last three games of the season, and I wasn't one of them. So I went in there and said some things I shouldn't have said—and I was on my way to Saskatchewan. If I had gone to Green Bay, I'd never have ended up in Calgary. If I hadn't got hurt, I'd have never ended up in Saskatchewan and met the girl I married and had the family we have."

Gotta was traded for Lovell Coleman.

After five years in Regina and seven games in Montreal, Gotta retired, joining the staff of Eagle Keys in 1965 and winning Saskatchewan's first Grey Cup in 1966. He moved on to Ottawa as Frank Clair's assistant, winning Cups in 1968 and '69. He succeeded Clair as head coach. When team owner David Loeb wouldn't renegotiate his contract after winning the Grey Cup in 1973, Gotta went to Birmingham of the World Football League.

Although there were several paths not taken in his life, he clearly regretted one of the choices he didn't make. "The one thing I wonder about," he said wistfully, "is when I was down in the WFL and I had been offered the head coaching job of the Chicago Bears by Jimmy Finks. This was just before we won the World Bowl Championship game down there. We won that game, and I talked to Jimmy again and said, 'Give me a little time to think about it', and I thought, Well, the group in Birmingham was lobbying to get into the NFL, and I would have had part ownership in an NFL franchise, which kind of blew my mind. When the World League folded,

I thought we were going into the NFL, but instead they chose Seattle and Tampa Bay.

"So I turned a job down to coach the Bears. The next year, I had a chance to go to Atlanta as interim head coach. You turn those down, and, of course, the door never opens again— and maybe it shouldn't. That was the only time I regretted a decision—turning down Jim Finks. I had the highest regard for him."

Clearly Jack Gotta was a winner with four Grey Cup rings and a WFL championship. The Stampeders were delighted to have him, as were Calgarians for whom he became and remains a beloved favourite son.

"After the WFL folded," recalled Gotta, "I was approached by a couple of clubs in the east and some U.S. universities, and I had a chance to come to Calgary. Well, I didn't even consider the other ones. They might have been offering more money or a longer contract, but Calgary is where I wanted to go. It was also crucial for my family. My oldest boy was only 12, my youngest ready to enter kindergarten. [My daughter] did all her schooling here, and the next youngest did all but kindergarten in Calgary.

"When I came here as a young player, it was a fascinating place. I saw a lot of advantages living in a great city and area. This is the place I wanted to be. I always felt good here."

Looking back on his days as a player, Gotta said, "I worked for the McMahons at Pacific Petroleum. I did some fishing and hunting while playing football. You'd go out goose and duck hunting, and then go back and practice. I thought to myself, it can't get any better than this. The city and I were made for each other."

Gotta was named general manager as well as coach. "I think having both jobs will avoid the conflicts that happened here in the past," he explained. "When I came here as a visiting coach, I'd hear the coaches on one radio show and the general manager on another show, and they would be contradicting each other and taking credit or assessing blame. I'd never been around a situation like that before."

Gotta's challenge was obvious amid the flagging fortunes of the Stampeders. "The fact that you're down for a long period of time, it's pretty hard to change a whole lot of people's minds. I'm talking about players. A guy's a loser instead of being a winner. You have to change that attitude so they believe they are winners."

He looked forward to the 1977 campaign. "I think we can do it here. We can turn this team around. Our players and coaches really give me a positive feeling. I just hope we can catch a playoff spot. For us to improve a hundred percent means we win four games."

Gotta clearly expected much better, but his tongue-in-cheek comment proved prophetic. The Stamps finished in last place at 4–12, the first team in CFL history to earn the dubious distinction of missing the playoffs for six straight years.

In truth, most of Gotta's problem resulted from injuries to offensive personnel like Forzani, Armstead, Linterman, Viccars and Burden. The Stamps had to field a makeshift line-up most of the season. Although they moved the ball well, the continuous substitution cost them dearly when they got into the red zone. Said John Hufnagel, "We were moving the ball, but when we needed that extra yard to get into the end zone we couldn't do it. We weren't a very mature team.

"I just didn't have the versatility with receivers I wanted," Hufnagel continued. "Tom Forzani broke his wrist and took awhile to get back into form. Willie Armstead broke his leg. Bob Viccars broke a wrist. We just didn't have any continuity at all."

The Stampeders won their home opener over Hamilton and then lost seven straight.

They tried everything, even allowing XL Radio to bring in Salem, Massachusetts, Wendell the White Warlock to put the whammy on Winnipeg. He spent the evening cruising the McMahon sidelines while muttering mysterious incantations and waving a magic wand menacingly at the opposition. Calgary won 16–10 when Ray Odums returned an interception for a touchdown. They beat Saskatchewan a week later, but Wendell's witchcraft waned as they lost four of their last five games.

Tom Forzani made All-Canadian, Burden All-Western.

For the first time in nine years, John Helton didn't make the dream team. Why not? "Dislocated my shoulder," he lamented. "They didn't diagnose it. I missed one game and played the rest of the year with it. After that I always had shoulder problems from about September on. I could get through the first part of the season, and then hitting would take its toll and I'd finish the season on one arm again."

A Calgary writer working on a tip from the coaches' room accused Helton of malingering for taking himself out of a game against Saskatchewan (the game where he sustained the injury) and not dressing for the following encounter against B.C. Helton phoned the broadcast crew long distance, stating unequivocally that the team doctor told him not to play. But the relationship between the team and tackle had soured and was never the same again. Despite a bum shoulder, Helton made All-Canadian three more times, two as a Blue Bomber, bringing his total to nine.

If questioning Helton's courage was one of Gotta's big mistakes, cutting gritty veteran Rick Galbos was another. After a career at Ohio State under the guidance of Woody Hayes, Galbos first tried to crack the Roughrider line-up, losing out to veteran Bobby Thompson.

The great John Helton. COURTESY DARYL SLADE

He arrived in Calgary in 1973. During his stint with the Stamps, he rushed for 1,017 yards, caught 162 passes for 1,965 yards and scored 11 touchdowns. More importantly, he was the lead blocker for Burden.

Every time Galbos stepped on the field, he gave 100 percent despite hamstring pulls, broken bones and concussions. Stampeder trainer Alex Rescky said, "He has the greatest attitude an athlete could ever have. He just doesn't know how to quit. Rick isn't capable of dogging it. If all the boys had his attitude, we'd never lose a game."

With Rudy Linterman out with a torn bicep, Gotta wanted a faster back to relieve the pressure on Burden. He signed B.C. veteran Lou Harris, who, unlike Galbos, preferred the training room to the field and averaged a mere 17 yards per game.

After 13 seasons in the league, the great veteran centre Basil Bark retired. A homebrew,

Bark played for Montreal from 1965–69, coming west in the Terry Evanshen deal. He made all-star four times, twice in each division, playing the most complicated position on the offensive line. Bark's company InterSport Alberta now runs the Stamp Store.

Jack Gotta not only turned his team around in 1978, he almost knocked off the high-flying Eskimos and got to the Grey Cup. It was one of the most remarkable transformations in CFL history.

Gone that year were defensive backs Ron Woodward and Dennis Meyers, defensive lineman Lorne Sherbima, linebacker/punter Bill Palmer, receivers Brian Gervais and Larry Leathem, fullback Bobby Joe Easter, offensive tackle Jody Medford and centre Basil Bark. Newcomers included defensive tackle Miles Gorrell, defensive back Rob Kochel, line backer Bernie Morrison, offensive linemen Bob Lubig, Dave Kirzinger and Tom Humphrey, wide receiver Kelvin Kirk and running back James Sykes. Harold Holton was moved to defence. Quarterback Ken Johnson arrived in August.

The starting quarterback was John Hufnagel. "I think this is a pivotal year for me and also for the team. We expected good things last year, and they didn't happen. I'm in this game to win. If I don't win, I'm not very happy about it."

Calgary knew the road to the Grey Cup went through Edmonton, then a league powerhouse. Early returns weren't promising with the Stamps losing the opener up north 33–17. They bounced back with a win and tie against the Lions before losing 28–14 to Montreal, followed by wins over Winnipeg and Saskatchewan and a defeat in Ottawa. Home to face the 5–0–2 Eskimos in the Labour Day Classic, halfway through the season with a mark of 3–3–1, the Calgary offense was giving opponents the willies— Armstead and Burden, that is.

A new atmosphere began to emerge at McMahon Stadium. The previous six years, a favourite pastime for Calgarians was guessing what new, imaginative way the team would find to lose a game. During those years, they chuckled with appreciation when a game winning touchdown was nullified because of 14 men on the field, when Pete Liske threw three incomplete passes from the B.C. 1-yard line or when QB Joe Pisarcik took off with the ball still in centre Basil Bark's possession.

Even in 1978, anxious aficionados of failure nervously confronted Stampeder executives wondering when they were going to trade Forzani and Burden. "Not going to trade 'em," Art Evans insisted. "We're going to make the playoffs this year."

Diehard fans didn't believe it, but those were words they could finally believe in. Added to the arsenal was a new weapon in the form of running back James Sykes, who would help Calgary lead the CFL in rushing with 2,159 yards that year.

Jocko was delighted. "When guys lined up against us and saw Burden and Sykes, I know they had to spend a lot of hours wondering how they were going to handle them. They'd say, 'We don't have a linebacker who can handle Burden, let alone that other guy. There's no way.'"

The healthier Sykes was the more productive of the two running backs, rushing for 1,020 yards and catching 50 passes for 614 more. Sykes also contributed 737 yards on punt and kickoff returns for a grand total of 2,371 yards, the most combined yards in the country. Burden had 627 yards rushing, 307 receiving. The Stamps had the fewest fumbles in the CFL, rare for a running team.

While Sykes caught the most passes, Armstead and Forzani had more yardage, making Calgary second to B.C. in total offense.

They tied Edmonton on Labour Day and two weeks later. After losing to Saskatchewan, they closed out the season with five straight wins to finish second with a record of 9–4–3. Edmonton was 10–4–2.

After trouncing the Bombers 38–4 in the semi-final, the Stampeders headed for Edmonton. It was the first time the two teams met in the Western Final.

Going into the final, the Esks were first in points scored, Calgary second. The Stamps were second in total offense, Edmonton fourth. Calgary was No. 1 on defence, led by Helton, Lewis, Jonassen and McEleney up front; Bakken, Morrison and Palazetti, the linebackers; and Odums, Burleson, Irvin, Falconer and Kochel in the secondary. Cyril McFall was the leading kicker.

The quarterback would be newcomer Ken Johnson, in relief of Hufnagel who hurt his hand in the semi-final. Born in Scottsdale, Arizona, the 6' 2" Johnson went to Colorado and then bounced around the World League. He signed with Calgary in September 1978.

Dave Cutler and McFall traded first quarter field goals. In the second stanza, the Stamps' Odums intercepted Tom Wilkinson and returned it 53 yards for a touchdown. The Esks evened it up with a Jim Germany major.

Although the Stamps had the considerable wind in the third quarter, they could only manage a field goal. In the final 15 minutes, Edmonton finished them off. Three penalties for 30 yards kept a 66-yard drive going, resulting in Germany's second TD. One of the penalties was a ridiculous roughing-the-passer call on Helton, who actually laid Wilkinson down like a feather. Cutler converted three turnovers into nine points. Edmonton won 26–13.

In 1977 only Burden and Forzani made All-Star. The following year, Helton, Harold Holton, Reggie Lewis and James Sykes were All-Canadian, while Al Burleson and Terry Irvin made the Western team. Jack Gotta won his third coach of the year award.

New to the '79 roster were kickers J.T. Hay and Mike McTague, defensive backs Doug Battershill and Robert Sparks, defensive tackle Ken Dombrowski, offensive guard Tom Krebs, wide receiver Darrell Moir and quarterback Bruce Threadgill. Gone were Harold Holton, Jim Baker and Doug Falconer. The biggest loss was seven-time All-Canadian and two-time Outstanding Defensive Player John Helton, who was traded to Winnipeg for defensive back Merv Walker, defensive end Lyall Woznesensky and running back Richard Crump. Little children tugged at Jack Gotta's trouser cuffs crying, "Say it isn't so, Jack!"

The rumour persisted that Jack Gotta had been waiting for his chance to move Helton since the big guy took himself out of that 1977 game against Saskatchewan. Helton had felt unappreciated from that moment on.

"I had a good job in the off-season," Helton recalled, "so, although my salary was important to me, it wasn't the primary thing. If my pay reflected my talent and my contribution to the team, I was happy. The year before I went to Winnipeg, I didn't feel there was a reciprocal feeling about the worth of what I had contributed. If it had been about money, I would have gone to Buffalo 10 years earlier."

Gotta learned his negotiating skills from Frank Clair, who tossed nickels around like manhole covers. Helton was not amused.

"Mr. Harry Cohen from the clothing store told Jack that he would pay the difference in what it would take to keep me," Helton alleged. "Jack wouldn't accept that. Mr. Cohen was a wonderful man. I wouldn't have allowed that to happen."

Rumour had it the difference Mr. Cohen offered to make up was $5,000. "No, no, no," replied Helton. "But you played 10 years," he went on, "and you know your salary was substandard to lesser players in the league and you're willing to understand that and

never move, but, when I was called down for my play when I hurt my shoulder in '77, I can honestly say I was not able to even lift my shoulder and get a fork on my table for dinner. At night I would have great pain and would often wake up.

"Still, I missed one game in 14 years because of that shoulder. I think for playing defensive line that wasn't too bad. And then to be called down for a game—that makes me laugh.

"When the people around you watch this kind of thing happen and don't have anything to say about it—whether it be media or detractors or anybody else—then that doesn't speak very highly of the company you're in. So I just felt like, 'Hey, it's okay, I can see my abilities aren't needed here.' I went to Winnipeg."

With Jocko, it was strictly business. "When I first got here," he countered, "we were short on Canadian talent. With the trade, I was going to get Lyle Woz as a starter, Merv Walker as a starter and a running back, Richard Crump, an American starter. At that time, we had other good imports, true, not at the level of John Helton. But we had Ed McAleney and Reggie Lewis. I felt we were covered at Helton's position. I'm picking up two Canadian starters where I didn't have Canadian starters. I also felt that McAleney and Lewis had six years ahead of them, whereas John was already intimating that he might retire if he had a good year. The key was getting two Canadian starters."

Gotta also replaced John Hufnagel with Ken Johnson at starting quarterback. "John and Tom [Forzani] were a good combination," explained Gotta. "The ball was going to go 50 percent of the time to Tom Forzani. But other receivers would never get the football. John kept looking them off until Tommy was open. So Armstead and Kelvin Kirk and the backs are ignored. With Johnson, you had so many other things going for you.

"I like to throw to the backs, not as alternates or safety valves but primary targets. We ran a lot of option screens to Burden and Sykes. Or you can fake the screen and give it to the other back. You can't defence everything.

"It was so important to our offense. We spent hours and hours working on it. So John goes in there and doesn't call any of that stuff and just goes to Tom running a hook or a slant or this or that. It seemed we were just going to repeat the year those guys had the season before I came here. They had the worst record in the history of the Calgary Stampeders.

"It was barnyard football with those two guys. John matured, and when he had the chance, he moved. Some guys hated Kenny Johnson. Tom Forzani I know hated him because Kenny was going to the backs, going to Armstead."

In 1978, with Hufnagel starting, the leading receiver was Willie Armstead in yards and James Sykes in receptions. Under Johnson in 1979, the guy with the most catches was Forzani.

With Johnson at the controls in 1979, the Stamps were 12–4, their best record in a dozen years, but still second to the 12–2–2 Eskimos. Tom Forzani led the team in total yardage with 1,472, receiving and returns. Defensively, the Stamps surrendered the fewest total yards. Al Burleson had nine interceptions.

Once again, they had no trouble in the semi-final, crushing B.C. 37–2. Once again, it was off to the igloo for the western final.

The prognosis was not good. Two of their regular season losses were to Edmonton, 44–9 July 31 up north and 27–1 on Labour Day in Calgary. They finally beat their nemesis 26–19 on September 30 at McMahon.

In the conference final, Edmonton made the most of two opportunities. In a span of 1:33, Warren Moon threw touchdown passes to John Konihowski and Brian Kelly. The Eskimos then fell back on their magnificent defence. Hay replied with two field goals and a single. The final score was Edmonton 19, Calgary 7.

The Stamps were victimized by questionable officiating. In the second quarter, Johnson hit Armstead with a long pass to the Eskimo 6-yard line. After making the catch, Armstead fumbled. While one Eskimo sat on him, another fell on the ball. The call should have been defensive holding or interference.

Armstead, Burleson, Fairbanks and Reggie Lewis were All-Canadians. John Helton—of Winnipeg—was the Western finalist for the Outstanding Defensive Player award.

Soon after the season ended, Gotta surprised the CFL by relinquishing his coaching duties in favour of assistant and long-time friend Ardell Wiegandt. Gotta felt good about his decision, he said. "When I was general manager and head coach here in '77, we started turning things around. In '78 and '79 we had really good football teams, and I thought we were really on our way. We went right into the fourth quarter in the finals, and that's when Edmonton had the best team ever and maybe Calgary had one of the better teams in the history of this club. We were 12–4 at the time the league was the best it has ever been."

Wiegandt had a strong staff with Stan Schwartz, Dennis Meyer, Marvin Bass and Walt Pozadowski. Gotta was ably assisted in the front office by Joe Tiller. They looked forward to ending Edmonton's two-year reign as Grey Cup champions with a contingent of veterans minus Ollie Bakken, Tom Humphrey, Richard Crump, Willie Thomas and Lyall Woznesensky. Merv Walker was the only player left from the Helton trade.

Bakken's toughness had been an inspiration to his teammates over the years. On September 17, 1977, the 1–8 Stamps entertained the Blue Bombers. Early in the first quarter, Jim Washington took a handoff and Bakken practically broke him in two. Inspired by that great hit, Calgary won 16–10, ending the seven-game losing streak. Bakken closed out his career in B.C. in 1980 but tragically died five years later at age 31 from a malignant brain tumour.

Following free agent John Hufnagel's signing with Saskatchewan, Ken Johnson became No. 1 quarterback, backed up by Mississippi State's Bruce Threadgill. Hufnagel would be back.

The star of the show was James Sykes, who rushed for 1,263 yards and 10 majors, caught 57 passes for 582 yards and led the team with 932 punt and kickoff returns yards. He led the league in combined yards, rushing and kickoff returns and made All-Canadian along with Reggie Lewis and Ray Odums.

A key to the success of both Burden and Sykes was the blocking of tight end Bob Viccars. The Calgary native and Bishop Grandin Ghost went from the junior Mohawks to the Stampeders. "I block on every running play, and we do a lot of running on first downs," he noted. "I'm held in to block on some kinds of passes, especially play-action stuff, so the faster guys can get open. It is a difficult position because you have to be both a blocker and a receiver. I like to see myself as both." None played the position better.

Offensively the Stamps were better in 1980 than the previous year, but they won three fewer games, finishing at 9–7 in third place behind Edmonton and Winnipeg. They slipped a bit defensively, but the big difference was their inability to win on the road, where they recorded only two victories. They lost the semi-final in Winnipeg 32–14.

Andy Jonassen and Robert Sparks left at the end of the season. Newcomers included offensive tackle Jeff Inglis, defensive tackle Franklin King, defensive back Harry Kruger

and wide receiver John Holland, who led the team in receiving with 56 catches for 1,017 yards before signing with Ottawa. Linebacker Danny Bass, Michigan State MVP and all-time tackle leader, arrived in town from Toronto later in the season.

Ed McAleney finally made the all-star team. He loved to get after quarterbacks. "All the way through the athletic system, a lineman could never touch the quarterback in practice," mused the man from Maine. "When you get one day a week when you can hit the quarterback, you're going to do so. Because of all that has gone on before, you're going to unload on the quarterback a little harder than you would another guy."

Although the offense had been second only to Edmonton's, Wiegandt brought in Jerry Williams as offensive coordinator in the belief that if it ain't broke, fix it. He implemented a system players openly criticized as too complicated. The team was most successful in 1981 when Johnson ignored the system and went with their bread-and-butter flair passes to Sykes. Still, they were 5–4 after Labour Day and in third place behind Edmonton and B.C.

After losses to Edmonton, Toronto and Montreal, the executive, concerned with falling revenues, ordered Gotta to fire his friend Ardell. "I'd known Ardell since he was a young coach," Gotta lamented. "He was a hard-working guy. You don't know how an assistant coach is going to be as a head coach until he gets there. He's a math major, he knows football, he's well organized. He just couldn't communicate with his players."

Jerry Williams took over the coaching duties. Johnson was traded to Montreal for Canadian quarterback Gerry Dattilio to back up Bruce Threadgill. They won their first game after the change 29–3 over the Alouettes, but then went winless in their last three to finish 6–10 in the cellar.

William's offence was last in the division in points and yardage, first in fumbles and second in penalties. Lack of talent wasn't the problem. Neither was the defence, which was the stingiest unit in the CFL. The problem was that the team was confused offensively and thoroughly demoralized when it came time for the stretch run. Cliques split the team and executive members interfered constantly. Meanwhile the media howled.

At the end of the season, Williams was fired. The executive insisted Gotta resume the dual role of coach and general manager. Economist, oil patch entrepreneur, professional football player, outstanding athlete and all-around good guy Bob Viccars retired. He would be back.

Also saying goodbye was the great Willie Burden, who was placed on the 60-day injury list the middle of September. The injuries he sustained in 1981 didn't prevent him playing, but he was in constant pain. Given that he was in the final year of a three-year contract that paid him close to $80,000 annually and that he was used mostly as a blocker for Sykes, he knew it was unlikely that he'd fit the team's plans for 1982. Besides, he was in his eighth year as a professional running back and was living on borrowed time.

When Burden had arrived in Calgary near the end of the 1974 season, Gary Hobson had to order coach Jim Wood to play him. After games, Burden routinely had an ice pack on a shoulder or thigh and usually a bandage on his foot. The artificial surfaces caused extremely painful turf toe. When asked about his injuries, he usually smiled, "Don't worry about me. I'm just glad we were able to win tonight."

The last game Burden played at McMahon was August 21, a 30–18 victory over Ottawa. After the game, he had a huge bandage on his knee, an ice-pack nursing a deep shoulder bruise and so much wrapping on his toes that it looked like he had the gout. This time,

when asked about his injuries, he replied softly, "It hurts all the time, man. It just isn't much fun anymore."

The greatest human dignity comes from true humility. Willie Burden had it. An unsophisticated country boy from North Carolina who loved his grits and his momma but hated Canadian winters was one of he finest athletes and gentlemen ever to grace the Canadian game. In many ways, he was the greatest Stampeder of them all.

In 1982 Jack was back. Jim Erkenbeck, Dan Daniels, Jerry Keeling, Mike Roach and Stan Schwartz were the assistants, Schwartz the only constant of the Gotta era. New players included linebackers James West, Larry Barker and Wayne Harris, Jr.; defensive lineman Randy Trautman; defensive back Darrell Touissant; and running backs Darrell Smith and Gerry Dattilio. The Stamps would go with four linebackers led by Danny Bass. Offensively their weapons were Sykes, Forzani, Armstead, Darrell Smith and Mike McTague, receiver and punter, as well as J.T. Hay, the best place-kicker in Canada.

Calgary opened the season in Toronto with a tie at 24 even though Datillio threw six interceptions. Fortunately they had 16 days off until their curtain raiser at McMahon. Things didn't go much better with John Hufnagel's Roughriders edging the locals 25–19. They then reeled off three straight wins with Threadgill at the helm and prepared to face Winnipeg in a showdown for first place. Gotta enthused, "It's kind of fun challenging for Number 1. The guys like that. I like it. It's good."

But his team wasn't and was trounced 35–4. Then it was three more wins, including besting Edmonton 32–20 on Labour Day. The Stamps were 5–2–1 at the halfway mark and finished 9–6–1 in third place. It was a mystifying season. In the first nine games, the defence yielded an average of 20 points a game; thereafter, 37. After getting hammered in Regina 53–8, Gotta was incensed, saying, "I've never been embarrassed like that before, and it won't happen again." Defensive coordinator Dan Daniel's days were numbered. Two weeks later, the defence gave up 48 points to Hamilton. Fortunately Calgary scored 55 in the highest scoring game in CFL history, a surprise because both defences were healthy, the offenses banged up.

Their final opponent was B.C. with the winner making the playoffs. The Stamps won 25–19, but lost the semi-final in Winnipeg 24–3.

Armstead had 1,081 yards on 61 receptions, and Sykes rushed for 1,046. Both were Western all-stars. Danny Bass, Ray Odums and Lloyd Fairbanks made All-Canadian.

During the off-season, the Stampeder executive decided Gotta should just coach. Jocko disagreed. "I controlled the numbers here for five years," he explained, "but I irritated a couple of people. The president of Air Canada, Howard Paillefer, was also president of the team. I made a deal with Pacific Western to fly us everywhere. It was like $100 a ticket and Air Canada charged $200 a ticket.

"We saved about $80,000 in hotel and meal costs by getting out right after the game on a charter. But when I did that, I irritated Howard. He said, 'You can't do that.' I said, 'I went to Air Canada and they wouldn't do it, and I talked to you and nothing happened', so I did it.

"Another executive member's close friends had the concessions in the stadium. I got beer in the stadium. We made a couple hundred thousand dollars. But the executive is upset with me, even though we brought in triple what we were getting for the marketing rights by going to Labatts rather than Molsons. I'm bringing in $350,000 clear that we weren't generating before.

"The new president, Bill Britton, was manoeuvring to get me out of town. Even

The CFL's premier place-kicker J.T. Hay. COURTESY DARYL SLADE

after we had such a good year financially in '82 and made the playoffs, Billy Britton's thinking we can't have one guy being both coach and general manager. I go to the board meeting and Howard brings this up. They brought his buddy Walter Prisco in as GM, the Crisco kid."

When Prisco was appointed, assistant general manager Joe Tiller left for Purdue.

Still, Jocko looked ahead to 1983. "I've been around for a long time and this is the most anxious I've been to get into the season. We've got some great newcomers. Even our veterans are impressed with them."

Quarterbacks were always Gotta's Achilles' heel, but he was particularly enthusiastic about his rookies Bernard Quarles of Hawaii and Danny Barrett of Cincinnati.

"It was rise or fall with Gerry Dattilio last year, and he did a pretty good job, but we won't go beyond making the playoffs with Gerry at quarterback," Gotta conceded. "We're hoping one of the new guys emerges and takes charge. Right now Quarles is doing that."

Lloyd Fairbanks left for Montreal. Ray Crouse and Craig Ellis were in the backfield. Mike Levenseller joined as a new receiver. Arriving in the secondary were Ron Hopkins and Richie Hall.

After four games, James Sykes was released and allowed to slip ignominiously out of town. In his five full seasons, Sykes had rushed for 5,135 yards, returned kicks for 2,308 yards and caught 216 passes for 2,182 yards. He scored 49 touchdowns, was the CFL rushing champion twice, four times a Western all-star and three times All-Canadian. He started 73 games, averaging 132 combined yards per game.

The Stamps were 4–3 going into Labour Day. Against the Eskimos, they scored 10 points in the final two minutes to win 18–15. They were winning on the strong defensive play of Bass, West, Morrison, Odums, Irvin and Moir. Rookie Richie Hall played so well he made the all-star team. The offense sputtered and died, quarterbacking again the problem. Coming into the final game of the season, they were 8–7, impressive considering they had 14 rookies in the line-up. They needed a win over Saskatchewan to advance to the playoffs. The Riders won 27–23 in Calgary in the last minute of play.

In a calculated scenario of You-Can't-Fire Me, I-Quit, Jocko launched a pre-emptive strike by demanding a new contract and a substantial raise. Despite the fact he deserved both, he got neither, and the Jack Gotta era came to a close. His record during his seven years with the team was 42–34–4. He made the playoffs four times. As general manager he left the team with a big bank account. Media, fans and players were sorry to see him go. After a brief stint in broadcasting, he coached the Roughriders for two years, after which he retired to Cochrane.

Removing Gotta from the GM's job was the first mistake in a decade characterized by executive interference and incompetence that brought about the demise of community ownership and almost the end of the team itself. The second mistake was firing Gotta as the coach. The third was hiring Steve Buratto to replace him.

A career coach with no pro playing experience, Buratto was 39 when he got the job after serving as a assistant in Saskatchewan and B.C. While he turned out to be a fine coach later in his career, he was in over his head in Calgary. Although short of receivers, he forced Tom Forzani into retirement. At a free-agent camp, he passed on Lionel James, who went on to star in the NFL. Also gone were Ray Crouse, Ed McAleney and Willie Armstead.

Buratto traded Danny Bass to Edmonton for receiver Tommy Scott. Danny Bass—six times All-Canadian and eight times a Western all-star—is regarded as one of the greatest linebackers in CFL history. He won the Most Outstanding Defensive Player Award in 1989 and was inducted into the CFL Hall of Fame in 2000. "It was at the end of the 1983 season," Bass explained, "and Jack Gotta said, 'Dan, we're going to re-do your contract. We're going to do it right.' At that time, I wasn't getting paid very much. They had some guys sitting on the bench making more money. I hadn't said anything because I always believed you had to prove yourself first.

"About two weeks later, Jack got fired, and the assistant GM, Ed Alsman, knew what was going on but denied everything. I asked to be traded, and it was the best thing that ever happened to me because I came to Edmonton. I wasn't asking for the moon, just a fair shake."

Bass wanted $80,000. The team said no, though they had to assume Scott's $85,000 salary. Scott was 32, Bass 26. Bass was a leader of great character, the kind of player you build a team around.

As always the key to success was quarterback. Buratto evaluated his talent. "Greg Vavra has shown great promise and has run the offense well. Danny Barrett has done well. Bernard Quarles has been the slowest of the three. Quarles isn't gifted with great learning skills. He has great athletic ability." Barrett started the season as No. 1 but soon gave way to Quarles.

The offense was dreadful, last in the league in points and total yardage. Defensively, they were eighth in fumble recoveries, interceptions and sacks. They were 3–6 after the 30–28 Labour Day loss to third place Edmonton and 3–4 the rest of the way.

The combination of losses with an unusual number of rainy day games resulted in attendance dropping like a stone. With neither American quarterback doing well, the team turned to a local boy, former Dino Vavra, hoping he would put fans in the stands. Winning a game or two would be a bonus. Vavra played more than the others the rest of the way, completing 161 of 324 passes for 1,901 yards and 10 TDs. He threw 16 interceptions. He didn't have much to work with. The schemes were unimaginative, the receiving corps slow, the running attack anaemic. The

only bright spot was J.T. Hay's 135 points. Nothing reversed the declining attendance, which fell an average of 8,198 between 1982 and '84. The team lost over $1 million.

A prime example of the tragedy of errors that gripped the franchise during the 1980s was the debacle over Tom Forzani's sweater. Calgary's last home game was October 20 against the Lions. Herm Harrison and other executive members had arranged to retire Forzani's Number 22. At halftime, Tommy Scott, who wore 22, would switch to 26. Forzani would be brought out and his number retired. That's what happened, even though the management of the team knew nothing about it because they were opposed to honouring Forzani.

During the off-season, a desperate executive reached into the past and hired Earl Lunsford as general manager. "Rogers Lehew urged me to apply for the job in Winnipeg in 1968, and next thing I knew, I was general manager," Lunsford recalled. "They wanted an administrative guy who would not coach.

Earthquake Earl Lunsford came to shake up the front office. COURTESY *CALGARY HERALD*

That was fine with me because I liked the management side. I enjoyed my time with Winnipeg."

An omen of things to come, Winnipeg president Ross Smith wanted him to fire his coach Ray Jauch in 1979. Lunsford resisted. "Yes, I did. Ray was the only thing we had going for us. I didn't agree with the executive and said so." The next three years under Jauch, the Bombers were 32–16 and in the Western Final twice. But as the old saying goes, "The boss may not always be right, but he's always the boss."

By 1982 Lunsford was ready to leave Winnipeg. "I think there was a little unrest with me, and I felt like it was time to move on."

In Calgary, Lunsford's first decision was to sign 34-year-old quarterback Joe Barnes.

The Million-Dollar Man, Joe Barnes. COURTESY DARYL SLADE

"Some people believe when you rebuild, you start with the defence," he said. "I've always believed the quarterback is most important. Without that, you won't win games or put people in the seats. We have to prove to people here we are committed to winning. Joe Barnes is an important part of that." Rumour had it Lunsford paid him a million dollars. "Yes," Lunsford conceded, but "strung out over three years."

As for Buratto, Lunsford said he "would take a look at him for a year. I don't believe in just coming in and firing somebody and then say, 'We're going to get a new coach right now.' I believe in giving a guy a chance to prove himself and then make a decision after I have inspected him for a year."

Lunsford made a couple of more deals, swapping offensive linemen Willie Thomas, Kevin Molle and Ken Moore to Jack Gotta in Regina for Bob Poley, Gerry Hornet and Greg Fieger. He traded Bernard Quarles to Ottawa for the talented but erratic Canadian receiver Dwight Edwards and linebacker Dan O'Rasovich.

Come June of 1985, Buratto was confident and defiant. "I think we are going to win, and I'm not overly concerned about whether I retain my job or not. We're going to win football games if we get any kind of break at all. Last year we were 6–10. This season we are going to be much better than that."

They weren't. After opening the season with five straight losses, Buratto was fired August 12. "The situation was such that he needed to go because I don't think he cared about anything," said Lunsford, "and when he lost all hope, that's when he needed to go. I hired Bud Riley on an interim basis to get through the rest of the season and then re-evaluate it. The best coaches are hired in the off-season." Riley had been his coach in Winnipeg from 1974–'77. The Stamps were 3–8 the rest of the way, finishing last.

What about the million-dollar man? Awash in red ink, after their sixth loss, Barnes was traded to Montreal. The quarterback the rest of he way was newcomer Rick Johnson. Calgary's leading rusher, Larry Mason, averaged a mere 15 yards a game. The only bright spot was Emmanuel Tolbert, who had 1,124 yards receiving, but that was it. No Stampeder made an all-star team.

Once again the Stampeders only major weapon was J.T. Hay. In 1985 Hay set a record for most consecutive converts, 363, and kicked the fifth longest field goal in league history, 57 yards. When his career ended in 1988, he was the CFL's seventh all-time scorer with 1,411 points.

Hay began his CFL career in 1978 with Ottawa. For the first half of the season, he put the ball through the uprights with deadly accuracy. For the rest of the year, he couldn't hit the broadside of a barn door. Ottawa gave up and traded him to Calgary, where his 1,275 points place him second all-time to his successor Mark McLoughlin.

The secret of his success? "The coach who helped me the most was a Medicine Hat boy, Stan Schwartz," Hay maintained. "He helped me a great deal. If it wasn't for Stan, I wouldn't have enjoyed the success I had."

It didn't take long for Lunsford to figure out he had inherited a mess, a greater challenge than any defence he ever faced. To operate in 1985, the team secured a million dollar line of credit, the reserves left by Jack Gotta being gone. To balance the books, the Stampeders needed strong fan support, dependent on the team's performance. But whatever could go wrong, did go wrong, and by Labour Day, the team had lost $400,000.

The team didn't perform, and the fans stayed away. "We budgeted back in January to average 24,000 fans over the season," Lunsford said. "We thought we'd lose 2,000 season ticket holders because of the negative attitude here, but instead we lost 7,000. Our overall attendance is averaging about 14,500 a game.

"We can make it back if we start winning during the last half of the schedule. But we're not going to turn around the attitude of Calgary people on the short haul. Getting the fans back will be tough. Many of them have a wait-and-see attitude, and they want to see a lot."

Losing wasn't the only reason the team was facing bankruptcy. "Maybe some of the faults we've had are because we've always been able to make money regardless of the quality of the team or marketing," Lunsford mused. "I think we got a little bit lazy. We have self-inflicted wounds. We got fat and sassy and didn't take care of business. When we were the only game in town, we didn't do a lot of marketing. Then the NHL came, and television increased at a great rate. People saw all sorts of marketing which focused on our lack of it."

But, he added, "If it's all marketing and no product on the field, you've still got a problem."

Indeed. For the inaugural Wall of Fame game honouring Wayne Harris, John Helton and Paul Rowe fewer than 12,000 fans showed up. For the final home game against the high-flying Blue Bombers, the smallest crowd in McMahon history, just over 11,000 were in the stands. The Bombers won 47–4.

Late in 1985, team president Pat Peacock approached the corporate sector of the city for $3.6 million to not only pay off the team debt, but also tide them over until fortunes on the field improved. The plan fell apart because the business community would not invest as long as the present directors were in charge, believing they had reduced a sound team to rubble in three years. The Calgary Stampeder football club was on its deathbed.

Former player Gerry Shaw joined Doug Hunter, Bill Tanner and Brian Ekstrom to save the Stampeders. They had $2 million. They approached City Council and Premier Don Getty to come up with a line of credit for $6 million more. If the money was approved, a bond would be bought with the interest part of the guaranteed repayment. Led by former Eskimo Getty, the province was on board with the promise to guarantee half the interest or $1 million. City Council said no, though Mayor Ralph Klein said the city might pay the team's $500,000 rent to the McMahon Stadium Society.

In the midst of all the deal-making, former Personnel Director Ed Alsman was fronting for a wealthy individual who wanted to buy the team. Alsman made it clear he would be the general manager and Lunsford would be out.

A meeting between the Alsman group and the executive was called off because the directors didn't show up. A second meeting was cancelled. The Alsman group finally met with the executive, but due to short notice and an unreasonable deadline, they did not have time to do business properly. The Alsman group withdrew.

A "Save Our Stamps" campaign began in earnest. With a telethon, contests, appearances by present and past Stampeders, 22,400 season tickets were sold. There was money in the bank for a couple of years. Lunsford remained as GM with entrepreneur Vern Siemens installed as a volunteer, unpaid president to oversee the business side of the operation.

With the financial wolf away from the door, Lunsford set about improving the

Coach V. COURTESY CALGARY STAMPEDERS

product on the field. His chose Bob Vezpaziani as the new coach. "I had a good feeling about him, and he did things I agreed with," said Lunsford.

Vezpaziani began his Canadian career at Acadia University. "Frankie Morris [legendary Eskimo scout] was one of the few guys who gave any attention to the Maritimes," Vespaziani recalled. "I used to rap with him a lot, and we struck up a friendship. Just before Ray Jauch went to Winnipeg, I asked Frankie to put in a good word for me to Ray about guest coaching. I was his guest coach in '78. The next year he hired me. In '85 I was with Don Matthews, Roy Shivers and Adam Rita in B.C. I had a good run, winning two Grey Cups in a row with Winnipeg in '84 and B.C. in '85. I had worked for Earl in Winnipeg. He interviewed me, and I became the head coach."

Hall of Famer Frank Morris's 14-year playing career began with the Argos after the Second World War and ended with the Eskimos in 1958. COURTESY CANADIAN FOOTBALL HALL OF FAME

1986 was the first year of the 18-game schedule. Vezpaziani had 11 newcomers in his line-up.

The Stampeders' Gary Allen led the league in rushing with 1,153 yards. Ray Alexander was second in receiving with 1,590 yards, and Tolbert was fifth with 1,286. Rookie Marshall Toner was Calgary's Number 3 receiver with 41 catches for 403 yards. Quarterback Rick Johnson made All-Canadian with a ranking of first in touchdown passes with 31, first in yards with 4,379 and second in completions with 302. When the University of Saskatchewan grad wasn't drafted, he wrote letters to each CFL team, asking for a try-out. Only Bud Riley replied. Toner became a Stamp for six years.

Rookie Harold Hallman's 19 sacks and Vince Goldsmith's 15 helped set a record with 85 sacks. The O-line gave up the fewest. Hallman won the CFL Rookie of the Year Award. Yet, in 1985 not a single Stampeder made All-Star. In 1986, seven made the dream-teams, including Gary Allen, Hallman, Rick Johnson and Bob Poley as All-Canadian, and Mel Jenkins and J.T. Hay, All-Western. Hay was Number 1 in field goals and second in CFL scoring.

The Stampeders opened with two losses, won a couple, lost a couple, won three and were hammered 42–19 on Labour day by Edmonton. They were 6–2 the rest of the way, finishing at 11–7.

What a team, what a final kick! But they finished fourth. However the league had revised the playoff structure so that if the fourth-place team in either conference had a better record than the third-place team of the other conference, then it would make the playoffs instead. Calgary would thus meet the first-place Eskimos at Commonwealth Stadium in one semi-final.

Edmonton had won all three meetings with the Stamps that year. However, in the season opener at McMahon, Matt Dunigan completed a Hail Mary pass on the last play of the game to win by a point. On Labour Day, the Stamps gave up a long-bomb major on the opening play, fumbled the ensuing kick-off for another TD and were down 14–0 with three minutes gone in the opening quarter. In the final meeting, Rick Johnson threw a costly interception late in the final frame.

Going into Edmonton, Coach V was worried. "I always thought, unfortunately, my locker-room talk was prophetic," he recalled.

All Canadian Rick Johnson with Stan Schwartz. COURTESY CALGARY STAMPEDERS

"I emphasized the fact that just to be here wasn't it, guys. Yes, you've turned it around and finally had a helluva season. And had the town excited, and the year before they were ready to fold, so everything turned around and it was very positive. But I thought there were too many guys that were satisfied about that, and my point was, don't be satisfied. We don't know what's going to happen next year. I said, 'Some of us may not be here next year.' And sure as hell, I wasn't, as well as a few of the others," he said with a laugh.

Though Gary Allen was hurt, the Stamps were moving the ball well against the Green and Gold when disaster struck in the second quarter. Rick Johnson chipped a vertebrae in his neck and lost the use of his arm. The Horseshoe Factory prevailed 27–18.

"Our quarterback had a great year," enthused Vezpaziani in spite of the loss. "I thought our defence played very simple but very aggressively. Our special teams did a helluva job. They were coached by Tom Higgins, the only carry over from Buratto's staff."

The Stampeders had gone from 3–11 and bankruptcy to 11–7 and a full treasury in 12 months. The future looked bright. But remember, this was Calgary.

Ray Alexander and Mel Jenkins went to the NFL. Gary Allen, arrested for shoplifting in the off-season, was a shadow of his former self. ("He could be a problem child," said his coach.) Vespaziani was being undermined by his assistant, Lary Kuharich. At Roy Jenning's annual Stampeder–media steak barbecue, Kuharich openly courted executive members and the press. If all that wasn't bad enough, Vespaziani's quarterback was in no shape to play. Speaking of Johnson, he said, "He had a great year in '86, but that was it. In the off-season, he got his shoulder operated on, unbeknownst to us. That thing wasn't ready when he came to camp.

"He wanted to be an actor, and he had to lose weight. So he wasn't ready for football when he came in. In fact, if you didn't know who he was and were looking at the four quarterbacks we had in camp, you would have rated him last. His arm just wasn't ready. He couldn't deliver the ball. We had a lot of other injuries, too.

"That was the year the NFL was threatened with a strike, so there was nobody out there because anybody who could breathe was signed as a replacement player until they settled it down there. So we had some problems."

Usually when you break out of a losing streak, there are sighs of relief all around, and you're given a chance to continue. Not this time. "We won the first game, then lost six in a row, won the next one, and I got fired," said Vespaziani. "I think the thing that hurt me was at the end of '86, my defensive coach, Rich Ellerson, went back to Hawaii,

and one of the guys he took with him was my secondary coach, Duane Akina.

"That's when I hired Wally Buono. When Montreal folded their franchise after the last exhibition game in '87, he was out of a job. Joe Galat called me and recommended him highly. I'd never worked with Wally and didn't know him from a hole in the ground. He turned out pretty well, didn't he?"

The writing was on the wall for Vespaziani when the Stampeders met Ottawa. Trailing by 26 points, Kuharich left the press box early in the fourth quarter and came to the sidelines to engineer a 39–38 win. The players presented him with the game ball, pointedly ignoring their head coach.

Assistant coach Tom Higgins disagreed about the players' intent. "I actually got a game ball as well." Giving the game ball to Kuharich wasn't an anti-Vespaziani act, he insisted. "The players liked Bob."

The man who pulled the trigger on Vespaziani was club president Jim Silye, who ordered Lunsford to do the deed. On August 18, when Lunsford refused, both were fired, along with O-line coach Ron Smeltzer. Personnel man Bud Riley quit. The whole event was dubbed the "Massacre at McMahon Stadium."

"I fired Earl Lunsford," Jim Silye admitted. "The team was losing. We felt there was no motivation from the coaching staff. The board talked about it. We thought we needed a change in philosophy. We were losing our fan base, and it was a business. We decided we'd ask Earl to let Bob go. Earl said, 'I won't do that. I honour contracts. He has to stay.'

"I respected that, but I said, 'Earl, it's not working.' Nevertheless, he still insisted. 'No, if you're going to fire him, you're going to fire me, too.' I took that back to the board. They said it was my job to let them go. So I did.

"Earl did say he would let him go at the end of the year. That was the kiss of death because if you let him go then but not now, you're agreeing with us that he had to go. But the club was bleeding, we were hurting, we needed to create a little new juice. . . . Whether we use the coach as a scapegoat or whatever, we need to bring the guy in who will scare the players because the new guy always scares players. . . .

"And we couldn't go through another SOS campaign. One game, there were fewer than 6,000 fans there."

Coach V was aware of Kuharich's manoeuvring. "When you're not winning, that happens. That's why I missed Ellerson because [he] was a very loyal guy. . . . If Rich had heard about it, he would have brought it to my attention, and I would have dealt with it. But Rich wasn't there."

Kuharich came out of the box and mutinied against his captain. He knew he could get away with it because executive members told him they were going to fire Vespaziani, and he would get the job.

"The win [against Ottawa] finally gave us some relief after losing six in a row," said Coach V. "But the plans to fire me were already in place. That win didn't make any difference.

"I didn't endear myself to Silye because of some of the comments he made after our first good year. He said, 'When you have time, I'd like to talk to you about your offense.' I told him, 'The guy I answer to is that guy right there,' and I pointed to Lunsford. And I think that kind of pissed him off and he got his due the next year.

"I certainly know this is a what-have-you-done-for-me-lately business. I learned that lesson really quickly. I found out later that there was stuff going on between Kuharich and Silye and Siemens."

Vespaziani wasn't surprised Lunsford refused to fire him. "He did the same thing in Winnipeg when the president wanted to fire Ray Jauch. Earl was a pretty good fellow who stood by you. He was from the old school. A handshake to him was everything."

Lunsford also knew his days were numbered in Calgary before the Massacre at McMahon Stadium. "Anytime the board doesn't agree with you, you've got a problem," he cautioned. "Things weren't going well at the meetings, and they were telling me to do certain things, so it was time for me to be gone. That last year in Calgary, the board of directors became a little overbearing. They thought they knew more football than the general manager did."

According to Silye, no commitment had been made to Kuharich prior to Coach V's firing. "We had a little committee that discussed who we should replace him with.

Greg Vavra in action.
COURTESY DARYL SLADE

At the end of the day, we compared Tom Higgins and Kuharich. We voted on it, and Lary got one more vote."

Usually firing the coach midway through the season doesn't accomplish much. Not in this case. The Stamps won 8 of 10 and made the playoffs.

Kuharich benched Rick Johnson and went with rookie Rick Worman. The Stamps finished first in rushing but were otherwise near the bottom in most categories offensively and defensively. But they played gambling, audacious football. Kuharich called it "Putting a sword in their hands."

On to Edmonton for the semi-final, where they lost 30–16.

The following year was challenging for the CFL. It began with the collapse of the Alouettes and was followed by poor attendance across the league. To combat financial problems, a salary cap was introduced.

In Calgary, Normie Kwong replaced Jim Silye as the president and general manager. "I had stepped down as a director to become the full-time president of operations," Silye explained. "We were trying to save on overhead until we could find somebody. One of our directors, Fred Peacock called me a lame duck president. I said, 'Well, if I'm a lame duck, I'm out of here and I resigned. That's when they got Normie Kwong to take over the team. They gave him a hundred grand, which they could ill-afford at the time."

The club could also ill-afford its poor standing in the community. Although Kwong needed neither the money nor the aggravation, his love for the CFL compelled him to take the job. His presence in the front office meant instant credibility and a boost in public relations.

After the strong finish in 1987, it seemed Calgary was finally a legitimate Grey Cup contender. But the salary cap forced Kuharich to unload several veterans, including Richie

The Honourable Norman L. Kwong, Lieutenant Governor of Alberta from January 20, 2005 to May 11, 2010. Photo by Fred Katz. COURTESY OFFICE OF THE LIEUTENANT GOVERNOR OF ALBERTA

Hall, Rocco Romano and Vince Goldsmith. Players were cut and resigned at lower salaries. To make matters worse, middle linebacker Bernie Morrison was hurt and the outside backers played with nagging injuries. Bob Poley got hurt, and Rick Johnson played badly and was cut. Veterans Rudy Phillips and Leo Blanchard were added to the O-line.

In a pre-season game, QB hopeful Erik Kramer tore up his knee. The team had planned to bring in a running back but opted for a quarterback to replace Kramer. The running backs name? Michael 'Pinball' Clemons.

The team lost the season opener up north 33–0 and six of their next eight games, including a 27–11 thrashing on Labour Day. As the losses piled up, the behaviour of Coach Q, as Kuharich was called, grew increasingly bizarre. He was a Jekyll and Hyde, charming and rational one moment and in a total rage the next. Two of his victims were popular veterans J.T Hay and Bob Poley. Kuharich cut both, blaming it on the salary cap. But he did it after September 1, meaning that as six-year veterans they had to be paid their full salaries to the end of the season. Coach Q also

Tim Petros. COURTESY DARYL SLADE

cut Rick Worman in favour of Carl Fodor.

The Stamps dropped five of their last six, finishing fifth at 6–12.

Emmanuel Tolbert and Larry Willis each had 1,328 yards receiving. Tolbert made All-Canadian. The leading rusher was local boy Tim Petros with 737 yards and nine touchdowns.

But Coach Quixote! Sports teams are excellent at acknowledging physical injuries, but when it comes to mental illness they are woefully behind the times. Observed his predecessor Bob Vespaziani, "He was a perfect manic-depressive type—up, up and other days really down. In hindsight I should never have hired him, but he had good credentials, and Joe Kapp called me everyday on his behalf."

Jim Silye admitted that he had been instrumental in making Kuharich head coach. "I could see he was paranoid, and I was working with him on that. Normie couldn't handle Kuharich. It just got worse. Lary became a tyrant."

When asked about Coach Q's wild mood swings, Tom Higgins commented: "Wow! Yes! It was truly a unique situation. Never before—and probably never again—will I be able to deal with that and be around another personality like that."

Kuharich was in the first year of a three-year contract as director of football operations. Making matters worse was the fact his six assistants had two year contracts, unheard of in the CFL. What was the club to do? Hope Kuharich is a misunderstood genius and send him to charm school? They couldn't afford to clean house. Although Coach Quixote treated Kwong shamefully at times, the China Clipper swallowed his pride and kept him on, a wise decision when they rebounded to 10–8 and second place, a result they had no reason to expect.

They did it without Tolbert who went to Toronto. They had a rookie quarterback in

Terrance Jones, drafted seventh over-all by San Diego. Jones signed with Calgary because the Chargers wouldn't give him a shot at quarterback. When Jones got hurt, Kuharich picked up Danny Barrett and guard Dan Ferrone from the Argos. Lloyd Fairbanks returned later in the season.

Jeff Fairbanks. COURTESY CALGARY STAMPEDERS

Defensively, the Stamps were tough. The line-backing corps with Doug "Tank" Landry, Lemont Jeffers and Ken Ford was spectacular. The secondary with Greg Peterson, Derrick Taylor, Larry Hogue, Dave McCrary, Ron Hopkins and Chris Major was the best. Stu Laird got hurt and was replaced by Kent Warnock, who combined with Eugene Bellevue, newcomer Will Johnson

and Mitchell Price for 39 sacks. Willis led the West in receiving, Landry in tackles. The Stamps would host their first playoff game in ten long years.

Throughout the season, Kuharich had continued to exhibit the bizarre behaviour that made him impossible to work with—not mention a public relations disaster. When the '89 Stampeders fumbled 41 times, Defensive Coordinator Wally Buono sagely observed that the reason was "Maybe part and parcel of the players being too uptight, too tense." Buono may have been onto something.

After one game, Kuharich threw a full can of beer at Normie Kwong's head. In the Western semi-final, a battered bunch of Roughriders ventured into Calgary, where they fell behind 26–23 late in the fourth quarter, but rallied for 10 points and the win. The usual large contingent of Rider fans, many of them Stampeder season ticket holders, cheered noisily behind the Calgary bench as their team took the lead. Kuharich turned and gave them the finger. They responded with a cascade of snowballs.

Bernie Morrisson.
COURTESY DARYL SLADE

A few days later, amidst rumours of his Calgary coaching demise, Kuharich hastily cleaned out his office in the middle of the night and fled to Vancouver, where he was quickly introduced as the new boss of the B.C. Lions.

A huge sigh of relief could be heard all over the burg by the Bow. But just as the darkest hour is before the dawn, the Golden Age was about to begin.

CHAPTER 7

Happy Trails

The Golden Era
1990–2001

ATTENDANCE DURING THE 1986 SEASON AFTER THE SAVE OUR STAMPS campaign averaged 27,286 per game. By 1989 the average had slumped to 22,003. Once again the team was in dire straits. Thankfully, Normie Kwong was so highly regarded in the community that he was able to single-handedly keep the team alive. If the Stampeders had folded, the future of the CFL would have in doubt. It is not an exaggeration to credit Kwong with saving both his team and the league.

Under tremendous pressure to sell season tickets, Kwong could have opted for a big-name coach who might provide a quick fix. Instead, he picked a man with no head-coaching experience. He chose Wally Buono.

Born in Potenza, Italy, in 1950, Buono's family moved to Montreal in 1953. His father died when Wally was a boy. His mother spoke neither official language. Because she couldn't afford to look after Wally and his brother, the boys were put in the Shawbridge Boys Farm and Training School (a reformatory) until she could reclaim them.

After playing minor and high school football in Montreal, Buono went to Idaho State. He played linebacker for his hometown Alouettes from 1972–81, appearing in five Grey Cups, winning two. After four years as an assistant in Montreal, he joined Bob Vespaziani's Calgary staff in 1987.

Going into the 2010 campaign, Buono's record was 235–122–3, the most wins in CFL history. As coach of the Stampeders, Buono finished first in his division eight times in thirteen years, including five in a row from 1992–96. His teams got to the Grey Cup six times, winning three.

125

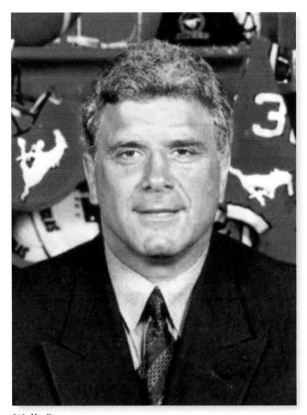

Wally Buono. COURTESY CALGARY STAMPEDERS

Buono's record speaks for itself, but it is more exceptional when viewed through the lens of the turbulent times he experienced in Calgary. There was the near bankruptcy of the club in 1991 and its purchase by the erratic Larry Ryckman, his collapse and the new ownership of Sig Gutsche. Every year Buono had to replace half a dozen starters. Coaching in Calgary was never easy, yet Wally Buono emerged as the greatest coach in Canadian football history.

In addition to Buono, Kwong hired the brilliant bird-dog Roy Shivers to scout American players. His acquisitions included Allen Pitts, Kelvin Anderson, Marvin Coleman, Alondra Johnson, Marvin Pope, Will Johnson and Darryl Hall. Kwong also

Bird Dog Deluxe, Roy Shivers.
COURTESY CALGARY STAMPEDERS

lured out of retirement the greatest personnel man of them all, Frankie Morris, a former teammate of the China Clipper in Edmonton and the architect of the great Eskimo dynasty of the 1970s and '80s. In 1995 Stan Schwartz became the team's Vice-president and General Manager, Administration. His rock-solid reputation for honesty coupled along with his common sense kept the Stampeders alive during the fall of Ryckman's financial empire and ensured a smooth transition to new ownership. The Medicine Hat native was appointed president of the club February 12, 1996. Thanks to Schwartz, Kwong and Buono, the Stampeders became the flagship franchise of the CFL.

Stan Schwartz.
COURTESY CALGARY STAMPEDERS

When Buono took over in 1990, he talked about what had to be done to bring a championship to Calgary. "One, you've got to work on attitude so everyone is thinking in the same direction. Two, you have to get the kind of people who respond to you. Three, you have to get good people, good football players, good athletes.

"People ask why we can't beat Edmonton. My direct answer is that the Edmonton organization has been at it for 30 or 40 years. You look at Hugh Campbell. He's the product of Norm Kimball, who was there for 25 years. That's why they are very successful. Their approach, their organizational skills are far better than those of anyone else. Get good people that you have confidence in, allow them to build the organization. That's one thing I really stressed when I talked to Norm Kwong and the board before I got the job.

"It's not so important who you hire, but be stable from the top down or be filtering people up so that if you do make a change at the top you do so without changing the philosophy or disrupting the organization.

"So hire good people, let them do their jobs, know what your role is, stay within your role, pick the best possible players, and don't screw them up. Let them play. The coaches we have are excellent in their field. They don't need me telling them what to do. They know more than I do. I know my role, and they know theirs. We're going to approach every game with the feeling we are going to win."

Asked why the team had such a troubled history, Buono responded thoughtfully, "Partly because of instability at the management level. You look at how many GMs and head coaches have been here. What philosophy or organizational plan were they following? Stability results in security, which usually results in a good team.

"Normie Kwong allows the coaches and scouts to do what they think is best for the organization. The present circumstances couldn't be any better for a head coach. We have the necessary stability to win in the future."

Improving the passing game would be a priority, Buono emphasized. "Our passing attack will get progressively better as the players understand our new system. The skill of the receivers we have in t raining camp right now is better than what we had last year. The veterans are doing a solid job. The young guys, Eddie Brown and Derrick Crawford, have been very impressive. Dave Sapunjis, our first-round pick has been a very pleasant surprise to us. He ran a 4.52 and has exceptionally good hands. On offense we

The youthful Frankie Morris who became perhaps the greatest bird dog of them all.
COURTESY CANADIAN FOOTBALL HALL OF FAME

feature the 3 Ms: movement, mobility and motion. My assistants—John Hufnagel, Jeff Tedford and Bob Swift—have an excellent understanding of the league, so we won't be a static team."

Any major concerns going into the 1990 season? "Coaching—me!" laughed Buono. "Young guys do make mistakes. But I have old, wily guys around to pull me out of the fire."

Buono's 1990 Stampeder team had nine rookies in the starting line-up, including an entire receiver corps of Derrick Crawford, Allen Pitts, Dave Sapunjis, Pee Wee Smith and Shawn Beals. Defensively, Buono went with rookie linebackers Joe Clausi and Henry Smith, as well as end Harold Hasselbach and defensive back Darryl Hall. Second-year men included defensive end Will Johnson and cornerback Junior Thurman. Johnson made All-Canadian five years in a row and should be in the CFL Hall of Fame. Veterans

Walter Ballard, Mitchell Price, Kent Warnock, Matt Finlay, Greg Peterson, Dave McCrary and Ron Hopkins rounded out the defence.

The O-line was anchored by 16-year veteran Lloyd Fairbanks in his tenth season in red and white. Leo Blanchard, who had spent nine seasons with Edmonton, and six-year veteran Mike Palumbo were the guards, 12-year veteran Kevin Powell the other tackle. Tom Spoletini was in his sixth year at centre. They protected the quarterback, Danny Barrett, who was backed up was Terrence Jones. The running backs were Keyvan Jenkins, Tim Petros and Andy McVey.

Calgary opened at B.C. on July 13 with an overtime tie. Buono chalked up his first victory as a head coach six days later at McMahon Stadium when the Stampeders defeated the defending Grey Cup champion Roughriders 30–25. The rookie was clearly delighted. "Saskatchewan is a good football team," he said after his inaugural victory. "That's why they won the Grey Cup last year—not because they were lucky, but because they were good. We're telling the people of Calgary and the CFL that we're a good football team, too. We're going to continue to win."

And win they did, taking three of the next four, including a rematch with the Roughriders on July 27. Part of the recipe for (Gainer the) Gopher pie is "Great green gobs of greasy, grimy gopher guts," so the childhood folk song goes, and the ingredient were in ample supply at Taylor Field as Calgary demolished the home team 54–16. The Stamps found themselves in first place. Veterans credited Buono with making football fun again.

"We're trying to instil confidence in our players," Buono insisted. "Don't be cautious, don't be scared. What's the worst thing that can happen? You can lose. Champions don't win by playing scared. Our players are starting to learn that. The great teams play hard, they take chances, they get after it."

For all the early confidence, the young coach's mettle was tested when his team lost four of their next five games, including both ends of the Labour Day week double header to the Eskimos, 38–4 at home and 34–17 at Commonwealth Stadium. But the Stampeders bounced back, closing out the regular season by winning five of six. Their record of 11–6–1 was good enough for first place and a bye into the Western Final. They accomplished their goal with 16 new starters and a rookie head coach and offensive coordinator. The last time they had finished first was 1971—also the last time they had won the Grey Cup. Another positive sign? In the Chinese calendar, 1990 was the Year of the Horse.

A key to Calgary success was overcoming impact of injuries through quality replacements. Keyvan Jenkins injured his knee in September and was replaced by Anthony Cherry. When Danny Barrett missed six weeks and backup Terrence Jones struggled, Buono picked up Rick Worman, who led the team to three key victories down the stretch. Blocking fullback Tim Petro was lost for the season, but rookie Andy McVey filled in admirably. When the line-backing corps broke down, homebrew Matt Finlay assumed a starting role and became a fixture for years to come.

Special teams were indeed special in 1990. Derrick Crawford was third in punt returns and second in combined yardage. Ron Hopkins set a CFL record with a missed field goal return of 128 yards. Allen Pitts had a sensational rookie year, catching 65 passes for 1,172 yards. Statistically the Stamps were average or below in most categories, but they played as a team.

Although they lost three out of four to Edmonton, they had eked out a 34–32 win over the Green and Gold at McMahon the last game of the season. Though Edmonton lost five of their last six games and was in disarray, they easily beat Saskatchewan in the semi-final and prepared to meet their doom at the hands of their provincial rival.

Not so fast. In what would become a familiar pattern, Calgary and Edmonton would both have trouble winning western finals at home. The trend began that year when the Eskimos waltzed into McMahon Stadium and beat the Stampeders 43–23.

Reminisced Danny Barrett 13 years later: "You knew we were on the brink of doing something big. First of all, we had to beat Edmonton late in the season to win first place. And then to be able to host that final. Calgary hadn't done that for a long time. There was a sense of we've arrived, we've got the Edmonton monkey off our back even though we lost that game. In that final game, which I remember vividly, we had a touchdown pass dropped, and we lost Derrick Crawford early. And that made a difference the rest of the day trying to penetrate their secondary."

Calgary hadn't won a playoff game since 1979. They still had to learn how to win the big game. "They've played in big games and won, and they lost a big playoff game," said Buono. "They understand there is a difference between winning and losing, and that there's really not that much. The winners learn to win, the losers learn to lose."

Most coaches when asked how to coach a winning attitude say if they knew that they would bottle it and make a million dollars. Not Buono. "Let me put it this way," he observed. "Supposedly we were a losing franchise, and now we are perceived as winners, so obviously somebody's doing something

Future Hall of Famer Allen Pitts in action against the Tabbies.

right. You don't coach it, but you have to stress it. You have to plant the seed in people's minds. You have to keep watering and fertilizing it so it grows. Winning doesn't happen by chance. A lot of things cause winning, and one of them is talking to the players about winning and letting them know it is there.

"We have some winners here now. Frankie Morris is a winner. Don Sutherin is a winner. All of a sudden your organization has winners—and guess what? They don't think about losing, they think about winning. Part of the process is to surround yourself with winners because they think positively. They know sometimes things don't go their way, but no big deal. They get around that and get it done."

As for the 1991 Stampeders, Buono insisted, "We should be a good enough football team that we should be thinking nothing but Grey Cup because we have enough skill, enough depth. The players have won enough to understand that winning is there and they just have to go out and get it."

Buono looked back on his first year as a head coach. "I learned that the things I valued the most—truth and honesty—paid dividends. Being able to look a man in the eye and know you haven't wronged him for any reason—I think that goes a long way.

"The emotional drain was a surprise to me. It is difficult always being in a position of authority where you're always making decisions. That gets very wearing."

The road to the Grey Cup had historically gone through Edmonton, but looking down the road at the '91 campaign, Buono felt that finally Calgary was the team to beat. "I feel that way. Maybe I'm the only one, but that's okay."

On defence, Buono added Karl Anthony and Erroll Tucker to the secondary. They were joined by veterans Darryl Hall, Greg Peterson and Junior Thurman. Matt Finlay, Dan Wicklum and Alondra Johnson were the linebackers, Stu Laird, Will Johnson, Kent Warnock and Tim Cofield the front four. Tucker and Cofield were new.

Derrick Crawford broke his leg early on and was replaced by rookie Carl Bland who caught 56 passes for 906 yards. Keyvan Jenkins overcame his injury and rushed for 801 yards, Calgary's best total in four years. The O-line featured Doug Davies at centre, Bill Henry and Lloyd Fairbanks the guards, and Ken Moore and Leo Blanchard at tackle. Danny Barrett returned at quarterback and had a career year. The other receivers were

Pitts, Beals, Marshall Toner and Sapunjis.

The Stampeders were led by Allen Pitts, one of the greatest receivers in CFL history. In 1990 the taciturn slotback had caught 65 passes for 1,172 yards. He was the first newcomer since Terry Evanshen in 1966 to rack up over 1,000 yards. In 1991 he would pick up 1,764 yards while setting a CFL record with 118 receptions. Nine times he would surpass 1,000 yards, third all-time behind Terry Vaughn and Milt Stegall. He ranks third all-time in receptions and holds the record for most receiving yards in a season with 2,036. He has the most 100-plus–yard games for a receiver at 64 and ranks second in career yards and touchdowns. He also holds the record for playoff receiving yards and is second in playoff receptions. Four times he led the league in receptions and receiving yardage. Pitts holds nine Stampeder records and was All-Canadian six times. His Number 18 has been retired. He was inducted onto the Wall of Fame in 2004 and into the CFL Hall of Fame, 2006.

Pitts was an impact player the moment he stepped on a CFL field. What is really remarkable is that he had been out of football for four years before arriving in Calgary. Graduating in 1986 from Cal State Fullerton, he attended two L.A. Ram camps but failed to make the grade. Then he got the call from Calgary.

"I attended an open camp in May 1990 in Irvine, California," Pitts recalled. "Roy Shivers was in charge of American personnel, and he knew me from my college days. Things went well, and I was invited up to Calgary, and they signed me to a contract."

Allen Pitts in action.
COURTESY CALGARY STAMPEDERS

Despite being away from the game, Pitts was convinced he could play professional football. "I made up my mind in May of 1989 to give it one more chance. I looked at it realistically and decided that I wasn't going to be ready in 1989 because I wasn't in the proper condition, mentally or physically, to give it my best shot. I prepared myself for the 1990 season. It was a slow process, but with a lot of determination, faith and prayer, things worked out for me."

Pitts described what it takes to be an outstanding receiver. "Never being satisfied, always looking for ways to improve," he counselled. "What also helps is that I've been very fortunate to be able to pretty much pick up on reading defences well, which helps me after the ball is snapped. I'm already on the run and reading whether they are in man coverage or zone. I have really good eyesight.

"To be a great receiver, you have to believe in yourself—that in tough circumstances you know you can get it done. It's that type of attitude along with God-given ability that carries some people to a higher level than others." Roy Shivers scouted many great players for the CFL but offered, "I would say I'm most proud of [Pitts]. . . . I think Jeff Garcia was a helluva find, but I think Allen, for the circumstances surrounding him, for being out of football for a number of years and for doing what he did in a short period of time. If he hadn't been hurt those two years—'93 and '97—he probably would have put the receiving records out of sight. Yeah, I'm really proud of Allen."

Throughout his career, Pitts was often regarded as surly and uncommunicative. When his number was retired in 2004, for example, he refused to do interviews. He got into trouble off the field on more than one occasion, caught at the border with banned substances and breaking his hand, according to the official explanation, in a bar fight in Los Angeles.

Shivers deserves most of the credit for keeping Pitts focused on the task at hand. "Most guys on the team, when they had problems," Shivers confided. "So, yeah, I talked to Allen. We talked a long time. Wally was good with him in that aspect, too. But I understood where Allen had come from. I stepped back and let him make his own decisions.

"But we talked. Allen would visit me in Vegas sometimes. We'd talk. I listened most of the time. Sometimes young people have to learn to let go of things. You can't do anything about the past, that's done. So you let go of it. I think that was one of Allen's problems. It took him awhile to let go of things."

In an interview with Dan Toth when Pitts was inducted into the CFL Hall of Fame, Buono said, "The fans wanted to get to know Al, but I don't know if Allen was going to allow that to happen. Allen could be very charming, but when he was in one of his moods, it was difficult. Allen fought some demons, some tough things."

But for all his demons, Allen Pitts had few equals in the history of catching passes. True, having a good quarterback helps. Pitts played with some greats—Danny Barrett, Doug Flutie, Jeff Garcia and Dave Dickenson—who were all special in their own way. Danny Barrett had to overcome a lot to get respect as a pivot. At the University of Cincinnati, they tried to make him a defensive back. In 1984 Calgary coach Steve Buratto converted him to wide receiver and then traded him to Toronto. After languishing on the bench behind Gilbert Renfroe in Hogtown, he asked to be traded. The only team that would take him was Calgary. Their quarterbacks were hurt, and they desperately needed someone to back up and guide their rookie, Terrence Jones.

Barrett explained how he landed in the CFL. "Jerry Keeling had an opportunity to see me play for the University of Cincinnati on

Cable TV against Miami, and he thought I had the skills to play in Canada. We ran a pro-type offense, but we also moved the pocket quite a bit.

"They gave me a free agent tryout in Las Vegas. Again, I wasn't one of the top guys they brought in, but I looked at it as an opportunity to join a pro football squad. As it turned out, I landed a contract. When I came out of university, I thought I had the skills to play in the NFL. Obviously I didn't because no one gave me a phone call about it."

The personable Barrett had a simple explanation for why, in 1991, he became a nine-year, overnight success. "Every time I've been given a chance to play longer than a few minutes, I've come through and really performed because that gave me confidence. If you instil confidence in a person, he's going to do what's necessary to win football games. I appreciate what the coaches have done for me as opposed to the past, where if you weren't spectacular in the first quarter, they yanked you.

"To be successful, you must be patient and don't turn the ball over. Don't hurt your team. If you can eliminate sacks and don't turn the ball over, you can dictate field-position and scoring. I've really learned a lot from John Hufnagel about reading defences. He's really helped me . . . be a smarter quarterback

"There is so much talent with you on the field. I just get the ball to my teammates, and they make things happen. I've been playing the game long enough that great stats and publicity don't mean very much. I'm past that now. I want to win a Grey Cup ring."

Unfortunately that goal eluded Danny

Danny Barrett.
COURTESY CALGARY STAMPEDERS

Barrett. Over the course of his career, he threw 3,078 passes and had 93 picked off, the best ratio in CFL history. In 1990 and '91, he had the fewest interceptions in the league.

When Doug Flutie became available after 1991, Barrett was traded to B.C. When the Lions acquired Kent Austin in 1994, Barrett headed for Ottawa. He rejoined the Stamps in 1996 and became their quarterback coach the following year. 1991 would be his best year.

With Barrett at pivot, the Stamps roared out of the starting gate in 1991 with six straight wins, their best record since 1971. After dropping two in a row to Winnipeg, they beat Edmonton 48–36 on Labour Day, then lost the return match 51–37. They split their remaining eight games and finished second to Edmonton and tied with B.C. Second place was awarded to Calgary because of their superior regular season record. In spite of a winning season, Calgary ranked fifth in points, seventh in total offense, last in rushing but second in passing. Defensively they ranked fifth. They were 11–7 because they made few mistakes while taking advantage of the miscues of their opponents, leading the league in the giveaway-takeaway category with +20. Danny Barrett missed five games with a broken finger, replaced by Steve Taylor and Gilbert Renfroe. Come what would be a wild and woolly semi-final, Barrett was ready to go.

"It was a shootout in Calgary," Barrett said. "We had to come from behind 16 points to win the game. We had to put the ball up. We put out our six pack and said, 'Let's go!' We came out on top."

Behind 31–15 at the half, Calgary's defensive coordinator, Don Sutherin, who played or coached in 12 Grey Cup games, read the riot act to his defence and did a gut check on the entire team. Questioning their manhood and ancestry, they returned to the field through the dressing room wall to score 28 points in the third quarter and send the Lions packing.

Trailing by two late in the game, Leo Lui Passaglia punted out of bounds at the Calgary 9-yard line. With three minutes left, B.C. had plenty of time to get the ball back in good field position and kick the winning field goal. Passaglia had been deadly all day.

He never got the chance. Though Barrett tied a playoff record by throwing five touchdown passes, it was the much-maligned running game that saved the day. Much to everyone's surprise, the Horsemen ran off nine straight running plays, moved the ball 63 yards and killed the clock. Final score: Calgary 43, B.C. 41.

Off to the northern field of broken dreams. If the natural provincial rivalry wasn't enough, the Eskimos added fuel to the fire by refusing to allow the Stampeders to practice on the Commonwealth turf, contrary to league rules. Calgary protested to no avail. The final would be another shootout and another of the great playoff games in CFL history.

Edmonton opened the scoring with a Tracy-Ham-to-Blake-Marshall 9-yard touchdown. Barrett hooked up with Dave Sapunjis for a 36-yard major, but Edmonton responded with a 60-yard pass-and-run from Tracy Ham to Chris Armstrong for the score. In the second stanza, Dean Dorsey kicked a field goal for the home team and Ham hit Craig Ellis for a 15-yard TD. The Esks had two singles, Calgary one. Keyvan Jenkins scored on a one-yard plunge, making the score at the half 26–15 in favour of Edmonton.

In the third quarter, Edmonton widened their lead on a Brian Walling touchdown and a Dorsey field goal. Calgary responded with three field goals by Mark McLaughlin and a one-yard quarterback sneak touchdown by Barrett. Trailing 36–31 with 1:02 left on the clock, Barrett hit Pee Wee Smith with a 67-yard pass for the major. Calgary won 38–36, advancing to the Grey Cup for the first time in 20 years. It was only the second playoff victory for Calgary in Edmonton since the Stampeders were born and the first time they had won a Western Final up north. Barrett loved every minute of it.

"I'll never forget it," he chortled. "They didn't want us to get on their field. We were trying to bang the doors down to get on their field. We were determined to get that monkey off our back.

"We just persevered. Guys hung in there believing in one another. The talk on the sidelines was 'Come on guys, we're a few plays away from winning this thing, let's step it up.' We stepped up and made some plays, and Pee Wee Smith hung on for dear life and ran it to the back of the end zone."

Their Grey Cup opponent would be Toronto. The 1991 Argos had been bought by Wayne Gretzky, the late John Candy and Bruce McNall. Understanding Torontonian's hunger for big-league status, the new owners signed the NFL's projected top draft pick, Notre Dame's Raghib "Rocket" Ismail to a contract estimated between $18 and $26 million. When the Argos opened their 1991 rookie camp, a large tent was erected for a press conference with the owners and the Rocket. The setting was appropriate to kickoff a year-long three-ring circus that was just the tonic a weary CFL needed to revive its sagging fortunes. Their pizzazz was also vital to Toronto because winning wasn't enough to attract fans to SkyDome.

Over 41,000 fans turned up at SkyDome on July 18 to see a glittering array of Hollywood personalities and the launching of the Rocket. He didn't disappoint, picking up 213 yards overall as Toronto won their home opener over Hamilton 41–18. They wouldn't taste defeat at home all year.

The 1991 edition of the Good Ship Argonaut finished first with a record of 13–5, despite quarterback Matt Dunigan being hurt in the home opener and missing 10 games. Pinball Clemons missed seven. With backup Ricky Foggie at the controls for most of the season, the Argos were second in scoring with 647 points but only fifth in total offense. Because of their dazzling special teams, they didn't have to go far to score. The Rocket Man picked up 3,049 all-purpose yards, the third highest total in CFL history, and was All-Canadian.

Dunigan return to action on August 27, but three weeks later, he broke his collarbone in several places. He returned again the last game of the regular season, but hurt his shoulder in the Eastern Final. He arrived for the Grey Cup with his arm in a sling. He was not expected to play.

But he did.

For the first time, the Grey Cup was played in Winnipeg, and all the fears about the weather came to pass. The temperature was –19°C at kickoff. Typical of the Stampeders' playoff fortunes, the team that showed up wasn't the team that played all season long. Although Barrett had but six picks during the regular season, he threw three interceptions. The usually stingy special teams came up small, surrendering the touchdown that broke Calgary's back.

With a minute and a half gone in the opening quarter, Argo Ed Berry intercepted and ran 50 yards for a touchdown. Lance Chomyc added the convert. "I can't remember the last time I threw an interception for a touchdown," moaned the disconsolate Calgary quarterback.

"We started off poorly," explained Dave Sapunjis. "Danny was a little nervous and threw a bad ball, and the receiver didn't do anything to knock it down."

Pee Wee Smith fumbled the ensuing kick-off. A minute and 16 seconds later, Toronto added a single when Chomyc missed a field goal. Sapunjis described the atmosphere at the Stampeder bench. "The players were quickly humbled. The offense gathered together. We got into a huddle on the sidelines, and we talked about what we were going to have to do on the next series. It is obviously discouraging when you go out in a big game and don't start off well. So we kind of gathered our thoughts and calmed each other down."

It worked. Barrett promptly marched the team down the field for a major score, a one-yard quarterback sneak. The teams traded field goals in the second quarter, making the score at halftime 11–10 in favour of Toronto.

Mark McLoughlin kicked the Stampeders into a 14–11 lead in the third quarter, but Matt Dunigan responded with a 48-yard touchdown pass to Darrell K. Smith. Toronto led 19–14 after 45 minutes.

Early in the final frame, Chomyc added a 19-yard field goal, set up when Reggie Pleasant intercepted Barrett on the opening play of the fourth quarter. Barrett brought the Stampeders back, completing a drive with a 13-yard TD pass to Pitts. Calgary trailed by one.

McLoughlin kicked off, and Rocket Ismail returned it 87 yards for a touchdown and an eight-point lead. With over 10 minutes remaining in the fourth quarter, Calgary had lots of time to recover. But on the ensuing kickoff, the ball bounced off Keyvan Jenkin's foot, and Keith Costello recovered his second fumble of the game for Toronto. Two plays later, Dunigan hit Paul Masotti in the end zone for Toronto's final major. In 58 seconds, the hopes and dreams of two decades of Calgary football were dashed.

Barrett didn't give up, marching from his own 31 to the Argo 2. A couple of running plays and Calgary would be eight points down with lots of time to even the score. Instead, they elected to pass. "On the touchdown before," Barrett explained, "I isolated Pitts on [Carl] Brazely, and I thought I could do it again." Barrett threw incomplete. Surely this time Andy McVey or Jenkins or Barrett would carry the ball. No. Barrett dropped back to pass and was sacked at the 11-yard line.

"I looked the wrong way, and by the time I saw my receiver, it was too late." Barrett lamented. "That series hurt us more than anything else. When I got sacked, that probably cost us the ball game."

John Hufnagel made the decision to throw. "We had a short passing play that we were pretty sure would work." It didn't. Final: Toronto 36, Calgary 21.

The victorious Argos hoist the Cup.
COURTESY CALGARY STAMPEDERS

Canadian Player of the Game Dave Sapunjis (4 catches for 45 yards) wasn't critical of the calls. "We were very confident with our receivers against their DBs. That was when using five or six receivers was coming into the league. We started it. Their defence wasn't used to that. So when we got to the two-yard line, we thought we could spread them apart and throw a quick pass. That was our game plan. It didn't work."

Dave Sapunjis, three-time Canadian Grey Cup MVP.
COURTESY CALGARY STAMPEDERS

All-Canadian defensive end Will Johnson wasn't so forgiving. "We're not coaches. We're just players, and we have to accept what the coaches do. With two yards to go, I'd have run a sweep or a quarterback sneak or quick hitting dive play."

Led by Johnson, Alondra Johnson and Matt Finlay, the Stampeder defence played well that day. "We played well, very well," allowed Big Will. They double-teamed me on both sides with a back and a tackle. Mainly, they'd spin it away from me.

"I hit Dunigan a couple of times. One time I hit him he coughed up the ball into the air, and Tim Cofield caught it and got a few yards before an offensive lineman grabbed him. They didn't really do anything to us. We defensively took control of the game. We

Will Johnson in action. COURTESY CALGARY STAMPEDERS

just should have scored on defence. Special teams killed us."

Mark McLoughlin discussed the impact of cold weather on the kicking game. "When you have weather like that, what happens to the ball is it hardens. It's almost like kicking a brick. It doesn't allow you to really have much control over the football, so what you do is just line up and try to kick it as straight as possible and hope it maintains its line. You just hope for the best."

He appreciated Argo coach Adam Rita's strategy of sky-kicking the ball. "That worked. When you're kicking hard footballs in that type of weather, you're not going to get a whole lot of distance on the ball, so if you try to kick it normally for depth, it is not going to happen. So that was a very good strategy, kicking the ball in the air and hoping the receivers have a hard time handling it."

The Argos were inspired by the return of Dunigan to the line-up, injury and all. The day before the game, he worked out in the

hotel ballroom. "I had my shoulder shot up to see if I could throw a football," he confirmed. "They shot it up with the medication and gave me a few minutes, and I was throwing the rock to Mike McCarthy. We were trying to get it right. I said, 'Hey, this is pretty good.' That's what happened."

According to Adam Rita, he decision to play Dunigan wasn't made until late Saturday. "Basically it was a decision made the night before the game. I had been told all week he wasn't going to play, so we had prepared Ricky Foggie."

Argo lineman Dan Ferrone remembered it differently. "We knew all along he was going to play. They just played it that way for the media, but we knew all along he was going to play. He had a sore shoulder, but they were going to freeze it. He wasn't going to miss that game no matter what."

Dunigan completed 12 of 29 passes for 142 yards and two touchdowns. He ran for 44 yards. It was a gutsy performance by one of the toughest men to ever play the Canadian game.

Sapunjis wasn't surprised Dunigan played. "You never know what's going on in the opposition dressing room. We didn't know how serious Dunigan was, and when he stepped on the field, well, it really didn't surprise us. I was surprised to hear after the game that he had a broken bone or separation, and he played with it."

To Sapunjis, special teams made the difference. "Absolutely. Ever since that Grey Cup I've always said when we've gone to the Grey Cup or playoffs, special teams be ready because sometimes it comes down to you guys. My first Grey Cup in '91, I believe we lost because of special teams. Rocket's touchdown sort of put us away. We still had a chance to come back and make it interesting at the end, but when you get beaten so badly on special teams, it starts to drain you on both sides of the ball. That really hurt us . . . . Your offense or defence is ready to go out, and then they return the ball for 70 yards. You start off poorly, [you do] some things fairly well. As the game goes on, you start to get your confidence back, and all of a sudden a guy like Rocket returns it all the way. Our emotions just drop and we lose our energy."

While special teams accounted for a good deal of Toronto's success, the name of the game was field position. While Argo special teams kept putting their offense in good position, Calgary punter Jerry Kauric's abysmal performance was the worst in modern Grey Cup history. Of all the injuries the Stampeders suffered during the year, including Barrett's broken finger, the most damaging in the end was the one to punter Brent Matich.

McLoughlin analyzed the defeat. "Special teams played a huge factor, but I think there was a lot of veteran leadership on that Argo team. For us as a fairly young team, we had just come off a very big emotional high in the Western Final up in Commonwealth Stadium. I think when we got to the Grey Cup, we said, 'Boy, we're here, let's enjoy this.' Maybe we approached it the wrong way. Maybe we thought we could carry on and let the emotions ride from the week before, but we weren't able to do that.

"The very first play was an interception for a touchdown, and there was a fumble. Those turnovers were very uncharacteristic of us. It's a mental thing when things like that happen. But we were down right off the bat. It was tough for us to come back. Plus Toronto was a very good team that year as well. They deserved to win it."

In Buono's first year as head coach, Calgary lost to Edmonton in the final. In year two, they beat the Eskimos but lost the Grey Cup. Looking ahead to 1992, Buono wanted his team to turn it up a notch and take that final step.

"The whole thing about the other notch," he explained, "is that the players have been there and . . . understand what the other notch is. Now they know that. Although the road is tough, the goal is attainable. It takes a lot of skill, but they have that. They know what must be done. The Grey Cup is now their focus, whereas in the past I don't think they believed they could do it."

Since the end of Buono's first year, 14 of the 24 starters had been replaced. He made eight changes to a line-up that had won the West, replacing Tim Cofield, Dan Wicklum and Erroll Tucker with Harold Hasselbach, Marvin Pope and Kenton Leonard. Lloyd Fairbanks, Leo Blanchard and Bill Henry were replaced on the O-line by Rocco Romano, Lou Cafazzo and rookie Bruce Covernton. Derrick Crawford was back after breaking a leg, and Dave Sapunjis became a starter at slot back. The biggest change was at quarterback, where Doug Flutie replaced Danny Barrett.

Doug Flutie in action.
COURTESY CALGARY STAMPEDERS

After playing in the USFL and backing up in the NFL former Heisman trophy winner, Flutie headed to B.C., signing a contract with flimflam man Murray Pezim, the owner of the B.C. Lions. When Pezim couldn't afford to keep him, soul brother Larry Ryckman signed the little guy to a personal services contract worth over $1 million dollars. He then traded Barrett to B.C. for Romano, the rights to Jamie Crysdale and $250,000 in stocks. Ryckman claimed the stocks were delivered late and were worth only $30,000. Pezim said tough noogies, a deal's a deal. Sometimes the value of stocks goes down. Ryckman wasn't satisfied and threatened to boycott their game at B.C. on July 23. Pezim called Ryckman a chicken and had ten thousand rubber "Chicken Ryckmans" made for distribution to the Lion faithful. Calgary won the game 37–19.

Said Roy Shivers, "When we made the deal for Flutie, Larry Ryckman called Wally and I, and took us out to dinner one night and said, 'I want to trade Danny for Flutie.' That was after Danny had thrown for 500-some yards in the Grey Cup.

Rocco Romano was inducted into the Canadian Football Hall of Fame in 2007.
COURTESY CANADIAN FOOTBALL HALL OF FAME

"I'm like, 'You're shitting me.'

"He said, 'I want to sell some tickets.'

"When we looked at it later, we never sold an extra ticket. Doug had a thing in his contract that he got a dollar for every ticket sold over a certain number. I don't think he ever got one. Football really took hold in Calgary because of Stan Schwartz, Ron Rooke and Wally, not Doug Flutie."

The Stampeders started the 1992 season with four wins in a row. Flutie, hailed as the conquering hero, was typically modest. "I've been on a roll," he allowed, "and the media and fans think it is all the quarterback, and it's not. You're dependent on the people in front of you. If you don't have time to throw the ball, you can't get it done. If you don't have guys working to get open and catching the ball, you still don't get it done.

Bob Woolf, Doug Flutie and Larry Ryckman. COURTESY CALGARY STAMPEDERS

There is too much emphasis on the quarterback. It takes 12 men to win."

Flutie and Pitts were made for each other. "We were watching film the other day," recalled Pitts, "and a situation came up where I was running a route, and me and Doug just clicked on that particular play. Normally I would have kept on going to the outside, but I stayed inside, and he was with me all the way and we were able to connect. I had a sixth sense where to go, and it worked out because the quarterback was on the same page with me. The main thing is just having the confidence in each other, believing in each other's abilities. The fact that the two of you out there working hard is going to make some positive things come about for the team."

How was Flutie different from Barrett? "The main difference is the velocity of the ball," Pitts replied. "Danny threw harder. What Doug brings is the creativity, which opens up other opportunities. With the type of mobility he has, we are able to do more things offensively."

The two formed a mutual admiration society. "Pitts was a big, physical presence," said Flutie. "Great movements. Great body position. Ran great routes. All the tools. I've never seen a player dominate a game the way Al could. When we were rolling, we'd walk the ball down the field. Second and 10, second and 15, third and a bunch—the idea was get Al the ball. I trusted him to make the play."

After their fast start, the Stampeders split the next eight before finishing with seven straight wins and a final mark of 13–5, good for first place. Typically the battles around Labour Day were the highlights of the regular season. The first game took place at Commonwealth in the rain August 28. Edmonton led 13–10 at the half on the strength of a Craig Ellis touchdown and Sean Fleming's kicking. McLoughlin tallied three field goals and a single for the visitors. Then the offenses got untracked, exchanging touchdowns and field goals into the final 15 minutes.

With the game tied at 23, Leroy Blugh scored for Edmonton. Flutie replied with a touchdown throw to Pitts. Tony Martino kicked a 66-yard single to give the Stamps a one-point lead with less than five minutes to go. But Tracy Ham wasn't done. He engineered a long drive culminating in a Blake Marshall touchdown, followed by a two-point conversion pass to Jim Sandusky. With 1:44 left on the clock, Edmonton led by seven.

Then it was Flutie's turn, marching his team to the Eskimo 14-yard line. With third and 15 at the 19, Flutie eluded the pursuit and rambled down to the 4. Andy McVey then crashed into the end zone to pull his team into a tie. With five seconds left in the first overtime period, Flutie found Pee Wee Smith in the end zone for the victory. Calgary 45, Edmonton 38, their first regular season win in Edmonton in 12 years.

Ham and Flutie engaged in another compelling duel before a record Labour Day crowd of 38,205 at McMahon. Each team scored two touchdowns and added field goals and singles. The Eskimos led 20–18 after 30 minutes. Ham engineered two more majors in the second half, Calgary added a field goal and Edmonton moved into first place with a 34–21 win. On October 24 in Calgary, Ham separated a shoulder in the second quarter, and the Stamps wrapped up the season series with a 40–23 romp.

The Eskimos scraped by Saskatchewan in the semi-final 22–20. Edmonton headed for Calgary and a third consecutive Western showdown.

As usual, it was a thriller, a marvellous duel between two great quarterbacks. With 1:30 left, the visitors were leading 22–16. Flutie then marched his Stampeders to the 3-yard line via strikes to Sapunjis and Pitts.

With precious seconds ticking away, Flutie audibled to tackle Ken Moore and slipped, minus a shoe, into the end zone behind him. Shoeless Doug Flutie had found a way to win. The final score was 23–22. After the game, Flutie said the comeback was his greatest moment in football, even greater than the play that made him famous, the Hail Mary touchdown pass that beat Miami 47–45.

In 1992 Flutie completed 396 passes for 5,945 yards and 32 touchdowns. He ran for 669 yards and scored 11 rushing touchdowns. He won the Most Outstanding Player Award and made All-Canadian along with Pitts, Romano, Will Johnson, Thurman and Hall. Buono won his first Coach of the Year Award.

The Blue Bombers were the Stampeders' Grey Cup opponent. The year before, Calgary

Stu Laird. COURTESY CALGARY STAMPEDERS

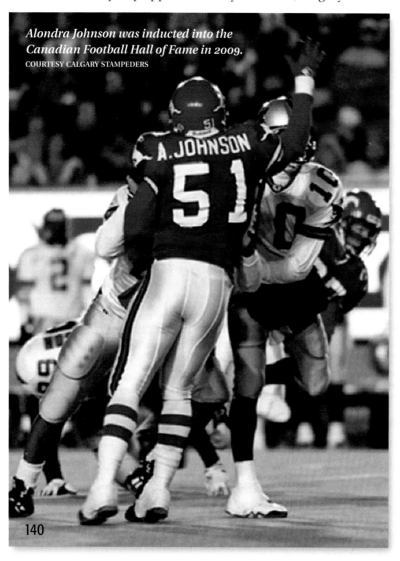

Alondra Johnson was inducted into the Canadian Football Hall of Fame in 2009.
COURTESY CALGARY STAMPEDERS

couldn't beat Toronto in Winnipeg. Maybe they could beat Winnipeg in Toronto. At least weather wouldn't be a problem.

All the attention was on the offense. Allen Pitts led the league for the second straight season catching 1,203 for 1,591 yards and 13 touchdowns, the first Stampeder receiver since Herm Harrison to have three consecutive 1,000-yard seasons. Dave Sapunjis caught 72 passes for 1,317 yards, and Carl Bland picked up 1,052 yards on 72 receptions.

A pleasant surprise was Calgary's first-round draft pick, Bruce Covernton, the rookie at left tackle. Nicknamed Tuna by his teammates, the big guy didn't play organized football until he was 20. The Winnipeg native played one year for the St. Vital Mustangs and then attended Weber State, where he made All-American. The 6'5", 294-pound newcomer learned his lessons so well that he was the West's nominee for Most Outstanding Rookie, losing to Bomber back Mike Richardson.

Complementing Flutie and friends

Dave Sapunjis makes the catch and goes on to score Calgary's first touchdown in 1992 Grey Cup action against the Blue Bombers.
COURTESY CANADIAN PRESS, HANS DERYK PHOTO

was a defence that led the league in most categories. Will Johnson, Kent Warnock, Harold Hasselbach, Srecko Zizakovic and Stu Laird were the best. The line-backing corps of Matt Finlay, Alondra Johnson and Marvin Pope was ferocious, and the secondary of Junior Thurman, Darryl Hall, Greg Knox, Karl Anthony, Greg Peterson, Kenton Leonard and Ken Watson was superb. Knox had been a sixth-round draft choice!

The Stamps would face a Blue Bomber team that had overcome significant adversity. They lost their coach and general manager when Cal Murphy entered hospital at the University of Western Ontario for a heart transplant. Urban Bowman took over the reins at age 55, his first head coaching opportunity. Quarterback Matt Dunigan was at the helm when they crushed Hamilton 59–11 in the Eastern Final. The Bomber's main weapon was running back Michael Richardson, who gained 1,123 yards.

Calgary's weakness was defending against the run; Winnipeg's, stopping the pass. If Calgary could jump into an early 10-point lead, they would force Winnipeg out of the running game and make their defence play cautiously.

That is exactly what happened. Calgary

scored on four of their first five possessions, forcing Dunigan put the ball in the air. Richardson picked up only 21 yards in the first half, 27 overall. Winnipeg ran once in the second half.

The Stampeders took an early lead when Mark McLoughlin kicked a 37-yard field goal and a single. Four minutes later, Flutie finished a drive with a 35-yard pass to Dave Sapunjis.

"It was a simple corner pattern," the Western Ontario grad recalled. "Their guy was one on one with me. I beat him inside. I know Flutie didn't see the ball after he released it. He just let it go to the area I normally am in. It was a perfect pass. It was a romp, really."

McLoughlin kicked two 17-yarders in the second quarter to give his team a 17–0 lead at the half.

The third quarter was scoreless, a tribute to outstanding defence by both teams. At 2:36 of the fourth, Flutie completed a 15-yard pass to Pitts for a touchdown. "It was called a 144X–Smash," Pitts explained. "I'm the receiver, and that's a corner route by me. They were in man coverage that play. I just beat the guy, and Doug did a real good job of putting the ball in a very good spot."

With 6:37 left in the game, Winnipeg finally got on the scoreboard when Troy Westwood kicked a 46-yard field goal. Four minutes later, Gerald Alphin scored their only touchdown. The final was Calgary 24, Winnipeg 10. The Stampeders had won their third Grey Cup their first since 1971.

Flutie was the Player of the Game. He completed 15 of his first 20 passes and 17 of 25 by the half. He finished the game with 33 out of 49 for 480 yards and two touchdowns, the second best performance in Grey Cup history. Dave Sapunjis was again the Canadian Player of the Game with seven receptions for 85 yards and a touchdown. Honourable mention should have gone to

Grey Cup champion Doug Flutie.
COURTESY CALGARY STAMPEDERS

Derrick Crawford, who, after a banner 1990 season, shattered his ankle in the first game of 1991. He was never quite the same until that Sunday at SkyDome, where he played brilliantly, catching six passes for 162 yards. It was his finest hour in a Stampeder uniform.

The 24–10 final score flattered Winnipeg. "We moved the ball a whole lot, yes," agreed Pitts, "but we didn't finish off drives like we should have."

Said Sapunjis, "Yeah, we absolutely dominated that game. We probably should have been up 42 points. We marched the ball down every time we had to. We just didn't put it into the end zone every time. Defensively we stopped them."

Blue Bomber defensive lineman Stan Mikawas agreed. "Yes, they did dominate. Flutie did a number on us. He's very elusive and very fast with his release and his speed.

Mark McLoughlin. COURTESY CALGARY STAMPEDERS

Jubilant Stampeders celebrate their 1992 Grey Cup victory in Olympic Plaza after a parade through the downtown. COURTESY CANADIAN PRESS, DAVE BUSTON PHOTO

We just couldn't stop him, and our offense couldn't get anything on the board."

Mark McLoughlin scored half of Calgary's points, demonstrating that no matter how dominant the offense, the place-kicker always has to be able to perform. "You do because any time you are put in a position to score points, you must do so," he said. "It seemed we just controlled the game from the very outset. And to me personally, the outcome was never in doubt. I knew we were going to win that game just by the way we were controlling the football. But when you look at the score, the score was a lot closer than the play indicated."

McLoughlin described how the team prepared for the Grey Cup. "We took a very low key approach during that week. We went into that game with a tremendous amount of confidence. We weren't really concerned about what Winnipeg was going to do, we were just concerned about what we were going to do. Once Doug got hold of the ball, that was it."

Winnipeg's healing Cal Murphy took it all in stride. When it was suggested that Calgary dominated on both sides of the ball, he laughed. "You're being kind. We were never in it. It was Flutie, Flutie and more Flutie."

Flutie was spectacular, Dunigan was not, Sapunjis concluded. "Dunigan didn't have a good day. They did not have good coaching that game. Their defence? We were surprised at how they played us. They were playing linebackers on guys like me, and we're going to beat them every time. Dunigan did not have all that good of a game, but our defensive players were pumped up and ready to go."

Future Hall of Famer and great Bomber linebacker Greg Battle also felt the Bombers had been out-coached. "We were put in bad situations. Several times I had to go and cover Derrick Crawford. That's definitely a mismatch. Now, if Flutie was running the ball up the middle, that would be my forte,

and I'd have the advantage. They were running a package that caught us off guard, and we didn't make any adjustments."

Matt Dunigan did not question Urban Bowman's game plan. "We had opportunities early, but we were just missing. It was just a matter of inches. If we had made some of those plays, it would have given the game a totally different complexion. You hear often that football is a game of inches. In that game, I believe it was. We were maybe an inch away offensively from making it happen. A receiver would stumble or let up. We did not make the plays. Calgary did, so you take your hat off to them and move on."

Just a matter of inches? "I don't think so," said Calgary's Will Johnson, "not in a Grey Cup game when you lose 24–10. Our guys were playing well. Winnipeg didn't score a point until the fourth quarter, and to be honest, I think they were given that touchdown."

McLoughlin described what it was like to win. "It was a great feeling, winning the championship. When you have an opportunity to do that and experience it, it's a great relief, and it really doesn't sink in for a while. When we got back to Calgary with the Cup and had the parade, that's when it started to sink in. When you have the off-season to enjoy that, take the Grey Cup around to different functions, different schools, let other people share in that, that's when it really hits home that you've accomplished a tremendous goal."

Wally Buono and his Stampeders had made two Grey Cup appearances in three years. Everybody was talking dynasty. But while they dominated the '92 Grey Cup, they got out of the West by

Hall of Famer Doug Flutie.

the skin of their teeth twice in a row. Buono was not concerned. "Some of the greatest games I ever had as a player were in the Eastern Final," he recalled. "When you play the final, the game is usually very close or it's a complete blowout. Did Edmonton's defence fail because they couldn't stop Doug Flutie in the last 38 seconds? I don't think so. You've got to give the players credit. Great players rise to the occasion and do great things. That is what Doug did."

That Grey Cup was the apex of Flutie's Calgary career. He wouldn't win another wearing red and white.

Yet Buono didn't think Flutie was the difference between being Grey Cup finalists in '91 and winning it all in '92. "It had nothing to do with Flutie, really. Not to say that he wasn't very important. The intention of our players from January 1, 1992, to November 29, 1992, was to be the Grey Cup champion. So the focus from the beginning of each workout until the end was to be the champion.

"Everybody in June has aspirations to go to the Grey Cup. They might be short-lived. You start struggling, and you realize it won't happen. That's not the way it was with us. Our theme was—and will be again—playing in and winning that big game in November. When you get that focus, your mind, your body, your actions reflect that. You could be lucky and accidentally win the Grey Cup. But I think that the teams that are prepared to win it and expect to win it have the advantage.

"What are the biggest things this team has? I think two things. One, they've got the skills. If you've got the skills, all you have to do is go out and do what is natural for you. The other thing you have to have is the determination to want to do it again. If you've got the skill, what prevents you from winning is yourself.

"The essential thing in the off-season for our veterans to accept pay cuts wasn't the desire to be nice to me—it was to return and win again as a team. The players would take a pay cut because they expect to make it to the Grey Cup."

The 1993 season would be extra special for the Calgary Stampeders. Not only were they defending champions for only the third time in their history, they were hosting the Grey Cup and wanted to be in it. In preparation for the upcoming campaign, Lou Cafazzo moved to defence, replaced by Todd Storme. Carl Bland gave way to Brian Wiggins and Will Moore. On defence Kent Warnock retired, overcome by chronic injuries. Eric Johnson took his place. Greg Peterson also retired, replaced by Greg Knox. Darryl Hall went to the NFL. Greg Eaglin and Gerald Vaughn were added to the secondary.

Buono was particularly high on Knox. "Tom Higgins and I went to the Vanier Cup and liked him. The knock against him was that he had some injuries. We had a priority list for the draft, and we felt if he was available in the fifth or sixth round, we would take him. He was and we did.

"Greg started 10–12 games as a rookie last year, and he played very well. His confidence level will be much higher this year, and he'll really feel like part of the team. Greg is competitive. He's a very tough kid. When there's an opportunity there, that's when you see what kind of player you have. If he seizes the opportunity like I think he will, his career will take off."

Knox made All-Canadian in 1994.

Another defender Buono held in high esteem was outside linebacker Matt Finlay, who made the Western All-Star team in 1992. The personification of what a professional football player should be, Finlay gives everything he has to the game, conducting himself with courage, pride and dignity. Born and raised in the Toronto area, Finlay graduated from Eastern Michigan and was drafted by the Alouettes in 1986. His coach then was Wally Buono. When the Als folded, Finlay was delighted to be picked up by his hometown Argonauts. That good feeling didn't last long. "I was there for one week," he said flatly. "Willie Pless was injured and they told me at that time I would be part of their system. A week later, Willie came off his injury, and they traded me to Calgary. I think Bob O'Billovich planned all along to only use me for the week.

"I was disappointed, being my hometown with my family being there, but it would have been difficult to play in my hometown. I've seen that in Calgary. For me getting out of Toronto was a good move."

Said Wally Buono, "I've watched the progression of Matt Finlay from a rookie to a very seasoned football player who right now is one of the premier linebackers in the league. The maturing of Matt Finlay has been very rewarding to me, not only as a football player but also as a leader. Matt is a consummate pro. He is well prepared. He leads not only by example, he keeps the other players motivated. He helps them to be sharp on the field. He's a good guy to be around, a good guy in the locker room. He's having a good career. He's worked extremely hard to get where he is today."

Finlay played the 1993 season in constant pain. "I tore a bicep," he explained. "It's going to be that way forever. That's not going to change. My knee is slowly getting better, but it will take some time. I'm wearing a brace now and likely will for the rest of my career. My Achilles' tendon is pretty bad right now. It's hard to run, so I don't do much of that during the week, only in games."

He was philosophical about the sacrifices made to play football. "Pain is part of the game. I've always played with pain. In college I had knee surgery and two shoulder surgeries. For me though, the cup is always half full,

so I believe I'm always going to get better and be able to play. When my injuries really do affect what I'm doing, that will be the time to hang 'em up." Finlay played two more years.

The Stampeders came out of the starting gate like Secretariat in 1993, winning 10 in a row. They hadn't lost since September 27, 1992, and their winning streak of 17 games was the fifth longest in league history. The streak ended in Edmonton on September 10 when the lost 29–16. Allen Pitts, Keyvan Jenkins and Junior Thurman sustained season-ending injuries.

The Stamps responded to adversity by winning their next four and five of the next seven to finish first with a mark of 15–3. But two of those losses were to the Eskimos in Edmonton, including losing 39–21 in the last game of the season. On the other hand, they were undefeated at home. They wouldn't lose a regular season game at McMahon Stadium until August 18, 1995.

The top four Western teams made the playoffs. Calgary beat B.C. 17–9 thanks to Tony Martino's punting on a windy day, while Edmonton destroyed Saskatchewan 51–13. The Alberta entries prepared to meet in the final for the fourth year in a row.

Calgary's record was deceptive. Besides losing Pitts, Thurman and Jenkins, Will Johnson was on the limp. The Eskimos mushed into Calgary on a six-game winning streak. While the Stampeders had lost at home only once in two years, Edmonton was the better team on a bad field. The days leading up the game were bitterly cold and with blizzard conditions. Long-time observers couldn't remember more daunting weather for a Western Final.

The Stamps started in dramatic fashion with Pee Wee Smith returning a punt 64 yards for a touchdown three minutes into the opening quarter. Mark McLoughlin added a field goal to give Calgary a 10–0 lead after one quarter of play. In the second frame, Edmonton scored on a 73-yard pass from Damon Allen to Jim Sandusky plus a single. McLoughlin replied with a field goal. Calgary led 13–8 at the half.

Halftime was extended to allow the stadium crew to clear snow off the field. That seemed to be all Edmonton needed. Damon Allen completed TD passes to Sandusky, Eddie Brown and Jay Christensen, while Calgary was held to a safety. Edmonton 29, Calgary 15. Flutie left the game in the fourth quarter complaining about cold hands. To lose the right to defend their title in their stadium to their archenemy was a bitter pill to swallow. The Eskimos took great delight occupying the Stampeders' dressing room come Grey Cup day. They won it all, beating the Bombers 33–23.

1993 was the Year of the Sponge when Dave Sapunjis became the first Canadian in CFL history to catch over 100 passes. He finished the season with 103 for 1,484 yards and 15 touchdowns. Sapunjis made All-Canadian and won the CFL's Most Outstanding Canadian Award.

Doug Flutie won the Most Outstanding Award for the third straight year, the only one to accomplish that. Flutie completed 408 of 677 passes for 6,003 yards and a record setting 44 touchdowns. He surpassed 15,000 yards passing faster than any quarterback in CFL history. And he wasn't the best of a bad lot. He competed against Kent Austin, Danny Barrett, Damon Allen, Matt Dunigan, Tracy Ham, Tom Burgess and David Archer.

Bruce Covernton was runner up for the Offensive Lineman award. Derrick Crawford was second only to Eskimo Gizmo Williams with 2,213 combined yards and 11 touchdowns. Flutie, Sapunjis, Will Johnson, Hasselbach, Karl Anthony and Covernton made All-Canadian.

In charge of getting the stadium ready for the Grey Cup was Stan Schwartz, the manager of McMahon Stadium since 1982. Stan was born on a farm near Brooks, Alberta, and moved to Medicine Hat, where he began Grade Three at Elm Street School. He graduated from Medicine Hat High School in 1963. Stan attended the University of Calgary and earned a Master's degree from Indiana State University. Stan was a high school teacher and counsellor in Calgary before joining the Stampeder coaching staff in 1979. When the Stampeders and Jack Gotta parted company, McMahon Stadium Society president Tony Anselmo asked Stan to manage the stadium. Always up to a challenge, Schwartz accepted.

"There's no such thing as stadium management school," he said. "I asked Tony why he picked me from the Stampeder coaching staff to manage the stadium given that I didn't know anything about it. He said he thought I had leadership qualities, could work with people and would put the time in required to do the job.

Life after football. Doug Flutie in 2009 as drummer of the Flutie Brothers Band.
COURTESY CRAIG MICHAUD

"It was a learning process. I have to credit my farm background with being able to handle the technical side of things. I was always good with my hands and could build things. I operated different kinds of equipment on summer jobs. Also, I've always been a fussy guy, demanding a high standard. Once I got the right staff in place, everything worked out well."

Still, hosting the Grey Cup was a challenge. "This is tougher than the Olympics because there is no structure," he explained the week before the big day. "In fairness to Larry Ryckman and everyone, they've had to put this thing together so fast. Larry turned to Bill Pratt and the COC [Canadian Olympic Committee] regime. They had access to a lot of credible people who are lending a lot to this project."

Schwartz oversaw major changes to the stadium during the fall of '93. "There were three main changes. We added 10,000 temporary seats in the north end. We had to remove the Olympic cauldron, which upset some people. The second change was the addition of the new press box area. Right in the middle of that will be the VIP box, which Larry Ryckman will occupy during the game. After the Grey Cup, the new press area will be converted to corporate boxes, which will be a source of revenue for years to come. "The third thing people will see is 72,000 square feet of tent shelters that will house corporate sponsors and a cabaret."

When the CFL changed its policy so teams had to buy the right to host the Grey Cup, it meant no stone was left unturned in maximizing profit, which was frustrating to a football man like Stan. "The biggest concern—the game itself—has been secondary," he lamented. "Some people don't realize that the only reason we're there is because of the game. So much that is happening has been driven by the almighty dollar."

The worst-case scenario was a repeat of the weather for the Western Final. "If you have [a blizzard] the night before, you at least have an opportunity to get the field clean. If you have time, you can clean out the aisles and stands. Once you get to game time, there isn't much you can do. We're looking at a work force of about 50 people. We'll all have a shovel and pick a line and clean it off. You can't use any equipment because that would pack the snow down. You'd end up with ruts. One good thing about artificial turf is that you don't need much sun for it to warm up. The synthetic fibres really absorb heat.

"We did the Grey Cup logo in the middle of the field in September. That cost $15,000. . . . If you get pellet-like snow, it operates like sand paper and takes the paint off. Re-doing it this week in cold weather would be a real problem. Painting the lines and numbers on the field is our priority, but you also have the corporate people who spent a lot for their logos. They have to be painted, too.

"You have two practices everyday starting Wednesday plus rehearsals for the parade, pre-game and halftime shows. You don't have much time to get the field ready. We'll be working from 10:00 PM until about 8:00 AM, and the weather can be extreme during those hours."

The field was in great shape come Grey Cup day, and the weather was beautiful.

The 1994 season saw three new U.S. entries, stocked by Americans only, Las Vegas Posse, Shreveport Pirates and the Baltimore CFLers. The Sacramento Goldminers had joined the previous year.

After squandering a 21–3 lead after three quarters and losing their opener in Regina 22–21, the Stampeders ran off eight straight wins—averaging 46 points a game—the most incredible eight games ever seen in professional football. They won in Baltimore 42–16, then beat the Bombers and B.C. at home

58–19 and 62–21. They avenged their loss to Saskatchewan, trouncing the Green and White 54–15, sank the good ship Argonaut 52–3 and took the measure of Edmonton on Labour Day 48–15. Calgary displayed the most productive offense in the history of the game, scoring 698 points, a record that still stands. It was no wonder the team had two horses on the injury list. The noble steeds that ran the sidelines when the team scored a touchdown were worn to a frazzle. It's surprising the Stamps weren't reported to the SPCA. Calgary was also the best defensively.

As usual, Wally Buono had to overcome adversity when he lost Harold Hasselbach to the NFL, Karl Anthony and Ken Watson to Baltimore and Andy McVey and Keyvan Jenkins to retirement. He was worried about Allen Pitts who had broken his leg the year before. "I went to L.A. on April 10 and worked him out," Buono said. "We were very much pleased with his progress. He reassured me he would be ready to go and be as effective as he once was. Tremendous speed has never been his forte. It's his size, his demeanour, his ability to get open. None of that has changed. He might be a step faster because of all the hard work and rehab he's done."

Pitts went on to have his greatest season as a pro, catching a record 126 passes for 2,036 yards and 21 touchdowns. He led the league in receptions, yards, yards from scrimmage and touchdowns. He made All-Canadian.

Flutie won the Most Outstanding Player Award for the fourth time. He completed 403 passes for 5,726 yards and 48 touchdowns. He led the league in passing attempts, completions, yards and passing touchdowns. In the big win over Winnipeg, Calgary scored 50 points in the first half with Flutie throwing for six TDs and running for two others. "It was one of those nights when everything works for you," he said, clearly delighted.

The legendary eight-game winning streak ended in a rainstorm at Edmonton on September 9 when the Stamps lost 38–12. A week later, Flutie came back to out-duel an unknown rookie named Anthony Calvillo and defeat the Las Vegas Posse 35–25. They won six of their last seven games to finish first with a record of 15–3.

In another four-team playoff, Calgary hosted Saskatchewan in one semi-final winning 36–3. The Stamps were jubilant when they heard B.C. had upset the dreaded Eskimos 24–23, ignoring the fact they had only beaten the Lions by a single point the last game of the season.

Still, it looked like a mismatch. Calgary hadn't lost a playoff game to B.C. in 30 years. The Lions were in no shape to play anybody, let alone the powerful Stampeders. Quarterback Kent Austin had a separated shoulder and their other pivot, Danny McManus, had torn a muscle. Defenders Less Browne and Barry Wilburn had a cartilage and rib injury, respectively. Even though they had squeaked by the Eskimos in Edmonton, they came into Calgary on a wing and a prayer, which was enough for Leo coach Dave Ritchie.

"Going into Calgary, no one believed in us anyway," recalled the Lions' Brady Browne, the CFL's all-time interceptor. "I think that benefits a team, knowing you are the big underdog, just bodies on the field. That makes people play above their ability. We did that."

Despite wintry conditions, the game was a shootout. With just over a minute to play, Calgary led 36–31. They lined up for a field goal. It was blocked. McLoughlin explained what happened. "Apparently Ray Alexander pyramided. The ball was hit well, but it was just a great play on his part." It was the first time in McLoughlin's career he had a field goal blocked.

Not to worry. With less than a minute to play, the Lions would have to move the ball 64 yards and score a touchdown to win.

With Austin on the sideline, the fate of the Lions was in the hands of Danny McManus. Just three completions later, the Lions were on the Calgary 4. McManus to Darren Flutie, touchdown. Final score: Underdogs 38, Overdogs 36.

"Darren was supposed to go to the back corner of the end zone," McManus recalled, "but as he did frequently, he just saw the open space. It was weird. He and I sort of made eye contact, and I had an idea he was going to sit there. I got lucky and just put the ball between two guys, and he was able to catch it. Calgary was playing so passive. I mean their secondary was just so soft during that last drive. You've got to play every play. One play can beat you."

Everything had to go right for B.C. and wrong for Calgary—and it did. For most of the Stampeders—especially McLoughlin—it was the most devastating loss of their careers. "We had a lot of opportunities and, personally, I had a lot of opportunities to contribute to a victory in that game and a couple of those drives," he lamented. "We could have ended them with field goals that probably would have given us the margin of victory. It didn't happen."

Once again a magnificent season had ended in crushing disappointment.

Approaching the 1995 season, Wally Buono was a frustrated man. He had the third-best winning percentage in CFL history. Doug Flutie and Allen Pitts were rewriting the record book. His Stampeders had finished first every year but one in the '90s. They should have been regarded as one of the best teams ever, but they weren't because they only had one Grey Cup.

Buono discussed his goals for 1995. "The biggest thing is, I'd like to win the games that are most important. In the last four years, we played in four Western Finals. Two we lost. We should have won all four. The tragedy of

our sport is the fact that you play one game to get to the next step and sometimes that isn't the game that you are at your peak. Last year defensively we played as consistently as anybody in the league for as long as I can remember, yet when it came to the Western Final, we didn't play anywhere close to the level we played during the season or in the semi-final, where our defence dominated a good Saskatchewan team.

"I don't know what happened. I wish I did. We talked to [the players] at halftime and mentioned that it was important to get back to being more dominant. Sometimes what you say doesn't happen.

"How can we improve? By winning the Western Final and Grey Cup. Can we win more than 15 games? We talked about that last year at this time. We won 15. I guess the issue for this year is, can we win three playoff games?"

The Stampeders lost key players to free agency and retirement. Gone were Junior Thurman, Douglas Kraft, Will Moore, Bruce Wiggins, Doug Davies, Ken Moore and backup quarterback Steve Taylor.

The O-line was revamped with Bruce Beaton, Denny Chronopoulous, Jamie Crysdale, Bobby Pandelidis and Rocco Romano. Bruce Covernton missed most of the season with an injury and never really recovered. Terry Vaughn and Tyrone Williams replaced Wiggins and Moore, and Marvin Coleman and Al Jordan started on the corners. Marvin Pope replaced Ken Walker at defensive end with Anthony McLanahan taking Pope's spot at linebacker. They still had Flutie—but not for long.

Again the Stamps got off to a fast start, winning their first seven games. In Game 8, at home to the Birmingham Barracudas, disaster struck. After breaking the 30,000 career-passing-yards mark, Flutie injured his elbow and was unable to answer the bell for the third quarter. The Barracudas went on to win 31–26, ending Calgary's record setting 27 home-game winning streak. Flutie had surgery the following week. He was out for the season. Surely the Stampeders were doomed.

When Jeff Garcia replaced Flutie in the third quarter of the Birmingham game, sports writers scrambled to find out something about the red-headed kid from California. No one had given the backup a second thought because Flutie had never missed a game in his CFL career. (After returning from his injury, he wouldn't miss another.)

Garcia, showing the self-assurance of an old veteran, proceeded to win six games in a row, including the Labour Day Classic against Edmonton when he threw six touchdown passes, equalling the record held by Peter Liske and Flutie. Calgary's newest hero took it all in stride. "Today was just a dream come true," he enthused. "I know it's a big game for the province, but I've been through big games in college, games where we were highly overmatched. But in this situation, we were not over-matched. . . . The main thing I try to do is play within myself. I have tremendous athletes around me, especially great receivers. The thing is to get the ball to them and let them do what they do best. With that kind of supporting cast, I don't need to go out and make everything happen. I feel confident with them and that helps me calm down and get comfortable."

Knowing how good he was, it must have been frustrating sitting on the bench behind Flutie. "I think that was something that I was dealing with early on," Garcia admitted. "I knew I was going to get opportunities to play late in games just because of the manner in which we were able to put teams away.

"Was I content with that? Not really. But I was in a situation where I was backing up the best quarterback in the league. I was learning and growing within the system. I pretty much felt that I was just going to wait out my remaining years on my contract. I never really saw what was coming, but I was prepared for it."

In addition to a strong arm, Garcia could run and did so with reckless abandon, usually paying the price. After a game against Toronto, a reporter noticed a blue smudge on his helmet. "That's paint from an Argo helmet," he replied. "I got hit so hard the paint came off." Ouch.

"I can't control him," said Wally Buono with a sigh. "I can't tell him not to run. If they only rush three linemen and leave that much territory open, he's going to take off and run."

Calgary again finished at 15–3 atop the division. In three years, Calgary's regular season record was 45–9, the best streak in CFL history in term of wins. The Eskimos, playing a 16 game schedule, lost only six games between 1979–81. Dave Sapunjis won his second Most Outstanding Canadian Player Award, and the Stamps dominated most statistical categories.

Come playoff time, the Stampeders wanted to leave nothing to chance. In the new playoff format to accommodate American expansion, all the Canadian teams were in

Jeff Garcia. COURTESY CALGARY STAMPEDERS

one division. Calgary faced Hamilton in the semi-final. Against all odds, Flutie was back but turned the ball over five times before being booed off the field at halftime. Garcia returned, winning a surprisingly close game 18–15. Was the horse collar getting tight?

Edmonton had been thoroughly whipped 51–24 and 33–17 by the Stamps during Labour Day week. But the Eskimos hadn't lost since, including their playoff win over B.C. For the fifth time in six years, the Alberta teams contested the Division Final. This time Calgary shucked King Kong off its back, winning 37–4.

Calgary scored on every first-half possession, Flutie playing the game of his life. He threw short over the middle to Vince Danielson, Sapunjis and Pitts. He went long to Terry Vaughn and Tyrone Williams. He ran with the ball, putting moves on defenders that would make a bullfighter green with envy.

The competitive fire burns deeply in Flutie. He had been stung by the booing the week before. He had been hurt by suggestions that Calgary lost the final in 1993 because he couldn't handle the cold. He looked forward to vindication in Regina against Don Matthews' Baltimore Stallions, who would be a formidable opponent.

The Stallions also finished at 15–3. They were led by running back Mike Pringle, who set the CFL rushing record in 1994 with 1,972 yards. He was runner-up to Flutie for the Most Outstanding Player Award. He found a home in Baltimore after being cut by Edmonton and traded by Sacramento.

In 1995 Pringle was rushing champion again with 1,791 yards, beating out Dave Sapunjis for the Outstanding Player Award, though Sponge's 111 catches for 1,655 yards and 12 touchdowns earned him the Canadian award.

While the other U.S. expansion teams struggled to master the Canadian game, Stallions' coach Don Matthews recruited the American cream of the CFL free-agent crop. Although his club had lost the Grey Cup to B.C. in their first year, Matthews was Canadians nightmare come true: a team stocked entirely by Americans with solid experience playing the Canadian game. To win, Will Johnson, Stu Laird, Marvin Pope and Gonzalo Floyd would have to win the war in the trenches against Baltimore's mammoth offensive line, which outweighed the Stamp's contingent by 55 pounds per man.

Calgary led the league against the run and had held Pringle to 50 yards when they beat Baltimore 29–15 on August 6. Calgary was first in total offense, points and passing. Baltimore's pass defence ranked ninth in yards and twelfth in completions. Baltimore's strength was rushing. Calgary had trouble with the run. The Stallions' weakness was pass defence. The place-kickers were equal, but Baltimore's punter Josh Miller was clearly superior to Tony Martino.

The Stampeder strategy would be to box in Tracy Ham, forcing him to throw, the belief being Ham wasn't a good passer but a dangerous runner. Ham had the third highest career percentage completion rate in CFL history!

Matt Finlay was playing his last game. His spirit was willing, but his flesh just couldn't take it anymore. He discussed getting ready for Grey Cup '95. "Experience is certainly going to help us cope with the jitters. Guys who have been there don't get as nervous. They'll be able to settle down quicker. But this is the second year in a row for Baltimore, so we can't use that as an advantage. About half our team has been to two Grey Cups. This is my third.

"The largest crowd in Canadian sports for the year is watching the game. If you think about it, it could get to you. A great number of people are watching you, and one wrong move could mean a loss for your team. The reality is there is a lot more pressure. But the game of football is pressure. It comes down to this game. You want to play in this game. Personally, I don't let the pressure get to me because I feel very fortunate just to be playing in it."

Finlay thought shutting down Baltimore's running attack and having good coverage on special teams was essential to victory. "That's basically been our game plan all year. By concentrating on the run, we try to make teams one-dimensional and throw the ball. If you can shut Pringle down that really limits what they are able to do. Even Ham running is not all that bad because he's not going to beat you alone.

"What we're really concentrating on is special teams. Baltimore is excellent in all aspects of special team play. They have the premier returner in the league in Chris Wright. If you're not careful, he'll blow right by you for a touchdown. Special teams are just as important as offense and defence, and I hope the guys realize that. Special teams are going to be a big part of the game, and we can't let them win that battle because that could make a difference in the game. They have the premier punter in the league. He gets the ball down the field in a big way every time. So we are going to need big returns on our side, and we're going to have to limit their returns."

After leading the team into the playoffs, Jeff Garcia was the odd man out. "Hopefully I'll get an opportunity to play in Sunday's game," he offered. "I'm preparing like it's any other game, not trying to over-emphasize it even though I know it's for all the marbles." Garcia didn't play a down.

His offensive coordinator, John Hufnagel, knew Garcia would be disappointed. In the 1984 Grey Cup when Tom Clements lost a contact lens and had to come out, Hufnagel went in and got the Blue Bombers untracked.

When Clements got another lens, Hufnagel returned to the sideline. He made sure Garcia understood that his value to the team wasn't diminished because Flutie was starting.

Hufnagel thought the team's Grey Cup experience was an advantage. "This is not a normal preparation week. The players are away for the whole week. They have all kinds of distractions to take them away from what really is the job at hand, getting themselves ready to play. It is tough to stay focused. That's what the players have to fight through, being focused enough to prepare themselves for the big game. The more experience you have at it, the smarter you are, and you'll be able to handle the distractions better.

"The worst thing is being too concerned about making a mistake. If you're going to be that concerned about it, you're not going to be flying around. This what the mental preparation part of it is all about. If you are confident about that part of the game, you are going to be flying around. If you make a mistake, just don't make it again—but at least you're flying around and creating havoc, hitting people and knocking people down. Grey Cup is a special couple of days. Come game time, it's an exciting moment, an exciting day."

To say Grey Cup day in Regina was windy would be an enormous understatement. Though the theme for Grey Cup '95 was "Huddle Up in Saskatchewan," the cold never materialized during Grey Cup week when the weather was unseasonably balmy. Early Sunday morning, however, a ferocious wind blew in.

A straight-faced commissioner Larry Smith downplayed the gale, saying, "The only problem I had was when the wind got up to about 85kpm. Our insurance on the temporary stands covered up to 90kph, and we had a backup plan to take 20,000 people into a hockey rink and watch it on the screens. The winds stuck about 75kpm, so we were okay." A lot of fans in the south end zone facing the torrent, however, weren't okay and had to leave the game by halftime.

Matt Finlay said they had to stop Mike Pringle and at least match Baltimore's special teams. Pringle picked up 137 yards rushing, and Calgary's special teams were a disaster.

The Stamps' Tony Stewart returned the opening kickoff 15 yards to the 40. With the wind at his back, Flutie completed a 13-yarder to Sapunjis. Stewart lost a yard, Flutie threw incomplete and Martino punted 43 yards to Chris Wright at the Baltimore 28. He returned it 82 yards for a touchdown, still the record. With 2:26 gone, it was 7–0 for Baltimore.

The Stallions had an opportunity to add to their lead when Stewart fumbled the kick-off, which was recovered by Tracey Gravely at the Calgary 47. Three plays later, a field-goal attempt went awry when Dan Crowley fumbled the snap. Flutie then engineered two field goals. At the end of 15 minutes, the score stood Baltimore 7, Calgary 6.

On the first play of the second quarter, Ham threw a screen pass behind Gerald Alphin. Will Johnson picked it up and raced to the enemy 3. Flutie fooled everyone in the ballpark by throwing to linebacker Marvin Pope for the touchdown. The Stallions replied with a 30-yard Carlos Huerta field goal.

Then special teams became the deciding factor. Set to punt five minutes later, the Stampeders, in total confusion, were looking at one other and throwing up their hands as O.J. Brigance blocked the punt. Alvin Watson picked it up and ran to the end zone. Baltimore 17, Calgary 13, both touchdowns coming on special-team breakdowns. The Americans added a brace of field goals to lead 23–13 at the half, one, a 53-yarder, a Grey Cup record.

Baltimore had the wind in the third quarter. Miller kicked an 80-yard single. Then Flutie went to work. Flutie for 9; Stewart for 10 and 2. To Pitts for 10; Stewart, 5. To Sponge

for 7, to Vaughn for 22. Flutie took it the rest of the way on three plays. The 65-yard drive ate up six and a half minutes into the wind. The score was Baltimore 24, Calgary 20.

Then came the finest moments in Tracy Ham's career. His intelligence and heart often questioned, Ham answered his critics. Starting at the 18, he completed passes to Robert Clark and Gerald Alphin. Will Johnson batted down a pass at the Stallion 52. Ham then threw to Peter Tuipulotu for nine. On third and one came the quarterback sneak. Ham was awarded the first down over the strenuous objections of the opposition. Four plays later, Ham eluded a fierce pass rush and ran in for a touchdown. Baltimore 31, Calgary 20.

Even with the wind at their backs, Calgary was shut out in the final quarter while Huerta added two field goals. Mike Pringle sealed the Stamps' fate by picking up 90 of his 137 yards in last quarter. The final score was Baltimore 37, Calgary 20. Canada's Grey Cup had fallen into American hands.

Tracy Ham completed 17 of 29 for 213 yards, ran for 24 and was named Grey Cup MVP. Dave Sapunjis, 8 for 113 yards, won the Canadian Player of the Game for the third time.

Everyone agreed that Calgary had trouble getting by Baltimore's 25-yard line. "Yes," said Sapunjis, "they stopped us down there quite well. They played a defence where they dropped guys back and let us try to pick it apart—and we didn't. We struggled on the 25-yard line in. It wasn't any one player, just as a unit we didn't move the ball when we had to. They outplayed us on special teams, offensively and defensively."

For Sapunjis, Chris Wright's punt return for a touchdown was déjà vu all over again. "It was just like that play in 1991 where Rocket returned it all the way. The guys on the sideline were trying to get going, and all of a sudden they break a big play. Our emotional

Doug Flutie in action against the Baltimore Stallions, who took the Cup south of the border.
COURTESY CALGARY STAMPEDERS

level dropped, and it hurt us. 1995 and 1991 were similar in the fact that the other team's special team dominated."

Buono analyzed the special team breakdown. "The first one, [Wright] found a crease and got into the open field. That happens with a good returner. On the blocked punt, there was missed communication. They were moving around, and one of our guys let somebody through. He blocked the punt. It's tough to spot any team 14 points on special teams and think you're going to win."

155

Doug Flutie completed 23 of 49 passes for 287 yards with one interception and one touchdown. Was the wind a major problem? "It was more of a factor in the first half than the second half," he replied. "I was disappointed that we couldn't move the ball when we had the wind in the fourth quarter. We had to be efficient. We didn't get enough yards on first downs."

Was the decision to go with Flutie rather than Jeff Garcia the right one? "Absolutely," insisted Sapunjis. "I think you had to go with Doug. We talked about that all week, and I said you have to go with his experience. Go with the leadership, go with the guy that has played in the Grey Cup and won. If he really struggles, bring Jeff in.

"Did he struggle? I don't think so. Doug played well enough to win. I think the guys around him didn't play well enough to win."

Winning the Canadian Player of the Game three times and the Outstanding Canadian Award twice were the highlights of Sapunjis's career. "I take great pride in playing well in the big games. Being named Outstanding Canadian not only in that game but for the season as well was great. I've been named the league's Outstanding Canadian twice, and that's not a feat many have accomplished. When I retire, I hope I'll be known as one of the best Canadian receivers ever."

Will Johnson disagreed with the strategy to contain Ham. "The plan was to box him in and let him throw out of the pocket. They didn't want to let him run. But any quarterback, no matter how lousy he is, if he stays in the pocket for a long time, is going to pick you apart."

Johnson thought they should be going after Ham. Why didn't he? "I did later on, but the other guys are more coach-conscious, whereas I'm more win-oriented, doing what it takes. I've been in the league a long time so I do what I think it takes to win.

"If you're pushing a guy back into the quarterback on almost every play and bumping him, then you've got him. If you're not getting any push up the middle, it's useless. So I've got to pass rush. I've got to get off what the coach is saying and do what it is going to take to win this thing. I've had my battles with Tracy Ham. When I first came into the league, we had our battles, and I ended up winning because he ended up leaving Edmonton and we ended up beating them often."

Don Matthews agreed with Johnson. "I'm always surprised when anyone uses that strategy. Tracy Ham or any scrambling quarterback hurts you when you get conservative on your pass rush. There's no question. When we played Tracy, we sent our front four with reckless abandon after him. We also played a lot of zone, so if he scrambled we were going to treat him like a flare back and just keep him under five yards with zone protection.

"We felt the worst thing we could do was play man coverage where your DBs have their backs to Tracy. Every time you do that, you have to slow down your pass rush, which affords him more time, and that's when he's dangerous. Tracy's very bright. He's a remarkable talent and a quality guy. If you say keep Tracy in the pocket and make him throw, he'll kill you. You've got to go get him."

Matthews followed his own advice against Flutie. "We played a lot of three man rush and kept everybody looking at him because we didn't want him to scramble. On man-to-man coverage, you have everybody run off, so when the quarterback scrambles, eight of your players never see him go because they are in coverage. In zone, those eight players are looking at him, and they go get him when he takes off." Flutie ran the ball 10 times for 45 yards.

"When the observation was made that Ham had lots of time to throw, Wally Buono said, "That was part of our plan for keeping Tracy boxed in. The defensive line was doing pretty much what we asked them to do, push the pocket, try to stay in front. Overall, the majority of time we did keep him in the pocket. There were times he did have the time to throw, but I don't think his throwing really hurt us. The key factors were the two special team plays and our inability to catch the football and keep drives alive.

"We let them score in the third quarter. We were trying to get momentum, and it was critical for our defence not to give up any points in the third quarter. But we did. We wanted to win the third quarter and put our offense in a position to get points in the fourth. But they put the ball in the end zone, which was a big demoralizer."

As far as Mark McLoughlin was concerned, the reason the Stampeders lost was simple. "We were outplayed. Don't make excuses for us. When they needed to make the big plays, they did."

Before opening the 1996 training camp, Buono looked back at Grey Cup '95.

"Maybe in Saskatchewan if the wind had waited three or four hours, it might have been a different game. We could have controlled our punting game better if that had been the case. (Miller averaged 49.5 yards for Baltimore, Martino 33.7). You've got to be at the right place at the right time. The circumstances have to be right for you.

"When we played the first part of the game, I knew we were not at our best. But I felt that as the game progressed, we started to come out of it. I thought in the third quarter we started to take control of the game— and then Tracy Ham broke away.

"But there was a play before that. It was third down. They went for it and made it by an inch, and they could easily not have made it by an inch on the spot. If they don't make it, we not only had momentum because we just scored, now we have the momentum because we had just taken it away from them. They get the first down, they go in and we're right behind the eight ball again."

After the game, when a reporter asked Doug Flutie if he expected criticism for another postseason failure, the usually unflappable icon showed a rare flash of temper. "We shouldn't but probably will. That crap comes from the media. We played our ass off all year long, played our ass off in the playoffs and played hard today. You lose some games. That's just the way it happens."

But it was a legitimate question. Four powerful teams led by the man deemed the greatest to ever play the Canadian game had earned only one Grey Cup. As events unfolded, the 1995 Grey Cup was the last time Flutie would don a Calgary uniform. The following year, he signed with Toronto after Stampeder owner Larry Ryckman reneged on his million-dollar contract.

Community ownership had ended October 23, 1991, when Ryckman bought the club. Described as a financier, Ryckman was the toast of the town for saving the Stampeders from bankruptcy. Five years later, Ryckman left Calgary in disgrace after securities regulators banned him from trading and from directing any publicly held companies until 2014. Ryckman was found guilty of stock manipulation. During his five-year stint as owner, he enjoyed five years of winning football, including three Grey Cup appearances. He also left a string of unpaid bills behind him.

Ryckman was a man who craved attention. He would corral the media and make an outrageous statement, which was dutifully reported to the public. When the reaction was predictably negative, he would swear off reporters forever. The next day he would round them up and start over again.

The public in the 1990s was conditioned to believe all CFL franchises had one foot in the grave. It was easy to believe the Stampeder's financial problems were the same as those in other CFL cities. But that wasn't the case. The Stampeders were very profitable, but Ryckman was spending money on things that had nothing to do with strengthening the franchise.

Anyone could play the role of Diamond Jim football owner if he didn't pay his bills. Ryckman used a personal services contract to avoid the league salary cap to sign Doug Flutie for $1 million, but he made only one payment in 1995 to Flutie—and then put a stop payment on the cheque. Not wanting to aggravate a crisis situation or let his teammates down, Flutie kept his mouth shut and basically played for nothing.

Where did Ryckman spend money? Some of the more egregious examples include flying a planeload of friends at the team's expense to the Grey Cup in Toronto in 1992. There were gifts for the players, fancy bags for the media, beautiful Grey Cup rings for his champions. There were the limos when the team was on the road. And there were mountains of debt. Larry Ryckman always went first class—usually with someone else's money.

Other examples included hiring NFL Hall of Famer Deacon Jones to do PR work, which cost the team about $75,000 although Jones did very little. Ryckman spent thousands of dollars on a Jumbo-Tron television for the 1993 Western Final,

even though he had to borrow a bundle of money to stage the Grey Cup. All the while, management repeatedly urged him to pay for the portable stands and other essential

Larry Ryckman with what someone else's money can buy.
COURTESY CALGARY STAMPEDERS

changes to the stadium. Ryckman wanted glory—or at least to bask in the reflected glare of it.

By 1995 there were times when the team was only hours away from failing to meet the payroll. Even finding the money to get the team to Regina for the Grey Cup was a struggle.

Heading into 1996, the club was over $5 million in debt owed to nine major creditors including the Government of Alberta, the Alberta Treasury Branch, a chartered bank, Doug Flutie and the CFL. Ryckman later said he lost $14 million owning the Calgary Stampeders.

In 1989 it was Normie Kwong who saved the Stampeders. In 1995 it was Stan Schwartz, who was appointed president and general manager, administration, on February 7. He was the only reason the bailiff hadn't carried away the club's physical assets and padlocked the doors. His unimpeachable reputation for honesty saved the franchise.

Schwartz agonized a long time before agreeing to take over the administration of the team. He had seen the books, both sets, and knew what a financial mess the Stampeders were in. When friends convinced him his reputation for integrity would not be compromised by his association with Ryckman, he accepted the challenge to clean out the Stampeder Augean Stables.

And what a challenge it was. There were sweetheart deals with various employees and companies that had to be ended. The cheque to Flutie hadn't been the only one retracted later by the flamboyant owner. Creditors had to be kept at bay with the promise of a brighter future. There was the matter of the tenuous negotiations with the McMahon Stadium Society for a new lease. But Schwartz did it.

When liens and litigation were resolved and the team could be sold, another local businessman, Sig Gutsche, owner of the Hard

Rock Cafe in Eau Claire, among other properties, rode to the rescue. Successful in oil, gas, computers, land development and restaurants, why would he buy the Stampeders?

Gutsche explained his reasons for wanting to own a professional sports franchise. "I enjoy living in Calgary. It is a very cosmopolitan city. We've got museums, galleries, theatre, the symphony, baseball, hockey and football. If we lost any segment of that, it would make us less of a city. Calgary was on the verge of losing the Stampeders and quite frankly, no one else was prepared to step up to the plate."

In two years, the team was back in the black in the hands of an entrepreneur who had demonstrated his business acumen at the tender age of 12. "I came from a very poor family," Gutsche recalled. "My mother and father came over to Canada as agricultural workers. Unskilled workers could only emigrate if they signed up as agricultural workers. We signed up on a sugar beet farm at Turin, Alberta.

Sig Gutsche. COURTESY CALGARY STAMPEDERS

"When we moved to Calgary, my mother cleaned houses, and my father worked for the city. I had to make my own spending money. I'd go to the local Loblaw's store, and I'd get some of the day-old stuff they were throwing out. I'd walk door to door with my wagon and sell it. I could make a lot of money doing it."

Gutsche and Schwartz were the odd couple of management, but their relationship worked. "I think the world of Stan," said Gutsche. "He's the world's biggest pragmatist. He's a pessimist, almost. I'm the world's biggest optimist. Stan and I are like little old ladies who natter at each other all the time. But the final decision is usually somewhere in between and it is usually the best one for the team."

With his many and varied business interests, where did his heart lie? "With the Stamps," he insisted. "You can't help but get caught up with it. I figured I'd end up working one or two days a week at it. Well, it's sort of a full-time job."

Besides Sig Gutsche buying the team and Flutie fleeing to Toronto, Matt Finlay retired, Marvin Pope tried the NFL, failed and came back and Tony Stewart was traded to Hamilton. After three years in the NFL, Darryl Hall returned. O-linemen Bruce Beaton, Bobby Pandelidis and Denny Chronopoulos were traded away for salary cap reasons. They were replaced by Jay McNeil and import Fred Childress. Running back Kelvin Anderson began his distinguished career in red and white with Duane Forde providing key blocks from the fullback position. Also back was defensive lineman Will Johnson, who had been All-Canadian the previous five years and was the all-time Calgary sack leader.

The 6´5´´, 245-pound gentle giant from Monroe, Louisiana, was drafted by the NFL Bears and played 11 games for Chicago in 1987. He then became a police officer in Dallas because, he said, "I was making the same amount of money as I did in the NFL." Missing football, he gave it another shot with the Saints.

"When I went to New Orleans, I didn't like it there. Lary Kuharich's brother was the GM. He got me fixed up with Calgary."

Despite his tremendous success, Johnson did feel he received the recognition he deserved, even though his coaches referred to him as a team leader. "That's what I don't get, " the always blunt Johnson said, shaking his head. "They call me a real leader, but I don't have a leader's salary or status. If I'm a leader, make me team captain. Let me go out there when they toss the coin. . . . Back in my younger days, they designed a defence around me and put me in a position to make plays. You have to give them credit for that, but you have to give me credit for making those plays. That's what got me the All-Canadian nominations. I developed a name for myself and just kept going."

Although Johnson can sound like a blowhard, he is not. The man is without guile, and simply states the facts as he sees them.

His playing style changed after arriving at McMahon in 1989. "When I first came into the league I relied on finesse," he recalled. "Then I gained weight and employed power and finesse. At first I used to sprint off the ball. I don't do that anymore because it gets you into trouble by causing you to jump offside. I'll give them a head start and then react."

Johnson was so quick and strong that he blew by blockers to the quarterback. Because of his savvy and experience, he was seldom trapped or pushed to the outside. He was also completely unpredictable. "If a guy concentrates on tendencies with me," he said with assurance, "he'll lose. I have no tendencies. If you watch game film, you'll see me pass-rush several different ways. I'm never the same.

Most players are nervous and restless before a game, unable to sleep. Not Johnson. "I don't think about the game until game day," he insists. "I don't preoccupy myself because all I need to know when the game starts is my assignment. It's not hard to learn. You play best when you don't have anything to think about. Football should be an instinctive game. Things should come naturally. If you think about it, you're going to mess up."

Despite the lack of official recognition from the team, Johnson preferred to play in Calgary. "I've been here a long time. I respect Wally and his decisions a great deal. He does choose players well."

Jeff Garcia was the starter in 1996. Danny Barrett returned as the backup, and Number 3 on the depth chart was Montana Grizzlie Dave Dickenson.

Despite the changes, the Stamps were picked to finish first for a fifth straight year, which they did with a record of 13–5. They won nine of their first 10 games but lost three out of the remaining five, including two to Edmonton. In the Western Final, Jeff Garcia sustained a knee injury in the second quarter, and Edmonton went on to win 15–12. Pitts set the record for most 100-plus yard receiving games at 46, and McLoughlin equalled the league mark by kicking eight field goals in an August 5 game against Saskatchewan. Kelvin Anderson ran for 1,068 yards and scored 10 touchdowns to win the CFL Most Outstanding Rookie Award.

Before the 1997 season began, Allen Pitts smashed his hand in a bar fight in Los Angeles and did not return to the team until September. Dave Sapunjis, Stu Laird and Rodney Harding retired. Hobbled by a chronic back problem, Will Johnson was released and signed with Saskatchewan. When the Riders came to town in August, Johnson blew out his knee and retired to the Calgary Police Service. Pee Wee Smith was cut.

Uncharacteristic of any Buono team, the '97 Stampeders lost four of their first five games before winning three in a row. They split the Labour Day week with Edmonton and won five of their final seven games to secure second place. They looked confidently ahead to avenge the events of 1993 by knocking off the Eskimos and representing the West in the Grey Cup to be played in Edmonton. Instead they were defeated by the Cinderella Roughriders, ending their most disappointing season of the decade.

"What stands out for me," recalled Dave Dickenson, "is Reggie Slack running all over the place. Jeff got hurt at the end of the first quarter. We played a decent game. I wouldn't say we were great, but I threw for around 300 yards in three quarters. Slack beat us with his feet." Slack 33, Calgary 30.

Jeff Garcia was runner up to Doug Flutie for the CFL's Most Outstanding Player Award, and Fred Childress came second to Argo Mike Kiselak for Most Outstanding Offensive Lineman. Mark McLoughlin won the Tom Pate Memorial Award, chosen by the Players' Association for the individual who most exemplifies sportsmanship, dedication to the league and service to the community. Childress and cornerback Marvin Coleman made All-Canadian.

When the 1998 campaign got under way, the Stampeders were the most talented team in the country. Wally Buono had signed a contract extension. Jeff Garcia had been the Western All-Star quarterback the past two years, and Dave Dickenson showed great promise. Number 3 on the depth chart was an unknown from Temple University named Henry Burris. Allen Pitts, Vince Danielson, Terry Vaughn and Travis Moore were the best receiving corps in the league, Kelvin Anderson was coming off two straight 1,000-plus yards rushing seasons, and the offensive line of Jamie Crysdale, Rocco Romano, Fred Childress, Jay McNeil and Rohn Meyer was first-rate.

The Stamps fielded a veteran defence with a front seven of Jermaine Miles, Ray Jacobs,

Bronzell Miller, Steve Anderson, Darry Hall Anthony McLanahan and Alondra Johnson, and a secondary of corners Marvin Coleman and Willie Hampton, defensive backs Eddie Davis and Jack Kellog, and safety Greg Knox. Tony Martino and Mark McLoughlin led formidable special teams.

But over the past five seasons, having the best players hadn't been enough. Something was missing. In 1997, in particular, little things seemed to go wrong all the time. The team was out of kilter. Some players, particularly on defence, seemed to believe they only had to throw their helmets out on the field to win. The 1998 Stampeders needed an attitude transformation to lead them to their fourth Grey Cup championship.

Mark McLoughlin recognized the attitude adjustment between '97 and '98. "One word that comes to mind is 'focused,'" he commented. "From the first day of training camp, the veterans were determined to get back to the Grey Cup and win it. The veterans stepped forward and provided the leadership."

Said Wally Buono on the difference in the 1998 campaign: "I think the veterans this year really felt they played good football pretty much the whole year, and when it was all said and done, we should be the team that would be hoisting the Cup because we were good enough to be able to do that.

"In 1997 there was a lot of turmoil which was unsettling all around, all the time. I spent a lot of time putting out fires, trying to mend fences, trying to create what really wasn't there, whereas in '98 the big thing we always talked about was keeping focused on the goal ahead, which was to be Grey Cup champions. I don't think the sell this year was anywhere as difficult as it was last year."

In particular, Buono cited the improved chemistry on defence of certain individuals. "Maybe the individuals that weren't here more so than the individuals that were here.

The guys I thought were key were Darryl Hall, Steve Anderson and Alondra Johnson. Obviously A.J.'s new attitude, his rededication to himself and his teammates was a big part of it. I think by changing one or two guys last year we took one or two thorns out of the sides of everybody, which helped everything to be just that more congenial."

Addition by subtraction. Gone was Alondra Johnson's sidekick Marvin Pope. Choosing his words carefully, Buono said, "Marvin Pope was not a positive force, especially last year. I don't know how many people he brought with him. I think it was a good separation because of that. That was one of the main reasons I had no consideration for bringing him back."

Although the Stampeders racked up their seventh first-place finish of the decade with a 12–6 record, including three wins over Edmonton, it wasn't clear sailing to Winnipeg. Safety Greg Knox was unable to overcome injuries sustained the year before and had to retire at the end of the season. His replacements, Dave Van Belleghem and Greg Frers, also missed several games due to injury. At one time, Vince Danielson, Travis Moore and Greg Vaughn were on the injury list together. Pitts was hurt at the beginning of the season, Marvin Coleman, Jermaine Miles and Bronzell Miller later.

In training camp, the Stamps looked invincible at linebacker, but the tremendously talented Anthony McClanahan sustained a spinal cord injury that ended his career. Canadian Raymond Biggs also went down for the count. Buono brought in Henry Newby and Shonte Peoples, and they soldiered on.

Seven Stampeders made All-Canadian in 1998 including Jeff Garcia, Kelvin Anderson, Terry Vaughn, Allen Pitts, Fred Childress, Alondra Johnson and Tony Martino. Four were finalists for league awards: Vince Danielson top Canadian, Kelvin Anderson Most Outstanding Player, Johnson for the defensive award and Fred Childress, the only winner as Most Outstanding Offensive Lineman.

The most talented Stampeder, Allen Pitts, never represented the West in the awards. In fact, only twice was he even his team's nominee. And yet in 1998, Pitts moved into second slot for all-time receiving yards with 12,297 yards on 792 catches. He set a new record for touchdowns with 101.

After easily disposing of Edmonton 33–10 in the conference final, the Stampeders headed for Winnipeg, carrying their new attitude into Grey Cup week. In 1995, in Regina,

Buono imposed no curfew, and several players were spotted returning to their hotel at 7:00 AM on the Thursday of Grey Cup week. By their own admission, they partied too much and weren't focused on the game.

1998 was different. A curfew was imposed. "That was my idea," said Buono. "I talked to the captains about it. Whether that was a big issue or not, I really don't know. Just the fact that they even were willing to listen showed that their intentions were better. Maybe the disappointment we shared in the middle '90s had a lot to do with their mental framework more so than a curfew.

High-flying Kelvin Anderson led the CFL in touchdowns in 1998 with 16. COURTESY CALGARY STAMPEDERS

"They came to Winnipeg wanting to win, and if that meant they had to be in a couple of nights, it wasn't going to be a big deal. A couple of them probably went out anyway after we checked. But enough of them cared. . . . If you get enough to care, they will discipline themselves."

Although Jeff Garcia publicly complained about teammates entertaining women into the wee hours of the morning, the 1998 edition of the Calgary Stampeders was a more disciplined, more committed club than the one that lost to Baltimore. And, given coaching errors, special teams breakdowns and the talent of the Stallions, in all likelihood the Stamps would have lost anyway even if they had been sequestered at St. Michael's retreat house in Lumsden.

Grey Cup '98 was an intriguing match up, pitting the Stampeders against Edmonton East, a.k.a. the Hamilton Tiger-Cats. The Stamps would face the dynamic duo that had broken their hearts in '94 and '96, Danny McManus and Darren Flutie. Add in old nemesis Ron Lancaster and the cast was complete.

The Westerners were loaded with veterans. Fifteen had played in the '95 Cup, seven in '92, six in '91. Only four Ti-Cats had been in the big game, including kicker Paul Osbaldiston. The Stamps knew what it took to win and how long the off-season was when you lose.

The teams were evenly matched. Calgary was first in points and total offense; Hamilton, second. Calgary yielded the second fewest yards; Hamilton, the third. Hamilton surrendered the fewest points, Calgary second.

Hamilton's offensive line gave up only 15 sacks in 1998, the second lowest total in CFL history. Calgary's Garcia and Dickenson went down 40 times. Tony Martino, Marvin Coleman and Terry Vaughn gave Calgary the edge on special teams. Osbaldiston and McLoughlin were great veterans, the Tabbie

fourth all-time in scoring with 2,130 points, Mark just four points behind.

If there was a dark cloud on the Steeltown horizon, it was their fifth place standing against the run. Also, the Stampeders would wear their black uniforms in which they had never tasted defeat.

Come kickoff, it was a balmy +10°C with a west wind of 28–37kph.

Wally Buono addressed the troops. "I told them that we had worked awfully hard to get here, and let's make the most of the opportunities. Let's not come back in here with any regrets. We talked about some of the key factors as far as field position and big plays."

In the Eastern dressing room, Ron Lancaster said, "We've probably got further than a lot of people thought. The opportunity to win a Grey Cup isn't there every year. That's basically what I tried to tell them.

"You get there one year. . . . I got there in my rookie year and it took me six years to get there again. It is hard to do, it is hard to get to that Grey Cup game, and when you get there, you've got to take the opportunity to win it. Even though . . . you think you've got a good team, it's not easy to get back there. It's hard. You've worked your tail off to get here. Let's finish it off right."

Calgary won the coin toss, keeping the wind in the second and fourth quarters.

The Stampeders opened the scoring at 3:02 when Orlando Steinhauer conceded a single after McLoughlin missed on a 48-yard field goal try. Four minutes later, his counterpart kicked the Cats into the lead with a 24-yarder, followed soon after by a 34-yard field goal by McLoughlin. After 15 minutes, Calgary led 4–3, but they were at the Hamilton three.

In the second stanza, whatever could go wrong, did. Calgary's Kelvin Anderson capped the 86-yard, eight-play drive with a three-yard plunge into the end zone. But the snap went awry, and the convert was no good. Calgary 10, Hamilton 3. McManus replied by marching from his 24 to the enemy 13, where Osbaldiston's 20-yarder reduced Calgary's lead to four points.

Six plays later, Bobby Olive clearly fumbled Tony Martino's punt, but the referee blew the call. On second and 11 at the Hamilton 20, Greg Frers intercepted McManus but was called for interference. Buono disagreed. "The referee called us for jamming. He said [Frers] hit him in the face. I couldn't see it. I thought it was a great play. We did a nice job of disguising what we were doing, but the referee made the call."

With passes to Darren Flutie, Andrew Grigg and Mike Morreale, the Cats drove to the Calgary 39. McManus then read the blitz brilliantly and hooked up with Ron Williams for a 35-yard touchdown. Hamilton 13, Calgary 10.

Calgary came back, moving the ball to the Ti-Cat 42, where they lined up for a field goal. But it was a fake! Dave Dickenson hit Kelvin Anderson right in the breadbasket, but he dropped it. When the Stamps got nowhere on their next possession and with the ball on their 24, Martino went back to punt. The snap was high, and Martino rushed to get it off. The ball dribbled 23 yards, where the Stampeders were called for no yards. On the final play of the half, Osbaldiston kicked a 40-yard field goal, making the score Hamilton 16, Calgary 10.

Buono was not concerned. "The issue we addressed was the fact that when you look at it, everything really went against us—not in the negative sense, but in the what-else-can-go-wrong sense. But we're only behind by six points. In my mind, six points was just one play. I felt very confident, and I challenged the guys individually to go out and do what they knew they could do. I thought they responded very well to it.

"At halftime some of the guys were getting a little bit edgy, but we calmed them all down until they just relaxed. 'It's no big deal, it's just six points and there's still 30 minutes to be played. Let's not come back in here regretting the next 30 minutes.' I thought the players recaptured their focus very well.

"I didn't feel there was any need to panic. . . . The big need was for us to understand what had occurred and to go out and do something about it. The only way I knew how to do anything about it was to go through the corrections, put them down on the board what needed to be done to get the thing turned around, and then, individually, everybody go out and do what they get paid to do—which is to make plays. I thought they did a very good job of that."

Was Lancaster concerned that the Tabbies only led by six, considering everything went their way? "No," he said emphatically. "The game's going to go 60 minutes, and Calgary didn't get to the Grey Cup by laying down. . . . I didn't feel at halftime that either team had control of it. There were still 30 minutes of football to be played. In our league, three minutes is an eternity, so 30 minutes is forever.

"You never make drastic changes at half-time," Lancaster cautioned. "You take the game plan you went in with and cut it down to the things you are executing well and that you think will be good for you the second half. You go in trying to cover all situations, and each quarter you cut it down a bit. If you execute your game plan better than them, you'll win. If not, you're going to get beat."

Hamilton continued to have the upper hand through the first half of the third quarter but came away with only two points. Then Garcia and Anderson went to work, marching 75 yards in 14 plays for a touchdown on plays that had not worked earlier in the game. Anderson picked up 25 yards on the ground and 15 through the air. Garcia took it in from the 1-yard line on the final play of the third quarter. With the convert, Calgary trailed 18–17.

Why did those plays work then and not earlier? "Sometimes it's the defence that's called," Buono explained, "or it's how they've adjusted, or it's the fatigue factor. That drive took about seven minutes. The longer the defence is on the field, the more at a disadvantage it is. The defence starts to worry about everything. They get tired. That's why you want first downs. One builds to two, two to four, four to eight—and pretty soon you're in the end zone."

"We did show them a couple of different formations, which worked to our benefit," Buono continued. "We put in a tight-end formation with a tackle over, which they hadn't seen. We took Duane Forde out of the formation and put him in at receiver, which made them adjust their front. Those were just the little things that went a long way to help us do things and hurt them."

Calgary took the lead at 4:28 of the final frame when Mark McLoughlin kicked a 22-yard field goal set up by Aldi Henry's 26-yard interception return. McLoughlin added another three points on Calgary's next possession, this one from 32 yards out. With 5:45 remaining, the Stampeders led by five.

Starting at his 35, McManus threw incomplete. He then hit Andrew Grigg for 15. Incomplete again. McManus rumbled for nine. Third down on the Calgary 51, a two-yard quarterback sneak. Danny Mac then threw a short pass to Archie Amerson, who took it 47 yards to the 2. On third and goal, Ron Williams scored. The two-point conversion attempt failed when Jermaine Miles batted the ball down at the line of scrimmage. Hamilton 24, Calgary 23.

There was 2:02 remaining. "I knew as soon as we scored, there was too much time left," lamented Lancaster. Buono agreed. "I wasn't concerned because we got the ball back with plenty of time."

The Stamps started out at their 20 with 1:57 to go. Garcia hit rookie Aubrey Cummings for 12 and Travis Moore for 9. After a quarterback sneak and a first down, Garcia completed the last pass of the game to Moore for 13 yards. First down at the Hamilton 44, 57 seconds to go. Garcia ran for eight and three, Anderson for two, Garcia for three. On third and 5 on the Ti-Cat 28, Calgary was right in front of the uprights. Mark McLoughlin and Dave Dickenson took to the field.

Like all great kickers, McLoughlin lived for the moment when the big game is on the line. He went down his mental checklist and prepared to kick. "I was calm. I'd known for about the last three minutes that I'd have to make that kick."

Hamilton called a timeout. Asked what he and Dickenson talked about before the kick, McLoughlin replied, "Nothing."

The ball was snapped, Dickenson pinned it and McLoughlin swung through and drove it through. Calgary 26, Hamilton 24. No time left on the clock. Calgary had won its fourth Grey Cup.

For Winnipeg native McLoughlin, it was the sweetest Grey Cup of all. Referring to his father who died suddenly of a heart attack the year before, he said, "If only Dad would have been here to see. But he was here. He helped me. Without a doubt, my dad was right by my side when I kicked it. I wish he could have been here physically to share this moment with me, but I know he was here in spirit."

The king of the quarterbacks praised Jeff Garcia. "He took care of the ball very well on that last drive," said Lancaster. "He hit open receivers. He didn't throw into any trouble, and when it wasn't there he ran with it. Especially when they got across mid-field and he was getting close to field-goal range, he did a great job protecting the ball.

"They didn't make any mistakes when things were on the table. We did not make the play when we needed to make it on the last drive. Now, you can say Calgary did an outstanding job and that's probably what happened. They didn't allow us to do the things we did so well. And yet it still came down to a last drive to win the game."

Romano saddles up in true western fashion to celebrate the Calgary Grey Cup win. COURTESY CALGARY STAMPEDERS

Aubrey Cummings, Aldi Henry and Rocco Romano celebrate Grey Cup '98. COURTESY CALGARY STAMPEDERS

"I was so relaxed on that drive," Garcia enthused. "I didn't feel any pressure on me. All the pressure was on Hamilton's defence."

"It was a perfect last drive," Buono said. "He seemed to be moving the ball at will."

Still all would have been for naught if Mark McLoughlin hadn't made that field goal. Garcia laughed. "I'll be the first to admit that I was pretty nervous when it was time for Mark to kick it. I was just praying, and Mark came through. The whole team came through today. It was truly a great game for the fans. They couldn't ask for anything more."

"Routine," said Buono of the crucial kick. "I can mention another field goal in 1991 up in Commonwealth Stadium that Mark kicked. That was a tremendous win because it gave this organization a lot of confidence that carried us into the '90s."

Dave Dickenson, the holder, never had a moment of doubt. "I knew he was going to make it. The funny thing is, he had a tough year. He had family problems with his dad passing away. He had a tough year with accuracy. [At 64.8 percent, 1998 was the worst year of his distinguished career.] No one will remember that because it doesn't matter now because he made the big kick. He's still one of my closest friends, so that was a good feeling. I know that he ran off. After I looked up and saw he made the kick, I was ready to give someone the high five, but he was 30 yards away by that time. As soon as he kicked it, he knew he made it, so he took off."

For such a competitive and talented athlete, it was hard for Dickenson to be Number 2. "In that Grey Cup, my only pass was on a fake field goal. I broke my wrist that year holding for McLoughlin, and actually, in the playoffs, I could barely grip a ball. I broke it with about two or three weeks left in the regular season. I didn't suit back up until the Western Final.

"Unfortunately, I was taking painkillers and shots to try and be able to play because I never knew if Jeff was going to make it. In theory it was a very good thing that Jeff stayed healthy because I don't know what sort of production I would have been able to come up with.

"I look back at 1998 as a real good year because we won it, but if you think about individual stuff, no, I didn't get a lot of playing time, but it makes it a little bit better when you're winning. When you're losing, it really starts grating on you," Dickenson concluded.

Although the MVP award could easily have gone to Kelvin Anderson—who averaged over five yards per carry on first downs, rushed for 105 yards on 18 carries, scored a TD and had three receptions for 27 yards—as usual, it went to the quarterback Jeff Garcia, who completed 22 of 32 for 260 yards, no picks, no TDs. He ran for 47 yards.

Clearly elated, Garcia said, "It just feels so good, finally being on a championship team. In all my years in football from high school to college to pro, I've never been on a team that has won a championship. It was particularly great being able to do it with this team. You can't even imagine how this feels until it happens to you." Garcia would not win another.

On the basis of six catches for 82 yards, Vince Danielson won the Canadian Player of the Game Award, easing the pain of losing the league Outstanding Canadian Award. "I wouldn't trade this for anything," he exclaimed, "To be a champion is worth so much more than an individual award. That's what football is all about."

A key play in the game came when Danny McManus tried the two-point conversion on the last touchdown. It failed when Jermaine Miles batted the ball down at the line. "That was a tremendous play," said defensive coordinator Mike Roach. "A lot of people didn't realize it at the time, but if we don't make that play, the field goal won't win it."

Wally Buono praised the Tiger-Cats. "They were a lot like us. I don't know that they were as explosive on offense as we were, but defensively they were every bit as good if not better than us. They played hard. On offense they had the combo of McManus and Flutie that has always hurt us. This time I thought we pretty much kept them in check."

If Calgary had lost the 1998 Grey Cup, the Stampeders of the '90s would forever be labelled the greatest team that never was. In the weeks following their victory, the team shared the Cup with the people of Calgary. Because of the enormous pressure to win, Grey Cup '98 was especially meaningful for Wally Buono. "For me, it was a very satisfying win for a lot of reasons," he concluded. "I was happy for the players, I was happy for the organization, but I was also happy for myself in a very non-selfish way. To see the city really enjoy the victory was tremendous. It is a pleasure to see people get so much joy out of touching and feeling the Cup. Sometimes we participants don't realize what a great joy it is to the average fan."

During the off-season, Jeff Garcia, Tony Martino, Most Outstanding Offensive Lineman Fred Childress, receiver Terry Vaughn and linebacker Anthony McLanahan moved on. Garcia, Martino and Childress were All-Canadians. Garcia took his time deciding to abandon ship and head for San Francisco, where he wouldn't be restrained by a salary cap that limited quarterbacks to $150,000. Once again the redhead from Gilroy, California, proved all the doubters wrong and carved out an impressive NFL career. For a while Dave Dickenson was in limbo.

"Well, Jeff was kind of going back and forth, so I had to make a decision," he explained. "Obviously if Jeff stayed, I'm gone. I know now, but I thought back then that Wally wanted to keep me around, and he was trying to force Jeff's hand by using me as a little bit of leverage. I didn't want that to happen with Jeff, so I talked to Jeff, more than anything to say, 'If you could be honest with me, I'd appreciate it because I need to know.'

And he was. I knew it looked like he was signing with San Fran, so that made my decision easier to wait for the starting job to open up. Once Jeff left, yeah, Wally made it pretty clear that I was going to get first go at that job, and that's what happened."

The University of Montana star described how he became a Stampeder. "My rights belonged to Toronto, and Calgary was in the process of releasing Doug Flutie because of financial reasons. Doug went to Toronto, the only team that could really afford him.

"I thought, I'm never going to see the field

Terry Vaughn in action for the Eskimos. COURTESY CALGARY STAMPEDERS

if that guy is still there, so I was hoping to try and get a trade. In Calgary at that time there was talk of Garcia going to the NFL. So they made a trade. I think John Hufnagel had a lot to do with it, actually. I came in '96."

Although he eventually tried his luck in the NFL, Dickenson wasn't using the Stampeders as a steppingstone to somewhere else. "No, no no," he said emphatically. "I was just happy to be playing. I thought I could play up here, and ultimately I thought I could play down there, but I think most athletes think that.

"I knew it would be tough coming out of a smaller school in Montana in Great Falls. I was obviously not highly recruited at college or highly recruited by any professional league. It has always been that way with me. I had to start close to the bottom and work my way up. If you're not the prototypical type guy, you've really got to do other things to stand out. For me it was just keep trying to win games."

Dave Dickenson.
COURTESY CALGARY STAMPEDERS

Dickenson related to how Garcia also had to struggle for recognition. "He is one of the more competitive and one of the toughest guys that I've seen play the position," Dickenson said of his predecessor. "Jeff and I worked well together. I thought we were similar players. I thought he had more athletic ability than I did, but I was able to manage the game a little bit better. He sometimes would get so emotional and so into games that he'd be almost too fired up at the start. . . . Anyway, just the competitive side of Jeff. He's been told no so many times that he just wants to prove people wrong. If people keep telling you that you can't do it, you want to prove them wrong. I think we both have that in common."

Dickenson began his CFL career under John Hufnagel. "Hufnagel definitely had great feelings for what this game was about and playing the position. . . . Huf had a work ethic, mainly. The guy was always in the office first, always putting that extra time in. He had fun with the game, too. It wasn't like it was work

for him. He was always keeping things light in the room. But he was also very detailed, and I've always been that sort of guy anyway. To really try to figure out the intricacies of an offense, I wish I could have had a few more years with John after I became a starter."

Dickenson's first start came October 18, 1997, in Toronto, a 48–17 defeat at the hands of Flutie and company. "We ended up getting hammered. It was a pretty tough loss. I took a beating. But I kept competing and kept staying in there and made a few plays in the second half. Without that game, I don't think I would have had the confidence to come into that 1997 playoff game and perform well."

"Dave's awareness and pocket composure are excellent," said Buono before the opening of training camp in 1999. "He's really good at going to the second or third receiver. He will make teams defend more of the field because he will come back inside more. We're hoping with Dave we can throw the quick game more. If we can do that, he'll be more dangerous vertically."

Dickenson characterized his greatest strength as not making "a lot of mistakes. . . . The 2000 season when I threw 36 touchdown passes and six interceptions kind of epitomized what I could do. I didn't turn the ball over. I put our defence in a position where if we didn't score, the other team had to drive a long field. I think that's real important in being successful.

"I've got to use the intellect to make up for some of the other things. And you know what? That's the part of the quarterback position that people underestimate. There are tons and tons of guys out there who can throw the ball well. It is who can figure out what's going on out there."

Dickenson's targets for the defending Grey Cup champions would be Pitts, Danielson, Moore, Marcus Dowdell and Cummings.

Pitts was the most formidable weapon in the Stampeder arsenal. "Allen is such a force," said Buono, "that your focus is stopping him. When you have to draw your coverage to him, everybody else gets single coverage and leverage is lost. Vince can only be leveraged inside or outside. Same thing with Moore. Pitts makes everybody better."

Kelvin Anderson returned in the backfield, coming off a 1,325-yard season, second only to Mike Pringle. Duane Forde would do the blocking. Dickenson, Henry Burris and Mike McCoy would be protected by a veteran offensive line that included Rocco Romano, Jung-Yul Kim, Jay McNeil, Jamie Crysdale and Rohn Meyer. Later in the season, Childress and Martino returned from the NFL.

Calgary had the West's best defence in 1999 with Marvin Coleman, Jackie Kellog, Greg Frers and Willie Hampton. Eddie Davis was injured in the fourth game and replaced the rest of the way by Shad Criss. Alondra Johnson moved to middle linebacker, flanked by Darryl Hall and Kevin Johnson. Jermaine Miles, Jeff Traversy, Mark Gunn and Steven Anderson made up the front four.

Overcoming injuries to the key position was the theme for 1999. On the final play of game two, a 37–27 loss in Vancouver, Dickenson dislocated his shoulder. He re-injured it the following week at home to Edmonton and was replaced by Henry Burris, who preserved a 41–37 win. After beating the Alouettes 36–17 in Montreal seven days later, Burris tore knee ligaments on August 5 in a loss at home to the Lions. He was gone for the season. But while some football teams couldn't find a quarterback at an all-star game, the Stamps seemed to have a never-ending supply. After losing two starters, Mike McCoy entered the picture.

With limited experience in NFL training camps and the World League, McCoy was rescued from a desk job in Salt Lake City after Dickenson went down. When Burris got hurt, he stepped in and won his first three starts.

Though not expecting to become a starter, McCoy was happy to be in the CFL. "I'm feeling more comfortable," he said of his games. "The last three weeks I've had a full game plan. We haven't held anything back."

Buono, awaiting the Labour Day Classic and the return of Dickenson said of McCoy, "Mike's an intelligent guy who picks things up quickly. We lost our quarterbacks and won four out of five. I think that's going to make this football club better."

The Battle of Alberta was a thriller with Calgary losing 33–30 in overtime. Back in the Igloo, a healthier Dickenson engineered a convincing 36–13 triumph. At home against Toronto, late in the first quarter, Dickenson hit the goalpost, and the Stamps settled for the first of five McLoughlin field goals. Near the end of the half, Dickenson injured his knee. McCoy played the second half. With 57 seconds left in the final frame, Toronto scored to lead 26–22. McCoy threw deep to Marcus Dowdell for 58 yards. Then McCoy hit the goalpost, but the Argos were called for interfering with Pitts. Duane Forde scored the winning major at 14:46. The Stamps concluded the regular season winning four of five, finishing second to the Lions.

One of the goals Buono set for the 1999 season was improving the return game. The Stamps hadn't had a return for a touchdown since 1995 when Marvin Coleman ran a punt back. In 1999 he turned the trick twice. In addition to being the best return man in the CFL, Coleman was an outstanding corner and an All-Canadian five times. Ironically, 1999 was one of only two seasons in Stampeder livery he wasn't an all-star.

Coleman was another of the diamonds in the rough discovered by Stampeder super scout Roy Shivers. "Coming out of my senior year at Central State of Ohio," Coleman said,

"I was projected to go in the third round of the NFL draft, but I had to have surgery on my knee, and after that I guess the teams just backed off. Roy Shivers gave me a call and asked if I wanted to come to Calgary and play. And I was like, sure!"

When the attributes of a defensive back are listed, speed is usually mentioned. Not necessarily so, said Coleman. "Speed can be overrated. A lot of times it's all about being in position. You don't have to be the fastest. . . . Junior Thurman taught me to read backfield sets and pass routes. Knowing that gives you a jump on what's going on, so when a play happens you're right there to pick it off or break on it."

Coleman retired in 2003 as the CFL's third all-time kickoff return man and fourth in punt returns. He is Calgary's all-time leader in kickoff return yards, punt return yards for a career, season and game, as well as for career punt return touchdowns (five).

The 12–6 Stamps would host the 6–12 Eskimos in the semi-final. With Dickenson at the top of his game, they rolled over Edmonton 30–17 into the Western Final in Vancouver. One week later, the Grey Cup would be contested at B.C. Place so the 13–5 Lions had an extra incentive to beat Calgary.

"We had some great battles with them," recalled Dickenson. "We played them six times. They won the season series 3–1, and we won the pre-season and the playoff game. All of the games were close, and the final was tight. We were dominating them, and then I got sacked by Johnny Scott. And that's when I broke that bone, the coracoid. We were up 21–1, and I got hurt and they came right back and took the lead. In the fourth quarter, Wally came over to me and said, 'Can you play?' I said, 'Yeah.' I went in and got that last drive to win it."

The final score was 26–24.

The eighty-seventh Grey Cup would be a rematch with the Hamilton Tiger-Cats. For the first time in his career, Allen Pitts was the Western nominee for the Most Outstanding Player Award, the only Stampeder finalist that year. He caught 97 passes for 1,449 yards and 10 touchdowns in 1999, becoming in the process, the CFL's all-time leading receiver in catches and yardage. He was up against Danny McManus, who had the best year of his career, although he was only the ranked sixth as a passer in the league. 1999 turned out to be the year of the Cat with McManus taking home the hardware. "No matter," said Pitts, "the most important trophy is yet to come."

The combatants were evenly matched. Both teams had excellent quarterbacks, defences, kickers and coaches. In the Western Final, Calgary had trouble with the noise inside B.C. Place. Sunday the crowd would be against them because they had prevented the hometown heroes from playing in the big game and because McManus was idolized in Vancouver for winning the Cup for them in 1994.

At the beginning of the season, Wally Buono had said, "We want to be the highest sack team." They were, but not in the category Buono expected. The Stamps gave up 59 sacks, the worst in the league, Hamilton, just seven, the best. By the same token, Calgary had the fewest sacks with 31, Hamilton the most with 48. Dickenson had taken a fearful pounding all year long.

Hamilton opened the scoring at 10:08 of the first quarter when running back Ronald Williams handled the ball six straight times and scored on a one yard plunge. Three minutes later, Paul Osbaldiston added a field goal, then a single on the second play of second quarter. Calgary didn't get a first down until 3:17 of the second stanza when Kelvin Anderson ran for 12. The Ti-Cats closed out first half scoring with another field goal and a McManus-to-Darren-Flutie touchdown. Hamilton led 21–0 at the half.

When play resumed, Osbaldiston made it 22–0 on the kickoff. Then the good guys went to work. Starting at the 35, Dickenson was incomplete, but then hit Cummings for 9. Third and one, McCoy ran for 2. Then Dickenson threw 57 yards to Travis Moore and seven to Vince Danielson for the touchdown. On their next possession, Dickenson threw to Marcus Dowdell for 13, Moore for 31, Pitts for 15. Dickenson scrambled for 10 and then hit Pitts for 18 yards and a touchdown. Hamilton responded with a 21-yard field goal to lead 25–14 after 45 minutes of play.

McManus threw a seven-yard TD strike to Flutie to open the final quarter. The Stamps added a touchdown by Duane Forde, but that was it. Final score: Hamilton 32, Calgary 21.

Dickenson analyzed the defeat. "I wasn't very sharp. I'm going to take a lot of the blame. They really played physically and were able to knock us out of our routes. What surprised me was they used a three-man rush a lot. Do the math. That's nine guys dropping back. It was tough to get open. We couldn't do enough to counteract that."

The reason why? "We couldn't run a run play to the right," Dickenson said, "because I couldn't hand off with my left hand. There was a broken bone in the back—the cora-coid—part of the shoulder blade. I got this sharp pain, and I knew something was wrong. It may not have mattered though, consider-ing how hot McManus and those guys were. They made more one-handed catches in that game than any game I've seen."

Dickenson resembled his old self in the third quarter when he engineered two touch-down drives. "We started to move the ball, and I just got back in the shot gun. We were behind, so there was no more of the run-game stuff. I felt better just trying to make quick reads and getting the ball into the hands of our guys."

Injuries made 1999 a miserable experi-ence for the gritty quarterback. "I dislocated my shoulder on the final play of week two against B.C.," he said. "Unfortunately that injury never healed until after-the-season surgery. I'm proud of myself that I played through it but I don't know if I'd do it again because I probably dislocated it ten or fif-teen times throughout the season.

"We were having trouble keeping anybody healthy at quarterback. So obviously you try to help the team and play. But some of those games I look back on, and I really didn't feel very sharp health-wise the entire season and through the Grey Cup.

"In the Grey Cup, I played with a dislocated shoulder and a broken bone in the back of my shoulder. I didn't miss much playing time, and I'm real proud of that, but I certainly didn't feel up to my capabilities or standards that year."

In the Grey Cup game, Dickenson did his best to protect his shoulder, but "there just weren't any ligaments holding it together. That whole game I didn't feel like the same player. My accuracy was terrible. I remem-ber throwing balls, thinking, Where did that come from? It was too big a game to miss, and I wasn't going to come out. I'm glad I didn't, but it was too bad I couldn't have felt a little better. I thought maybe adrenalin could carry me through."

Though Dickenson shouldered much of the responsibility for the loss, he was too hard on himself. He completed 24 of 28 passes for 321 yards, two touchdowns and one interception. That's a great performance by a completely healthy quarterback. In the shape he was in, it was unbelievable.

And so the most successful decade in Calgary Stampeder history came to an end. Under Wally Buono's direction, the team was 127–52–1, didn't miss the playoffs, fin-ished first seven times, got to the Grey Cup five times and won it twice. Stampeders won seven Most Outstanding Awards. Ninety-four made Western All-Star, 49 All-Canadian.

Roy Shivers had been a big part of the team's success. After the 1999 campaign, he left to become the General Manager of the Saskatchewan Roughriders. When asked which was the greatest Stampeder team, he replied, "I would probably say the 1993 or 1994 team. Will Johnson was at his apex. AJ was playing good football. Allen Pitts was in his prime. We had the defensive backs in Anthony and those guys. I liked the '92 team, too. We had the receivers—Allen, Sapunjis, Crawford, Carl Bland."

In 2003 Shivers paid tribute to iron-man Alondra Johnson's contribution to those early '90s Stampeder teams. "Alondra's been a helluva ballplayer. He's played—what?—13 years now and can still play at a high level. I'm proud of him. He's gone through a lot of problems and stuff. I think he deserves all the accolades that he's gotten and that he will get. He's a heckuva football player and a heckuva person. I'm very happy for AJ. He ranks right up there with Allen in terms of some of things they've gone through to get to where they've come in their careers and in their lives.

"Will Johnson was a heckuva player. He's a big-time policeman now."

What else made those teams so good? "There was a businesslike atmosphere," Shivers insisted, "and I think our players took it as a business, too. It was their job, and they worked at it. I'd say this for Allen and Doug Flutie, as big stars as they were, they were the hardest workers I've ever seen. Same with Harold Hasselbach. They took the time to better themselves. Allen would stay after practice with Doug and catch passes—or with Jeff. Whatever drill we had, they crossed the line first.

"And that separates the average guy from

Alondra Johnson. COURTESY CALGARY STAMPEDERS

the great guy. They were leaders. That's what you're looking for, especially if you've had a guy for three or four years. You could see it when Allen or Sapunjis came into the huddle—the guys looked for him, the quarterback looked for him. On defence they looked for AJ or Will or Pope to make the big play. Marvin Coleman stayed in the secondary longer than the other guys. That's what you've got to have to solidify your team. Those are the intangibles the veterans bring to winning. We were fortunate to have had that for quite a while. We got into a situation where we had a great nucleus and we had them for a number of years. We were able to do things other people weren't able to do.

"I remember all the quarterbacks went down, but our receivers were so in tune with the offense that the guy who stepped in—Henry or Dickenson or McCoy—never had a problem. When Jeff stepped in for Doug, he never had a problem. The receivers knew the offense as well as the quarterback did.

"We had stability over the years. We would tinker with the jets just a little. And that benefited us simply because our guys knew what we expected of them."

Roy Shivers hired as his head coach former Stampeder Danny Barrett. His quarterback was Henry Burris. The games between the two teams would be the most interesting of the regular season.

Wally Buono thought his 2000 team had the potential to be his best yet. Only five newcomers cracked the line-up with rookie receiving sensation Marc Boerigter from tiny Hastings College in Nebraska being one of them, replacing Marcus Dowdell. Former Blue Bombers Joe Fleming and Shonte Peoples and NFL veteran Ray Jacobs joined Jeff Traversy on the defensive line, Buono being determined to get more pressure on the quarterback. Ray Biggs joined AJ and Darryl Hall at linebacker. The Stamps went from worst to best in sacks in the West.

A healthy Dave Dickenson would throw to Boerigter, the ancient 37-year-old Pitts, Danielson and Moore. He would be protected by Romano, McNeil, Crysdale, Childress and Thomas Rayam, the finest O-line in the country. Special teams were excellent with Coleman, the premier return man in the CFL, McLoughlin and Martino.

The Stamps started the season at 6–0–1, the one being a bizarre 52–52 tie in Regina. The Riders' Henry Burris was as hot as the +32°C weather, completing 25 of 45 for 381 yards and five touchdowns. Dave Dickenson was better, hitting on 24 of 35 for 476 yards and six touchdowns, tying the club record of Liske, Flutie and Garcia.

"I was sharp that night," said Dickenson. "For me that was a big game partially because it was against Saskatchewan, but also because some people in Calgary were saying, 'Hey, you should have kept Burris.' . . . The weird part about that game was the turf.

We went into a third and fourth overtime, and the humidity was such a factor that the turf turned really slippery. On our last possession, I had a guy wide open, and he slipped on the throw and it went incomplete."

After going undefeated through seven games, Calgary lost three in a row, including a 48–13 thrashing in Montreal, the team's worst loss in 10 years, and back-to-back Labour Day week defeats to Edmonton by a combined scored of 61–28, partly due to Dickenson being hurt and his backup, Troy Kopp, being inadequate. When Dickenson returned, they won six of eight to finish first. Two of the wins were against the Burris boys.

After the three losses and an overtime win against champion Hamilton, Calgary pundits were saying the Stamps (at 7–3–1) would have to play a lot better to stand any chance of beating Saskatchewan (at 4–6–1 but on a four-game winning streak). Rider receiver Curtis Marsh said his team would crush the Stampeders. After the tie game, Burris told Buono the Stamps were lucky to get a tie. Before their next encounter, Smilin' Hank said there wasn't any big dog in the league right now, so it might as well be his team. Buono's bone chasers begged to differ.

In a surgical display of football September 22 at Taylor Field, the old dog taught the new pup new tricks, sending the prairie dogs to their dressing room, tails between their legs. The final score, 40–17 for the visitors, flattered the Roughriders. It wasn't that close. No old dog played better than Pitts, who caught 12 passes for 173 yards and a touchdown.

Two weeks later, they were back at it on Thanksgiving when the rivals served up a turkey of a football game before the shivering spectators at a sold-out McMahon Stadium. Calgary came out on top 28–18, clinching a playoff spot for the eleventh straight year.

Did they win ugly? "I don't know what pretty is," Buono responded. "I don't know what ugly is. I just know what winning is." Two weeks later, his Stamps beat B.C. to clinch first place for the eighth time.

But, oh, those playoffs. Edmonton finished second at 10–8 and hosted the 8–10 B.C. Lions in the semi-final. Although they had dominated the season series, B.C. came into Commonwealth Stadium and won a nail-biter 34–32. Was this 1994 all over again?

Calgary had won all three games against the Lions, outscoring them 127–66. Yet, despite their losing record, the Leos led the league in total offense. Calgary was second. Defensively it was the other way around. The Lions had the great Damon Allen. Wunderkicker Lui Passaglia was retiring, and they wanted him to go out on a winning note. Calgary was hosting the first Grey Cup of the millennium and desperately wanted to play in front of the hometown fans a week later.

The final was played on a gorgeous, sunny day, albeit a bit windy. After 15 minutes, the Lions led 4–1. When the second quarter started, they were in the middle of a 75-yard, 12-play drive culminating in an Allen-to-Jimmy-Cunningham touchdown. Scrimmaging at their 38 after the kickoff, Eric Carter picked off Dickenson and took it to the house. Determined to pour it on, the Lions recovered the short kickoff and added a 42-yard field goal. In the space of 3:25, B.C. had scored 17 points to lead 21–1. The Lions coasted home 37–23 and moved into the Stampeders' dressing room to await the Montreal Alouettes. They won that one, too, 28–26.

Said Dave Dickenson, "B.C. was a much different team by the time the playoffs rolled around. They had really come together."

The following Friday, Dickenson won the CFL's Most Outstanding Player Award. "It was a dream season in many ways," he commented that night. "I just wish the team had been with me when I received the award." Dickenson, Travis Moore, Marvin Coleman, Eddie Davis,

Greg Frers, Alondra Johnson, Shonte Peoples and Joe Fleming made All-Canadian.

Individual awards couldn't obscure the fact that 2000 was the fifth time Buono's Stamps had finished first and lost the Western Final. So began Wally's winter of discontent. The pain in his voice, the look of devastation on his face after the defeat were in marked contrast to the you-win-some, you-lose-some attitude of several veterans in the dressing room. Marvin Coleman complained that their great teams hadn't won more Grey Cups because Buono didn't treat his players fairly. Months later Coleman signed with Winnipeg.

When Buono released Allen Pitts, the grousing reached fever pitch. Even though Pitts would turn 38 on June 28, 2001, and was less productive, he was not prepared to take a cut in his $142,000 salary. Travis Moore made $77,500; Danielson, $72,000; Boerighter, $34,000; Kelvin Anderson, $70,000. Anderson, Moore and Danielson were free agents. To keep them, Buono had to pay them more. Therefore, Pitts had to go, a lousy personal decision, but the right football decision.

Also gone were Shonte Peoples, Darryl Hall, Eddie Davis and Dave Dickenson. Dickenson, off to San Diego of the NFL, reminisced about playing with Allen Pitts. "Gee, it was an honour. Al was good for me. Al coached me up even before I was playing from '96 to '98. He would talk over why he was doing something, so when I did get in there, I felt real comfortable with him. I always felt he thought I could play, which was a big deal because he was the go-to guy.

"Obviously he matured and was definitely one of our main leaders those Grey Cup years. The guy was awesome. I mean, he worked. People don't realize how hard he worked. Everyone thinks Al was a natural. This guy worked in practice. He had a work ethic I've seen in the NFL but I rarely had seen in the CFL. That's why he was as good as he was. Obviously he was talented, but there are lots of talented guys out there. I was very privileged to play with Al."

Speaking of other leaders, Dickenson was quick to praise the likes of Rocco Romano, Alondra Johnson, Darryl Hall and Kelvin Anderson. "Rocco liked to speak up. Everyone kind of looked after their group. You don't spend a lot of time meeting as a whole team, so you have your leaders in the position meetings, and they need guys who are going to step up.

"On defence, AJ was a leader through the years. The quiet leader was Darryl Hall, who just pretty much went out and performed every game. Those are the sort of guys I like better anyway. I don't need someone telling me what to do. I always tried to be the guy everyone on the team can count on. You knew I was going to be prepared, you knew I was going to do my job, and I felt Darryl Hall was a perfect role model for that.

"Kelvin Anderson was a rock for the team. With Kelvin you didn't get a lot of flash, but you got that consistency. He wasn't really hurt his entire career, although he had ankle and shoulder problems he just quietly played through. He helped build that continuity. He could block, he just kind of fit in. He didn't try to step on anyone's toes. He didn't turn the ball over. He was just a good, solid player."

When training camp opened for the 2001 season, a new attitude prevailed. Referring to the loss to the Lions, Buono said, "Some players said they were frustrated, but the guys who said they were frustrated were the guys who made all the mistakes. The players can't say they weren't well prepared. They were. We gave them every opportunity to win. They just played terribly. Some of those guys aren't here. I'm not saying that out of revenge. If they don't want to be here, move on. And we're going to make some more moves."

Buono's coach and mentor had been Marv Levy, who got the Buffalo Bills to four Super Bowl appearances. With Levy, veterans with a job had to play themselves off the ball club. Buono did that in Calgary. Now, Buono was no longer Mr. Nice Guy. "Players who think they've got the team made are going to realize when it's all said and done that they didn't."

Otis Floyd replaced Darryl Hall. New to the secondary were Ricky Bell and Joe Barnes. The quarterback would be Marcus Crandell, formerly with Edmonton, seizing his first opportunity to be a starter. Buono was impressed. "He fits our system. He's a better thrower than most people give him credit for. He is athletic, but he's not a scrambler. He does the things we want him to do."

That said, Buono opted to start Ben Sankey, who broke his hand in the first game. Crandell came on in relief. Crandell was hurt in August. Travis Moore and Vince Danielson each missed five games with injuries. "There are no excuses for losing," said Buono. "If I use an injury to the quarterback as an excuse, what kind of message would I be sending the rest of the team? Everybody has to step up and get the job done. Sometimes we've done that, sometimes we've fallen short."

After losing to Edmonton on Labour Day, the Stampeders were 3–6 and tied with Saskatchewan for last place. They were an excellent example of how statistics are for losers. They led the division in points scored, rushing and total offense plus percentage pass completion. They had the fewest interceptions. They were first or second in most defensive categories. But only Saskatchewan had more turnovers, which was the reason why the Stamps were struggling.

Crandell got hurt on Labour Day. Sankey engineered wins over Edmonton and Saskatchewan, followed by three losses. Crandell was back at the helm to win three of the last four games of the season, including the last game in Winnipeg, which they needed to guarantee a playoff spot.

"The lights went off before the game started," recalled Crandell. "The kickoff was delayed. When the lights came back on, we played well. It was an exciting game. They made a comeback, but we won. That gave us the confidence we needed going into the playoffs and eventually the Grey Cup." The win gave the Stamps second place and a home semi-final date with the B.C. Lions. Time for revenge.

"Before the playoffs started, said Crandell, "Vince Danielson made a photocopy of a Grey Cup ring with the word FOCUS in big, red letters. He put one in everybody's locker. I think that kind of gave us the direction we wanted to go."

Alondra Johnson had also played a role in getting the team on the right track. "This is crunch time," he said before the end of the season. "You know your best players are going to rise when the pressure's on. This is when you find out who you can depend on and who the mice are. It's easy to turn tail and run and hide when it gets tough. To step up and be accountable is a different story. It takes more of a man."

Johnson was proud of his contribution. "I'm not going to say all defensive players are better than offensive players, but 75 percent of them are. Offensive players know where they're going. Defensive players don't know where they are going. They have to read and react. They have to do two things, whereas the offensive player only has to do the one thing: get open. [On defence] you're backpedalling and then you break. Out of the break, you've got to catch up with a guy who is running at you full speed. You tell me which one's got the toughest job."

Coming into the semi-final, the Lions had won only two games the last half of the schedule, but one of them was a 34–16 victory in Calgary on October 28. Which Lion team would show up? The losing Leos or the ones who had dined on horsemeat nine days earlier?

The Leos continued their slide, while the Stampeders were rounding into shape at exactly the right time. But it was close. The Stamps didn't take the lead until the first minute of the fourth quarter when Crandell hooked up with Marc Boerigter for the big slotback's second touchdown. B.C. struck back with a 47-yard field goal to move ahead 19–17 with 8:42 remaining. A brilliant punt by Duncan O'Mahony pinned B.C. at their 7. On the ensuing punt, Calgary was on the Lion 50. Crandell then engineered a brilliant eight-play drive capped off with a four-yard touchdown throw to defensive tackle Marc Pilon. The two-point convert worked. Calgary 25, B.C. 19. Calgary added a field goal.

Edmonton had finished the season ahead of Calgary by two points. Like the Stampeders, they were inconsistent. Calgary was brimming with confidence, aware their northern rival hadn't won a final at home in 15 years, plus the fact the home team had lost seven of the last 10 finals.

Playing the finest first half of his Stampeder career, Crandell administered a thorough 34–16 licking on the blubber eaters. In those 30 minutes, he threw for 287 yards and four touchdowns. "George Cortez changed the game plan and threw in a six receiver package," Crandell explained, "and they definitely weren't expecting it. That caught them off guard. They brought in a new defensive back, and the six-receiver package kept him on the field, and we definitely hit seams on him. They had a very aggressive defence, which meant there were holes, and we were able to exploit it. And we were all clicking."

The Calgary defence came up huge. The Eskimos turned the ball over a mind-boggling

12 times, eight consecutively. The Stamps were error free. "Yes," recalled Crandell, "that was a main reason why we got to the Grey Cup. Whoever wins the turnover battle usually wins the game. We not only didn't turn the ball over, we didn't have any fumbles either."

Safety Greg Frers recovered one Edmonton fumble. Drafted out of Simon Fraser by Calgary in 1993, he moved on to Winnipeg after three years being stuck behind all-star Greg Knox. He was traded to B.C. in 1997 and then cut after the first game of the 1998 regular season. Then his luck changed for the better.

"I had been working for Canada Post in the off-season," he recalled. "I was going back to work with them when I got the call from Wally to come to Calgary He phoned on my birthday, the fourth of August." During the five more years Frers played, he was a Western All-Star three times, All Canadian once.

It seemed the Stampeders had much better luck coming from second place. On to Montreal to face the Blue Bombers, the team they had defeated 22–15 to make the playoffs but had lost to at McMahon in the season opener 48–20.

It seemed Winnipeg only remembered the first game. They yapped incessantly about how good they were, which made the Stampeders even more determined to shove the ball down their collective throats. "You know, it did," Marcus Crandell admitted. "We felt like they were talking like they'd already won the game—and we hadn't even played yet. That gave a few guys extra incentive to beat them."

Crandell went on. "A team's already in the playoffs, and they are playing their starting quarterback the whole game? That means they were trying to win the game. Khari [Jones] stayed in the whole game, and we felt they were really trying to put us out of the playoffs. They did everything they could to beat us, and they didn't succeed. That was an emotional lift for us."

Greg Frers. COURTESY CALGARY STAMPEDERS

After the league awards when the players mingled with the great unwashed, the Bombers made it clear Sunday's game wouldn't even be close. While that angered the likes of Alondra Johnson, Ray Jacobs and Jamie Crysdale, Mark McLoughlin just shrugged. "It's nice to be confident," he said with a smile. Stampeder defensive coach Jim Daley said, "I feel really good about Sunday. The guys are ready, they've worked hard, they're well prepared and they believe they're going to win."

"Somebody's got to win," Wally Buono observed sardonically. "It might as well be us, right?"

Greg Frers felt the media helped supply incentive. "The whole week I had reporters coming after me asking how we were going to stop this basically unstoppable receiving corps. We took it upon ourselves to really challenge ourselves to get the job done. We came out and proved we did have some skill."

The Bombers were heavily favoured. Winnipeg's defence gave up the fewest points, first downs and total yardage. They were second in interceptions. Calgary's offense scored the most points and was second in total offense. Winnipeg had the best give-away-takeaway ratio at +8°C, Calgary the worst at -8. But other key statistics were telling: Winnipeg was the most penalized team in the league, Calgary second least. Mark McLoughlin's field-goal percentage was 74, his counterpart Troy Westwood's was 61 percent, the worst in the league. Still, the Bombers were 14–4, Calgary 8–10.

It was +17°C on Grey Cup Sunday, the warmest day on which the game has ever been played—not that it mattered since the contest was inside the cavernous Olympic Stadium. The Big O was packed to the rafters with the second largest crowd in Grey Cup history despite the fact Les Alouettes were not the Eastern champions.

During the playing of "O Canada," the old Winnipeg veteran Bob Cameron and Stamp safety Greg Frers had tears in their eyes. The roar of the crowd promptly reached an ear splitting crescendo inside the great stadium. The good people of Canada's second largest

Calgary defensive back Kelly Malveaux tackles Winnipeg Blue Bombers slotback Milt Stegall in 2001 Grey Cup action.
COURTESY CANADIAN PRESS, ANDRE FORGET PHOTO

city turned out in spectacular numbers to watch two teams from Western Canada battle it out for Earl Grey's old mug. There was no doubt football was back in Montreal. Two more-than-interested observers were Mr. and Mrs. Michael Feterik of California, the new owners of the Calgary Stampeders.

During the early going, it looked like Winnipeg could walk the talk. After returning the opening kickoff to their 36, Charles Roberts ran for 14 yards. Jones hit Milt Stegall for five, ran for 7 and then completed a 22-yarder to Robert Gordon. When the drive stalled at the 22, Westwood kicked a field goal.

Calgary's first possession wasn't promising. Doug Brown sacked Crandell, who then went incomplete. Aided by a no-yards call on Ricky Bell and a 15-yard strike to Gordon, the Bombers made it to the 31, where Westwood was wide on a field goal try. Two possessions later, Kelvin Anderson's fumble set up a Westwood 40-yarder, but it hit the post. After 15 minutes, the Easterners from the West led 4–0. The Bombers had 93 yards offense; Calgary, 33. Calgary was on the march when the second quarter began, but all for naught, when McLoughlin missed from 36 yards out, and Charles Roberts returned it to his 38.

On the next play, Jones completed a 33-yard pass to Stegall, nullified when Joe O'Reilly was called for roughing. Undeterred, Jones put together a nice march to the enemy 35. Eric Blount picked up a yard, and in a turning point in the game, AJ sacked Jones for a 13-yard loss, forcing a punt. Instead of being hemmed in deep, Calgary started at the 25 when Lukas Shaver was called for no yards. Crandell completed five in a row, missed one, setting up a successful 37-yard field goal. Winnipeg 4, Calgary 3.

Three and out for Winnipeg put Calgary first down on the 30. Crandell missed, then hit Marc Boerigter for 12 yards. He then found Boerigter

streaking down the sidelines and laid it in perfectly for a 68-yard pass and run for a touchdown and a lead they would not relinquish.

"That was one of the plays George Cortez put in the week before," explained Crandell. "We noticed that every time we ran a post pattern, the DB would turn and run after the guy. We had Boerigter run kind of a lazy pattern to the flat, and then he turned it up the field and ran down the sideline." The blazing Boerigter could not be caught.

AJ's crew forced three and out, the Stamps starting at their own 22. Crandell threw to Antonio Warren for six yards, but Lamar McGriggs brought him down by the facemask, giving Calgary field position and room to manoeuvre. Mixing his plays, Crandell got them to the 28, where he completed a 10-yarder to Danielson. Brian Clark was called for face-masking, so it was first and goal at the 9.

"We flooded the zone thinking they would leave one guy open," said Crandell, "and Travis [Moore] did a great job hiding himself coming out of the backfield. They got confused with all that motion. It was up to me to find the guy who was left open, and that was Travis." Touchdown with 54 seconds left in the quarter. Halftime score: Strong Silent Types 17, Undisciplined Big Mouths 4.

After Dave Ritchie peeled the paint off the dressing room wall, the Bombers marched 47 yards on their first second-half possession for a touchdown, a pass from Jones to Arland Bruce III. Later Westwood missed on a 53-yarder, scoring the single. After three quarters, Calgary led 17–12.

It takes all three phases—defence, offense and special teams—to win most football games. The Stampeder defence turned the game around in the second quarter. Crandell was on fire with Boerigter and Moore scoring a brace of majors before the half. Time for special teams to make a contribution.

On Winnipeg's second possession of the final fifteen, Bob Cameron dropped back to punt. Aldi Henry roared in and blocked it. Willie Fells picked it up and ran for the touchdown. Calgary 24, Winnipeg 12. The Bombers added a touchdown, Calgary a field goal to make the final score Stampeders 27, Blue Bombers 19.

Coming off their worst record of the Buono era, Calgary had won their most unlikely Grey Cup, the fifth in team history. Marcus Crandell was voted Grey Cup MVP, going 18 for 35, 309 yards, no interceptions and two touchdowns. The award was particularly gratifying to Modest Marcus. "Considering everything I'd

been through to get there—finally becoming a starter in the CFL, overcoming three years of disappointments—it definitely was a great feeling to win the Cup and the award." Aldi Henry was outstanding Canadian.

No one would argue with the writers giving the awards to Crandell and Henry. But it should be pointed out that no one was a bigger star that day than Alondra Johnson, who almost won the game single-handedly. The equally overlooked offensive line of Fred Childress, Jay McNeil, Jamie Crysdale, Dave Heasman and Thomas Rayam outplayed the Bomber front seven. Calgary's leading

Calgary defenders Joe Barnes (left) and Alondra Johnson take down Bombers wide receiver Robert Gordon in 2001 Grey Cup action.
COURTESY
CANADIAN PRESS,
FRANK GUNN PHOTO

Winnipeg punter Bob Cameron strains to tackle Willie Fells in 2001 Grey Cup action.
COURTESY CANADIAN PRESS, JACQUES BOISSINOT PHOTO

offensive performer was Marc Boerigter, who caught four passes for 114 yards and a touchdown. McLoughlin made two of three field goals; Troy Westwood, one of four.

Strategy also played a role, according to Frers. "We thought they were going to get Charles Roberts more into the game, you know—swing him out of the back-field. They didn't do that, which I think was a downfall for them."

The Bombers were unrepentant. "They remained mouthy," recalled Frers," even when the game was over. They never showed any respect for the ability we had. They were a very confident bunch who won a lot of games, and they

Jamie Crysdale.
COURTESY CALGARY STAMPEDERS

were a very good team, but obviously you don't play with your mouth."

The following spring, Bomber boss Dave Ritchie was still at it. "I really believe we were the better team," he said wistfully. "We had breakdowns on special teams, like the blocked kick. Defensive backs blew coverages twice, which led to Calgary touchdowns, and Troy Westwood missed three field goals."

Michael Feterik must have felt he couldn't have picked a better time to buy. It looked like Wally Buono was about to write another great chapter in the history of the Calgary Stampeders.

Instead, darkness and despair would soon descend on McMahon Stadium.

Grey Cup MVP Marcus Crandell. COURTESY CALGARY STAMPEDERS

CHAPTER 8

Varmints

Football Follies
2002–2004

WHEN MICHAEL FETERIK BOUGHT THE STAMPEDERS FROM SIG GUTSCHE, the key stipulation in the deal was that Feterik's son, Kevin, a quarterback, had to be on the roster. The demand was contrary to everything Wally Buono believed, but for the sake of his friend Sig, who desperately needed the money, he swallowed his pride and agreed.

Since the Stamps were already in a state of transition when they parlayed an 8–10 record into the 2001 Grey Cup championship, the identity of his third string quarterback was the least of Buono's worries. As the new season approached, he had to replace 16 starters, including his entire defensive line. Notable defections included Marc Boerigter, James Cotton, Otis Floyd and Antonio Warren to the NFL, Marc Pilon to Edmonton and Ray Jacobs to Saskatchewan. Vince Danielson and Joe Fleming retired.

Joining holdovers Travis Moore and Kamau Peterson were Don Blair and Rob Johnson. Marcus Crandell was the quarterback, Kelvin Anderson lugging the mail. "Offense will be a strength," said Buono. "We've lost a little bit at receiver, but we do have the guys who can step in and do the job. Having Marcus Crandell back is a big plus. Having the offensive line intact is a big, big plus. Our defensive line is our biggest problem. If we can get that stabilized, we'll be fine."

As Buono predicted, the O-line of Fred Childress, Jay McNeil, Jamie Crysdale, Bobby Singh and Jeff Pilon was superb. Getting the defensive line playing well as a unit proved difficult, however, and the Stamps opened the season with four straight losses, surrendering an average of

32.5 points a game. After winning the next three, it looked like their problems were behind them, especially after Cotton and Floyd returned to bolster the defence.

Buono then experienced the longest losing streak of his Stampeder career—five games—including a 28–20 Labour Day setback to Edmonton. By that point, half the 16 newcomers who opened the season were replaced. When Calgary lost to Winnipeg on October 18, they were officially out of the playoffs, the first time in Buono's head coaching career. They finished 6–12, fifth.

"A lot of people put a lot of effort into making the thing work, and it didn't work," Buono reflected. "It has been a very emotional, tough season for all of us. When the 18-game schedule is over or you've lost the Western Final and you're packing your bags instead of preparing for the next week, it is a lonely, depressing feeling."

Buono may have had some inkling that things would get worse.

As the losses piled up, Kevin Feterik remained glued to the bench while his dad inwardly seethed. After the Stamps lost to B.C. 37–14 on October 11, Michael Feterik publicly blasted offensive coordinator Jacques Chapdelaine. The owner of a quarterback school in the States, Feterik criticized Marcus Crandell and said he wanted his business partner to work with the quarterbacks during the off-season. He had business associates breakdown game film and make suggestions, which he passed on to the coaching staff.

"I don't buy a business if I don't know anything about that business." Feterik maintained. "If we're not doing well in one of my box factories, I know

Otis Floyd in action against Edmonton.
COURTESY CALGARY STAMPEDERS

how to fix it. Well, I'd better know how to fix this organization, too. If you go 18–0, I'm not going to say a word. But if we're 6–12, we've got a problem, and it has to be corrected. It's not going to be corrected by letting everything go as it was last year. It's not going to happen. So I'll correct it.

"A lot of the time people do something for so long they think that's the way to do it," Feterik ranted. "Time out! That's not going to happen anymore. We've done it wrong. How do I know? We were 8–10 and 6–12. Times change, people have to change. Sometimes coaches have to change. People get complacent."

As for Chapdelaine, Federik concluded that "He isn't ready for the job. I said, 'Wally, you put him in a position to fail. You're the best defensive coach in Canada, but you're not the best offensive coach.' He replaced the veteran George Cortez with Jacques. It wasn't my decision. But now it is my decision what we're going to do with the coaches. I've got an offense that's going to work that I want Wally to look at. It's like a BYU wide-open offense, a West Coast offense. And quit running Kelvin Anderson off-tackle. I said, 'Do we *only* have one play? Anderson off-tackle?'

"Now what we need is a couple of new assistant coaches that don't have the mindset of Canadian football to come here and put some new plays in. So that's my contribution. Fortunately I understand the game.

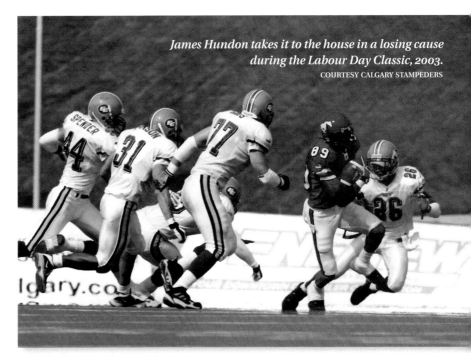

James Hundon takes it to the house in a losing cause during the Labour Day Classic, 2003.
COURTESY CALGARY STAMPEDERS

"My problem is I'm spread too thin. I just put a new person in charge of the organization, Fred Fateri. I need a guy in Calgary helping the organization get us to the next level. The communication is going to be incredible."

Problem was, Fateri didn't know if a football was blown up or stuffed.

When the 2001 season ended, Feterik and Buono negotiated a new contract. Come August Buono learned the owner was trying to get rid of him. Although Buono was the general manager, Fateri constantly interfered, making it clear to his boss that if he were in charge, son Kevin would be the starter. Feterik had bought the Stampeders to give his son a team to quarterback. Buono kept the kid on the roster, but he wouldn't start him. Buono had to go.

In an interview with the *Herald*'s Michael Petrie, Fateri said, "Wally wanted to make decisions with the offensive

Fred Fateri. COURTESY *CALGARY HERALD*

coordinator and all these players. I told him, 'I'm trying to help you. I'm trying to bring your supporting cast to where it was when you were the guru. No longer are you the guru because Bob O'Billovich [Stamps director of player personnel] isn't bringing in the right players. Or maybe he is and you're not coaching them right.'

"I told him, 'Wally, you had the supporting cast when you were the best coach at the time. You had a Roy Shivers who brought players in, and you got all the credit.'"

During the 2002 Grey Cup game in Edmonton, Feterik could be seen in close conversation with Bob Ackles of the B.C. Lions. Earlier in the week, Feterik said he couldn't in good conscience stand in Wally's way if he wanted to go to the Lions. A few feet over, Fateri—who usually called Buono "Bono"—said there was no way Buono would be given permission to talk to B.C. It turned out Feterik wanted players from the Lions in exchange for giving Buono his release. Fateri asked for three of Ryan Thelwell, Jason Clermont, Carl Kidd, Bo Lewis and Cameron Legault. Ackles refused.

"There's no question we were mislead from the beginning," Ackles said. "We were told they wanted Wally out of there, they shopped him around, they gave us permission to talk to him and told us they would even be prepared to pay a portion of his salary. Then the rules of the game changed."

Feterik wanted Buono gone, no matter what. On January 13, 2003, a press release was issued. "Sunday, January 12, the Calgary Stampeder Football Club officially accepted a letter of resignation from General Manager and Head Coach Wally Buono."

Feterik and Fateri interviewed Jim Barker, Matt Dunigan and Dave Arslanian in Las Vegas. Barker, a former Alouette assistant, got the job. He would also be the offensive coordinator. The only holdover from the Buono

Jim Barker. COURTESY CALGARY STAMPEDERS

era was his defensive coordinator Jim Daly. Personnel man Bob O'Billovich was replaced by Lannie Julias.

Barker, no Marcus Crandell fan, wanted to sign Dave Dickenson, who was about to return from the NFL. In May Fateri announced that Dickenson had been offered $200,000 but was out of their price range. In fact, the offer was for $125,000 to play football and $50,000 to work in marketing, a deal they knew Dickenson would refuse. They didn't want competition for Kevin.

While Crandell remained the starting quarterback, Barker pleased the boss by freely substituting son Feterik. In 2002 Feterik threw one incomplete pass. In 2003 he completed 119 of 186 passes for 1,497 yards and six touchdowns. Kevin Feterik was a good guy in an impossible situation. No football miscue was more embarrassing than when he got his bell rung and his mother raced from the press box to the sideline to comfort him.

To his credit, Barker shored up a shaky defence by getting Joe Fleming out of retirement and signing veteran Demetrious Maxie. He had an excellent line-backing corps with Alondra Johnson, Otis Floyd, Willie Fells and George White, a veteran secondary and an outstanding kicking game. But he took a chance on some shady characters, including Lawrence Philips, an All-American with a rap sheet as impressive as his credentials. Banished from Montreal, Philips was given a last chance in Calgary, and Barker cut Kelvin Anderson to do so. Phillips loudly criticized the game plan at practice October 8 and then barely went through the motions two days later, forcing Barker to cut him. On the other hand, receiver Darnell McDonald, banished from the NFL with legal problems, kept his nose clean in Calgary, where he caught 67 passes for 1,002 yards and was a leader in the dressing room.

The days of Calgary's all-time leading rusher Kelvin Anderson were numbered anyway. Said Barker May 2, 2003, "The downside on Kelvin is his age and his contract. I'd like to be better than Kelvin at that position. And I think Saladin McCullough is better than him. It's just like Travis Moore," whom Barker traded to Saskatchewan. "He was a fifth receiver in the XFL at San Francisco. In the XFL, Kelvin was just a guy. Saladin was the top running back in that league."

"Just a guy" Kelvin picked up 1,048 yards with B.C. in 2003, "the top running back" Saladin, 734 with Calgary. Moore had 70 receptions in Regina. (Said Barker of Moore, "I don't think any receiver deserves to get paid $180,000.")

Before the season started, Barker was optimistic. "The priorities when I got hired and I studied this team were improving the depth and quality of our Canadian content

and making us younger, faster, with better players on defence. We've done that."

The man Feterik thought would make Calgarians forget about Wally Buono went 5–13, 12 points behind fourth-place B.C. His offense and defence were the worst in the West in just about every category. Calgary averaged just 15 points a game. The only bright spot was Joe Fleming, who made All-Canadian and won the CFL Outstanding Defensive Player Award. To be fair, Barker lost Crandell for a month, Kevin Feterik sustained a concussion and third-string Scott Milanovich had no CFL experience. Still, the 2003 Stampeders were a joke on the field and a laughingstock off the field. Michael Feterik reaped what he had sowed.

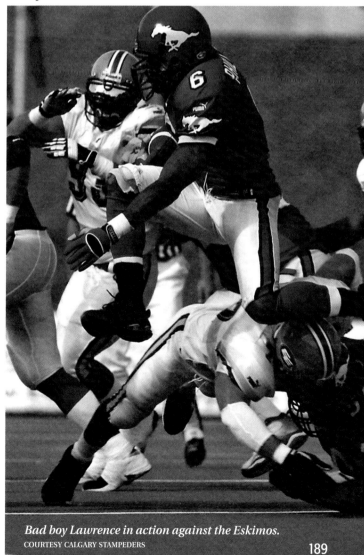

Bad boy Lawrence in action against the Eskimos.
COURTESY CALGARY STAMPEDERS

Throughout it all, Barker retained the loyalty of his coaches and players. When it was rumoured in October that Feterik was courting Matt Dunigan to replace Barker, players reacted with dismay. "This season has been full of bad decisions," said McDonald, "but that would be one of the worst decisions," he told *Herald* reporter Allen Cameron. "He's been here for one year and had a lot of injuries with his quarterbacks. I'd really consider not coming back if he didn't. He's a great coach, a great man, I love him to death."

Jamie Crysdale.
COURTESY CALGARY STAMPEDERS

During the year, although Stan Schwartz was president, Fateri and Feterik, characterized by *Herald* reporter Michael Petrie as the bumbling dimwits of the television series *F-Troop*, dodged him, going to team marketing man Ron Rooke and player Mark McLoughlin on club affairs. The dressing room was rife with rumours that Schwartz would be fired and replaced by McLoughlin as president. The players regarded their teammate as a management stooge, a sad way for the all-time leading scorer to go out. But that's what happened.

On August 28, Fateri told *Calgary Sun* reporter Dan Toth, "I put this organization together with great names, negotiated great contracts with some great players." The day before on the radio he had insulted the offensive line. He made it clear the team's 2–8 record wasn't his fault and that the players and Barker were to blame. The next day, receiver Wane McGarity taped a copy of the article to his back. "It's embarrassing," he told Toth. "It's embarrassing for everyone on this team to go through that, and it's not fair."

The great veteran Jamie Crysdale went further. "We need to stick together as a team and a franchise," he told Toth, "but maybe it's easier to put the blame on the players than to stand up and be accountable for actions you've taken. Normie Kwong on the radio summed it up best, saying it's like a peewee hockey team that the mothers have taken over. That hit the nail on the head." Crysdale went on to say that local ownership was the only way to save the team from destruction.

On September 2, 2003, Feterik fired Fateri and announced that McLoughlin had retired as a player to accept the position of president. When the football community learned Schwartz was being forced to the sidelines, they were outraged. Petrie reported the comments of several.

CFL Hall of Famer Tony Anselmo.
COURTESY CALGARY STAMPEDERS

Wally Buono: "Stan has been rock-solid, tireless and he has always put the interests of the organization ahead of his own. For him to be treated this way is really poor. When you look at the success of the Stamps, you have to realize Stan has been a big part of that."

Tony Anselmo: "They're taking another step in the wrong direction. Everything they do is negative. Stan has been a valuable asset to that organization for many, many years and the one person that kept that franchise together through two or three owners."

Normie Kwong: "Do you think McLoughlin can run the team better than Stan because he worked with a soccer team? I don't understand what they're doing."

Don Luzzi: "For a number of years, it was Stan that kept the franchise alive. The clock means nothing to him. He'll work from 6:30 in the morning until 8:30 at night, six or seven days a week to make sure things get accomplished."

Wayne Harris: "Nothing really surprises me anymore down there. It's unbelievable. I can't comprehend getting rid of Stan."

In the face of this firestorm of protest, Feterik asked Stan to stay as the C.O.O. Rooke, McLoughlin and Feterik were terrified Schwartz would walk and take all his knowledge and reputation with him. For the sake of the team, Schwartz said he would think about it and agreed to remain with the organization. McLoughlin soon realized he was in over his head. Feterik was in California, but Rooke thought he could run it without Schwartz. Six weeks later he struck.

After Labour Day, McLoughlin, Barker, Schwartz and Player Personnel Director Lannie Julias met to discuss the future. McLoughlin wanted to minimize ownership interference, but Julias disagreed. Later Julias was fired after he was overheard talking on the phone to Feterik, promising that if he were director of football operations son Kevin would be looked after.

In the middle of October, some players demanded that McLoughlin get rid of Kevin Feterik. Shortly thereafter, Feterik asked for a trade and was released.

McLoughlin lasted 47 days as president and special advisor. He returned to kick footballs when his successor, Duncan O'Mahony, struggled, and then retired, along with his Number 13, as part of his settlement. Schwartz was forced out by the end of October. The new president, Ron Rooke, worked with McLaughlin to convince Feterik to get rid of Fateri, Schwartz and Jim Barker. Why McLoughlin quit remains a mystery, though he must have quickly realized he wasn't prepared to be president of a football club. Perhaps he saw the writing on the wall when Fateri continued hanging around the office advising the owner.

On September 14, 2004, Michael Feterik discussed the circus that the Calgary Stampeders had become.

Why did he renegotiate Buono's contract? "He had a contract. I was taken completely by surprise that he wanted to negotiate a new one. I suggested he should get paid only for wins."

Was he unhappy with Buono? "I was unhappy with the offensive coordinator. I told Wally that. I told him I thought he should hire someone else but that it was his call. B.C. wanted Wally, and I told Braley that if Wally wanted to go, I wouldn't stand in his way."

Was he surprised at Fred Fateri's behaviour? "Oh, yes. He was a family friend. He actually approached my wife about the job."

How did McLoughlin become president? "Fred had been discussing it with him all that year. I told him I was against [McLoughlin] retiring. I thought he should wait until the end of the year. Then Fred quit and Mark became president. He didn't like the job, so he resigned later. It was a mess. He had no experience with administration matters. It was too much for him."

Were concerns raised when McLoughlin went back to playing? "Yes, it was a problem."

Did he offer Lannie Julias the position of vice-president of football operations? "He was hired by Jim Barker. He and Fred talked to him about it. I didn't know him. That's been a real problem for me. I'm down here, they're up there making decisions about people I didn't know. I had to take other people's word for it. My advice was seldom taken. I was expected to put up the money and keep quiet."

Why did you sour on Stan Schwartz? "I didn't sour on Stan. I liked Stan. He did a good job and was very easy to work with. But Fred wanted Mark."

Did you buy the team so your son had a place to play? "No, Kevin was on the team before I came along. He was a Heisman Trophy candidate, he went to a great passing school. Wally begged him to leave the Seahawks camp and sign with Calgary."

Fateri was gone, McLoughlin resigned after Thanksgiving, Schwartz left at the end of October. Days earlier, Rooke rounded up a few disgruntled employees whom, he told Feterik, wanted Stan out, ignoring the great majority who supported his leadership. Left standing were President Ron Rooke and Head Coach Jim Barker.

As the season drew to a close, Ron Rooke and Michael Feterik, publicly and privately, gave Barker a vote of confidence. When Feterik said October 18, "It's in [son Kevin's] best interests and in the club's best interests he plays somewhere else", he also said, "Jim Barker will be back next year." At the same time, they were courting Saskatchewan's Danny Barrett and Roy Shivers, as well as continuing to talk to Matt Dunigan. During Grey Cup week in Regina, Rooke and Dunigan were seen deep in conversation at the Hotel Saskatchewan. In the meantime, Barker had no idea what the future held, but since he knew what was going on behind his back, he knew it wasn't good. The knives were out.

Then all was quiet on the western front until three days before Christmas when Barker was told to go into the office to work on a trade. Mark McLoughlin took him into an office and put him on a speakerphone to Rooke in California. Rooke fired him.

The next day, December 23, Matt Dunigan was announced as the new general and coach of the Calgary Stampeders. Why hadn't Rooke fired Barker earlier? Because the deadline for season-ticket holders to get a discount when renewing was the day Barker was fired. Rooke knew if he fired him earlier, ticket sales would suffer.

Matt Dunigan played 14 years in the CFL and established a reputation for the spectacular. He was the only quarterback to lead four teams to four Grey Cup games, Edmonton in '86 and '87, B.C. in '88, Toronto, in '91 and Winnipeg in '92. He drank champagne from the mug in '87 and '91. His '93 Bombers also got to the big game.

The Louisiana Tech graduate signed with Edmonton in 1983. Four times All-Canadian, five times All-Division, Dunigan set the record for most passing yards in a game—713—when Winnipeg beat Edmonton 52–33 on July 14, 1994. He is the fifth-ranked passer of all-time and Number 5 in quarterback rushing yards. He was inducted into the CFL Hall of Fame in 2006.

Dunigan was traded twice in his career for a total of 12 players. The man was a warrior, a great quarterback with incredible courage who showed talent as a football analyst for TSN. He is also a genuinely nice guy.

That said, with the exception of a short stint as an assistant at Valdosta College, Dunigan had no experience as a coach and none in football management.

When he was introduced to the media December 23, he said, "We have to get away from the backstabbing and the agendas that were here last year. You can't have that on a team. You have to be able to trust that someone's got your back, and that didn't happen last year."

After reporting for work January 18, his first order of business was to fire all Barker's assistants. He brought in Denny Creehan as defensive coordinator and John Jenkins to run the offense, along with Mike Roach, Craig Dickenson, Carl Brennan and Trey Junkin.

It soon became clear that when son Kevin left, father Feterik had no interest in either providing a strong supporting cast or owning the team. To make the franchise more attractive to buyers, he wanted the payroll slashed. Allowed to leave were Demetrius Maxie, Duncan O'Mahoney, Otis Floyd, David Sanchez, Kamau Peterson, Steve Morley, David Heasman, Michael Dupuis, Mark McLoughlin and Bobby Singh.

When free agents became available, Dunigan passed. He did trade Kai Ellis and Anthony Malbrough to Ottawa for Fred Perry, John Grace, Seth Dittman and Romaro Miller, and he got Omar Evans from Montreal for Kelly Malveaux.

After a month on the job, Dunigan had lost a lot of the goodwill he had coming into the job. It would get worse.

You think Horatio had a tough challenge defending the bridge? Child's play compared to the next five months of Dunigan's life. In charge of everything, the only advice he got was when he talked to himself. Because they averaged only 18 points a game in 2003—the fewest of any team in 20 years—offense had to be a priority. But with defections and the retirement of Fred Childress from the offensive line, there was no depth. Although McCullogh had performed well, he was replaced by Vic Ike, who would soon be replaced by NFL cut Joffrey Reynolds.

The receivers were Albert Connell, Wane McGarrity, Mike Juhasz and the rookie Nik Lewis, who would lead them with 1,045 yards on 73 receptions. The quarterbacks were Crandell and Tommy Jones. In spite of difficulties Dunigan, also the personnel guy, was laying the foundation for future success.

The defence, led by Joe Fleming, George White, John Grace and Joey Boese would play well, ranked second in total yardage surrendered, interceptions and passing yards yielded.

Dunigan knew expectations were unrealistically high. Feterik said he would be disappointed if his team won fewer than 12 games. Before training camp opened, Dunigan said, "I've been with successful football teams and

A man of principle, Mike Roach, assistant coach.
COURTESY CALGARY STAMPEDERS

learned from what they've done and haven't done. It was clear to me this organization was starving for accountability. They needed more character. You have to pay the price."

Actions speak louder than words. In training camp, Dunigan had Alondra Johnson taken off the field in front of everybody and fired him, a man who had paid the price every time he wore the horse. It was a disgraceful way to treat a Calgary icon. Three times All-Canadian, six times All-Division, three Grey Cup rings, Western nominee for Outstanding Defensive Player in 1996, AJ was rightly regarded as one of the greatest linebackers of all time. He was inducted into the CFL Hall of Fame in his first year of eligibility in 2009.

The Stampeders season opened promisingly with a 33–10 win in Regina. After that they lost 11 of 12. Some losses were worse than others, and sometimes a single play can seal a man's fate. Offensive coordinator John Jenkins was Dunigan's friend, mentor and coach when he was with Winnipeg, Birmingham and Hamilton. Considered a creative thinker, Jenkins lived and died with the pass, eschewing the running game almost entirely. After four straight losses, the Stamps were leading Ottawa by two points with 50 seconds left. All they had to do was call three running plays and kill the clock. Jenkins called pass, Kelly Wiltshire stripped the ball from rookie pivot Tommy Jones, and the Renegades kicked the winning field goal.

Fans and sponsors erupted in white-hot fury. No one with even the most rudimentary football knowledge could understand why you would operate an offense without a running attack. Calgary had 160 yards on the ground after six games. Hamilton's Troy Davis ran for 167 yards against Saskatchewan the same week. When Dunigan told Jenkins to run more, he refused. Dunigan pointed to 16 Avenue and fired him. Now the rookie

coach and GM was also the offensive coordinator *and* quarterback coach.

The following week, the team responded by beating the Bombers 49–27. Then, came six straight losses and an unexpected 22–21 victory over the league-leading Lions at McMahon. Not withstanding the last minute heroics by rookie quarterback Michael Sousa and FG kicker Clinton Greathouse, the game was won by the defence. In another baffling move, Dunigan ripped the heart out of the defence two days later by trading Joe Fleming and Wes Lysack to Winnipeg for quarterback Khari Jones, fullback Randy Bowles and a draft choice. Scott Regimbald was tossed into the deal. Earlier, Fleming had gotten into a shouting match with Dunigan during a team meeting.

A former All-Canadian, Jones had been recuperating from a shoulder injury. Since nobody gives up a bona fide starting quarterback if he can still play, suspicion had it that the Stamps got damaged goods. That turned out to be the case. They had one more win and finished fifth at 4–14. Buono had won six in his last year, Barker five.

Negotiations between Michael Feterik and local businessmen Ted Hellard, John Forzani and Doug Mitchell had been going on throughout the season. On January 12, 2005, they were concluded. Two days later, Dunigan and Rooke were fired with two years left on their contracts.

In an exit interview with *Sun* sportswriter Randy Sportak, Feterik said he wanted to be remembered "For winning the Grey Cup. I was officially owner when we won. You can't take that away from me. I've got the ring." Of course, he had absolutely nothing to do with the Grey Cup win of 2001.

In four short years the F-troop had sent Canadian football's flagship franchise to the bottom of the CFL sea. Could Hellard, Forzani and Mitchell raise the *Titanic*?

CHAPTER 9

When It's Springtime in the Rockies

Smilin' Hank and Hufnagel
2005–2009

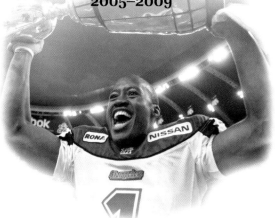

On January 12, 2005, it was announced that a group of Calgarians had bought the Stampeders for about $6 million. The driving force in the deal was Critical Mass Founder and Chairman Ted Hellard, along with former player and sports equipment czar John Forzani, former players and oil and gas entrepreneurs Bob Viccars and Dave Sapunjis, as well as Doug Mitchell, Matt Brister of Storm Exploration, Rob Peters of Black Diamond Land and Cattle Co. and five partners who wanted to remain anonymous.

Dunigan and Rooke were out, Stan Schwartz and Jim Barker back. Jamie Crysdale was ecstatic. "I'm looking forward to this," he told Mike Petrie of the *Herald*. "It's great they're guys from within the Calgary community. Some have played with the team, they live in the city, they have a vested interest and they'll be more passionate about seeing this succeed."

At the press conference announcing the deal, Hellard reminisced about going to Stampede Wrestling with his dad, something a family could afford and share. He added, "And that's what the CFL is about, what the Calgary Stampeders are about. About families being together at a football game—about moms and dads bonding with their kids. And you don't have to pay an arm and a leg to do it. It's much more than a sport to people in this country. It's part of our social fabric."

Ted Hellard was born in Nova Scotia in 1954, the son of air force mechanic Art Hellard. The family moved to Calgary when Ted was 10. He graduated from Central Memorial and the University of Calgary, where he starred on the basketball team and played for Canada's national team. After graduation he taught high school in Lacombe, Alberta. From there it was into business, where he parlayed creativity, hard work and luck into a financial empire.

"I've been extremely lucky," he told the *Herald*'s George Johnson. "I've been successful in business. So I don't have to worry about life. I know it sounds corny, but you have to give back, you have to make a difference. As you get older, you realize this. If I see one kid smiling at a Stampeder game, it will have been worth it.

"Eventually, the bell tolls for all of us. Do you want to go out saying, 'I did something good for the community'? And the Calgary Stampeders are good for this community."

Ted Hellard.
COURTESY CALGARY STAMPEDERS

John Forzani.
COURTESY CALGARY STAMPEDERS

John Forzani founded The Forzani group in 1974 and grew it into one of the largest sports enterprises in the world. No stranger to gambling in the fourth quarter or business, when his company took over Sports Experts, three times the size of his own, the economy went south, and after 22 years, the black ink turned to red. He lost $5 million in 1996 and $33 million the next year. Two years later, after streamlining his operation, the company made $8 million.

Forzani described his motivations for wanting to buy the Stampeders. "There were several motivations," the former Calgary native and player said. "First, I was disappointed with what was happening to the Calgary Stampeders' name. I thought with a more commonsense approach you could keep the tradition of the Stampeders alive and well. Secondly, having played, I thought it would be fun to be part of a group that acquired the team. Thirdly, I've spent my whole life in the sporting goods business, and I thought I had something to contribute.

"The two main guys in making it happen were Ted Hellard and myself. There were two or three groups making false starts to buy the team. We merged with another group of principally chaps from the oil patch."

He found things had changed since his playing days. "There was a whole different set of requirements then. Those guys like Frank Finn and Roy Jennings did a great job. All of those early Stampeder directors did. But in today's day and age, to have the best team in the league, you have to cover so many bases. You have to be good at so many different things. There are two distinct divisions: one is the football side. If you get a great quarterback and a great head coach, you're well on your way to success. And then you've got the operational side, and there are so many aspects of that. If the operational side succeeds, then you can provide the football side with the resources so they can succeed.

"When I played we had three coaches and that was about it. There wasn't a lot of infrastructure. Today the coaching and support staff amounts to close to 20 people. We have four or five guys on the video side. We have a computer program that can break down the game into 30 divisions. It's unbelievable."

The third member of the executive triumvirate was Doug Mitchell, a prominent lawyer, a former player, a CFL Commissioner from 1984–88 and member of the Order of

Doug Mitchell.
COURTESY CALGARY STAMPEDERS

Canada and the Alberta Sports Hall of Fame. Indefatigable and wise, Mitchell has been a treasured Calgary icon for many years.

Add in the others and you had a group with deep pockets dedicated to the team. After the reckless abandon of Ryckman, the financial juggling act of Gutsche and the three-ring circus of Feterik, the new owners came to their task having already established themselves to Calgarians as winners. Hellard became president; Forzani, chairman; Mitchell, governor. Stan Schwartz was appointed the Executive Vice-President and Consultant to the Executive Committee. Former player and COO of Critical Mass Darrell Moir was the Senior VP of Club Operations. Jim Barker was general manager.

This distinguished group was soon joined by former Stampeder player, assistant GM, Eskimo GM and coach Tom Higgins as head coach and director of football operations. As honest and decent a man as any who ever graced a Canadian gridiron, Higgins left

Tom Higgins. COURTESY CALGARY STAMPEDERS

the Eskimo front office in 2001 when Don Matthews was fired during training camp. His teams finished first three times and split two Grey Cups with the Alouettes. He was Coach of the Year in 2003 and fired when he lost the 2004 Western Semi-final.

Higgins faced the daunting task of cleaning up the mess left behind by the previous regime. Requiring immediate attention was restocking Canadian talent. He also needed a quarterback. The team told Khari Jones they wouldn't pursue anyone else if he agreed to agreed to a smaller contract than the $375,000 he was being paid. He could make that much by earning performance bonuses. Jones refused. Fortunately, former Stampeder Henry Burris was available. Signed by the Stamps out of Temple in 1997, he saw little action behind Jeff Garcia and Dave Dickenson. So he left for Saskatchewan in 2000 and then spent two years in the NFL before returning to Regina in 2003. Stuck behind Nealon Greene and Kevin Glenn, he threw 11 passes. His opportunity came the following year when Nealon Greene broke his leg in the first quarter of the first game of the season. Burris started game three, leading the team to 9–9 finish, a semi-final win over Edmonton and an overtime loss to the Lions in the Western Final. A free agent, he was ready to re-sign with the Riders. They offered the most money, but, according to Burris, refused to designate him Number 1.

Henry was delighted to don the white hat. "This was a no-brainer. To go back to where I started in 1997 as a snotty-nosed, diaper wearing quarterback from Temple and finish off some big things here in Calgary—you can't ask for anything better." He signed a three-year deal in the $900,000 range.

The Stamps were taking a chance. Burris hurt his shoulder in the NFL, and it took him a long time to recover. He was inconsistent in Saskatchewan and would not be an overnight success in Calgary. But he was a significant upgrade over Khari Jones, and Higgins was confident a mature Burris would be the cornerstone of the franchise. And, after the Feterik fiasco, Smilin' Hank was pure gold in the public relations department.

Helping Henry were free agents Alexander Gauthier on the O-Line and receiver Jermaine Copeland.

Higgins and Barker had a great CFL draft, picking Miguel Robede, Godfrey Ellis, John Comiskey and Brett Ralph. Impressive off-season signings included wide receiver Ken-Yon Rambo and defensive lineman Rahim Abdullah, as well as kickers Sandro DeAngelis and Burke Dales.

Once bitten in Edmonton, twice shy in Calgary, Higgins approached the 2005 campaign with caution. "I believe we're going to be a lot better. I believe we have a shot at making the playoffs, and when that occurs, anything is possible."

With 22 new faces in the line-up, Calgary opened the season at home on Canada Day against the defending champion Argonauts. The starting offense included receivers Ken Ron Rambo, MarTay Jenkins, Jermaine Copeland and Nik Lewis. Joffrey Reynolds, Scott Deibert and Burris were in the backfield behind a line of Alexander Gauthier, Jay McNeil, Jamie Crysdale, Taylor Robertson and Jeff Pilon. While Higgins tinkered with the fullback position, with the exception of Godfrey Ellis replacing the injured Crysdale at centre, the same line-up started the Western Semi-final.

Defensively, the front three were Demetrious Maxie, Rahim Abdullah and Sheldon Napastuk.

Henry Burris.
COURTESY CALGARY STAMPEDERS

The linebackers were Scott Coe, John Grace, Brian Clark and George White. The secondary was in flux all season due to injuries, the only constants being Wes Lysack and Ben Kelly.

DeAngelis and Dales were excellent kickers, and Randy Chevrier was an outstanding long snapper.

The Stamps lost the opener 22–16 after being down 22–3. They could have won except for an untimely Burris interception. Alternating wins and losses followed for the next eight games. Included in the wins was a 44–18 thrashing of Saskatchewan at McMahon, where over 10,000 Rider fans showed up to make Smilin' Hank's life miserable. After losing 25–23 to Edmonton on Labour Day, they closed out the campaign by

Jermaine Copeland.
COURTESY CALGARY STAMPEDERS

winning seven of eight for a record of 11–7 and second place, two points behind the Lions.

Big on the calendar was the October 23 game in Regina, the first time the Rider Nation would have an opportunity to directly vent their spleen at the man who done them wrong. "I expect to see all my family and friends there from Regina and be greeted with nothing but cheers," Burris laughed. "I'm looking forward to it. It's going to be a lot of fun. Hopefully we'll get a victory." Burris led them back from an 18 point deficit to win 29–21, knocking Saskatchewan out of the western playoff race in the process.

After beating Edmonton in Calgary 43–23, the Stamps looked forward to hosting the semi-final against those same Eskimos. On a beautiful afternoon, Calgary opened up a 9–0 lead by the end of 15 minutes. In the second quarter, Terrence Wilkins returned a kickoff 54 yards to the Eskimo 39. Reynolds ran to the one and then over. With 3:57 left in the half, Burris engineered a five-play touchdown drive, the key strike a 33-yard pass to Stallings. Edmonton had three field goals. Calgary led 23–9 at the half.

After the break, Jason Maas replaced Ricky Ray, and the Eskimos scored 21 unanswered points, winning 33–26, their first victory of the year over their southern rival. Calgary lost three fumbles, gave up three interceptions and turned the ball over on downs.

"We gave them the game," said Burris. "We moved the ball at will, then turnovers and penalties killed us."

"There is a lot to be learned from that game," said Higgins months later. "What happened was a lack of focus, of finishing the game. I believe people's minds were drifting. They were thinking about playing B.C. As a coach, you'd like to think you can control that, but you can't. I believe if we had been behind at halftime, we would have had a better chance of winning the game. One of my challenges in the second half was there were so many people that were happy. They were almost giddy. We told them to keep playing, don't let up. But they did. Sometimes you have to lose before you can win. I hope that will be a springboard toward this season."

In his first full year, Reynolds rushed for 1,453 yards and made All-Canadian, along

Chevrier and DeAngelis.
COURTESY CALGARY STAMPEDERS

with John Grace and Sandro DeAngelis. Grace won the Outstanding Defensive Player Award. Higgins was Coach of the Year. The new regime was off to a great start.

2005 saw the retirement of Calgary's great centre, Jamie Crysdale, after a distinguished 13-year career. Throughout his tenure as a Stampeder, Crysdale was a leader in the dressing room, a positive force. A Western All-star and President's Ring recipient, he played 210 consecutive games. Approaching 37, the constant pounding and nagging injuries had caught up to him. He would devote full time to his drilling services company, as well as to his daughters, Grace and Annabelle Faith. Jamie and his wife, Adrienne, learned when Grace was three she had leukaemia. She overcame the dreaded disease. A man of great character, Crysdale was impossible to replace.

Higgins approached 2006 with optimism. He discussed his goals, which he listed as: "To get into the playoffs and win the turn-over battle. We were minus six last year and turned the ball over seven times in the semi-final. The one thing we couldn't give our athletes was playoff experience. They have that now.

"Continuity is the biggest reason we have a chance to be successful. The coaches are the same, as are the offensive, defensive and special teams systems. The nucleus of the players is the same. They've got a chance to be special."

A big part of Higgin's plan hinged on Burris. To assist the young quarterback in his development, the club signed Danny McManus, who had three Grey Cups and a Most Outstanding Player award on his resume. Said Higgins, "Henry has so much going for him. But he has to be better at securing the football. He has to have a better ratio of touchdowns to interceptions. And the bottom line? A quarterback will always be judged on his ability to win, especially come playoff time. The addition of Danny McManus

Markus Howell. COURTESY CALGARY STAMPEDERS

might be what Henry needs to take him to an elite level in the CFL."

Other key off-season acquisitions were receiver Elijah Thurmon, also wide receiver Markus Howell and defensive back J.R. Ruffin, both excellent return men.

The Stampeders opened the season at home against Grey Cup champion Edmonton. A thunderstorm delayed the kickoff half an hour. Rain fell intermittently throughout a game that was sloppy and boring for 55 minutes. It wasn't until then that Calgary scored their first touchdown of the 2006 campaign, thus awakening Quick Six, the wonder horse from his slumber. The TD came on 10-play drive ending in a 33-yard pass to Nik Lewis with 1:31 remaining, putting the good guys into a 17–14 lead. Brian Clark picked Ricky Ray seconds later, and Burris found Jermaine Copeland in the end zone. Final score: Calgary 24, Edmonton 14.

Higgins told the team he was proud of them. "It's about winning. It doesn't matter how you win. . . . The bottom line is, we came back and got the 'W.'" But he cautioned that the win didn't mask the errors. "There were some bad decisions made by Burris. Sometimes he has to be reminded not to turn the ball over when you're in the scoring zone. At the end, Henry had the ability to stay alive and throw into the end zone and come home smiling."

Burris agreed. "This win will be important down the stretch. Anytime you beat Edmonton, it's big." The Stamps lost the return match a week later 18–14.

After edging Hamilton at home 23–22, it was off to Regina. Once again the boobirds bombarded Burris. Once again he rose to the occasion and won 53–36. After losses to Hamilton, B.C. and Saskatchewan, they beat the Riders at McMahon and defeated Montreal twice, the first when Sandro DeAngelis kicked field goals of 52 and 53

yards in the last 48 seconds on the day J.T. Hay was inducted onto the Wall of Fame.

Calgary then won the Labour Day Classic 44–23 to go 7–4. Burris was brilliant against the Eskimos. Ahead 20–13 with nine seconds left in the opening half, with the ball on the enemy 16, Higgins told Burris to throw it away if nobody was open. Instead Burris took off and with one second left, hurled himself into the end zone. Leading 23–13, the Eskimos were theirs.

Said Jay McNeil about the Burris run to pay dirt, "That was a huge motivator for us. What a way to lead by example. It's a smaller guy selling out with no concern for his body just trying to get the touchdown. Even an older guy like me gets excited when I see something like that."

Jay McNeil Blocks for Burris. COURTESY CALGARY STAMPEDERS

Having lost earlier in Hamilton when Burris had miscalculated the time left, Higgins was not nearly as impressed. "Okay, [he] did it. But what if [he] didn't? He made good, but learn the lesson that goes with it."

Though their winning streak stood at four, the Stampeders were terribly inconsistent. Believed to have the best receivers in the league, they trailed the West in passing with Burris having the worst percentage completion rate. John Grace was benched. The secondary was rebuilt for the fourth time in two years.

Calgary's games with B.C. were made more difficult by magpies Jermaine Copeland and Nik Lewis. Before losing 39–13 to the Lions, a team they hadn't beaten in two years and at B.C. Place in four, the Stamp receivers not only questioned Geroy Simon's ability but his manhood as well. The league sent a memo to the Stampeders to cease and desist such unsportsmanlike behaviour. After a great catch in front of the Calgary bench, Simon threw the ball at Lewis's feet. Higgins said he didn't like what his trash-talkers were doing and wished they'd stop. In the end, his inability to rein in Lewis and Copeland contributed to his downfall.

The ownership was so concerned about the listless performance in B.C. that Ted Hellard took the unusual step of addressing the team following practice. They bounced back the following week, beating Buono's boys 32–25 at home. With Joffrey Reynolds' rushing title on the line, they ended the season with an embarrassing 28–15 setback in Winnipeg, finishing second at 10–8, six behind the Lions.

Before the semi-final, controversy erupted when the Stampeder executive banned Gainer the Gopher from McMahon. Several fans showed dressed like the Roughrider mascot, including two-and-a-half-year-old Russell Kelly from Airdrie, who was there with his green-clad dad, Rob, and his red-and-white-clad sister, Kassidy, and mom, Stacy, typical of the divided loyalties the Stampeders have endured from the beginning. After the game, Saskatchewan coach Danny Barrett laughed and said the little guy was the Rider's good luck charm.

Not that they needed one. Their ferocious defence caused five Burris turnovers while shutting out the Stamps in the second half to win 30–21. Burris ended the season as he began: unable to realize his potential.

Reynolds, DeAngelis, Clark, Coby Rhinehart and Jay McNeil made All-Canadian. McNeil was completing his thirteenth season in the league. Growing aches and pains and the needs of his autistic son, Cuyler, were such he would retire after one more year as one of the truly all-time great Calgary Stampeders.

The 300-pound 6´ 4˝ native of London, Ontario, went to Kent State and was drafted in the fourth round by Calgary. A three-time All-Canadian, McNeil was the Western nominee for Outstanding Offensive lineman in 2001. He discussed the myths surrounding his position. "Offensive linemen are often portrayed as big, dumb football players. I think it is exactly the opposite. While we are big, along with quarterback, it is the position you have to be the smartest to play. There's a lot going on, a lot you need to know. You have to be able to think quickly and react well in situations."

One of McNeil's jobs is to open holes for running back Joffrey Reynolds. "He's an unbelievable runner," said the admiring lineman. "He just needs a little opening to run through. It's easy blocking for him because you don't have to put the defender on his back for him to make yards. He's the nicest guy, always positive. Guys want to do well for him."

Reynolds, a Tyler, Texas, native, graduated in 2003 in kinesiology from the University of Houston and then bounced around the NFL. Released by the Giants in 2004, he came north. "After I left New York, I was really down about playing football," he recalled. "I was thinking about getting a nine-to-five job when my agent told me about Calgary and convinced me to give it a shot. I'm glad I did."

In two full seasons he ran for 2,994 yards. He had 495 receiving yards and 360 returning kickoffs and 18 touchdowns. He was twice an All-Canadian and Calgary's nominee for Outstanding Player in 2006. In 2010 he would become the Stampeder's all-time leading rusher.

Losing two semi-finals didn't sit well with management, and the pressure was on Higgins, who was being undermined and second-guessed to the Executive Committee. An excellent coach who didn't have to prove anything to anybody, Higgins was unafraid to make the tough decisions. He knew what was going on, but there wasn't much he could do about it except win football games. A better Burris was required. "It goes without saying your fortunes go as your quarterback

goes," said Higgins during training camp 2007. "Everybody knows he has the ability to improvise and scramble. But the challenge when he does that is some of the decisions he made weren't good. Our coaches are working to improve his decision-making process. There have been times when Henry has looked like the best thing since sliced bread and other times he has reverted back to things we don't like."

Burris's backup would be former Cincinnati Bengal first-round draft choice Akili Smith.

Higgins looked ahead. "We need consistent play from our offense, which starts with

Joffrey Reynolds, Labour Day 2006.
COURTESY CALGARY STAMPEDERS

the quarterback. We need to continue to be special on special tams. If we are better defensively, we will be a better team than last year with a chance to get where we want to go."

Although they had excellent receivers, prodigal son Marc Boerigter returned after five years in the NFL and Ryan Thelwell came aboard as a free agent. Boerighter was a bust.

Just before the season started, Higgins traded surplus running back Wes Cates to Saskatchewan for veteran offensive lineman Rob Lazeo, a good deal for both clubs.

The Stamps opened the 2007 season at home by killing the Ti-Cats 37–9 and then suffered the worst back-to-back losses in the team's history. After being run out of Regina to the tune of 49–8, they lost four days later in Toronto 48–15.

The club had three days to prepare for the Argos. Considering they arrived in Hogtown at 4:00 AM, really they had only two days. Combine a bunch of rookies with little preparation time, unfamiliar high humidity and fatigue, and the Stampeders didn't stand a chance. Their 10 turnovers were indicative of a team mentally drained.

While the team was down east, secret discussions began between the owners and John Hufnagel, fired months earlier as the offensive coordinator of the New York Giants. Even though the team bounced back, going

Smilin' Hank in a losing cause against the Argos.
COURTESY CALGARY STAMPEDERS

5–2–1, including three wins over Edmonton, the talks continued.

In a July 28 home loss to the Lions 32–27, the Stamps had twice as many yards and should have won, but Burris had four turnovers. After the game Higgins said, "Henry has to get better." The reporter from Medicine Hat replied, "Tom, coaches have been saying that for six years. Will he ever get better?"

Visibly upset, Higgins replied, "Don't know yet. I'd like to say yes, but when we have these setbacks, I guess that's why I've lost hair and the rest is turning grey."

The old mantra in sports—"We win as a team and lose as a team"—didn't seem to apply. Burris was being blamed for Calgary's 2–3 start. Outwardly he was still Smilin' Hank. Inwardly he seethed and vowed to silence his critics by winning in Edmonton a week later. Taking matters into his own hands and feet, Burris rushed for crucial first downs to keep

The Men of the Horse.
COURTESY CALGARY STAMPEDERS

a last-minute drive alive that finished with a 33-yard field goal and a 34–32 victory.

Henry was happy. "Everybody's been yelling at me and trying to pillage my village. But the more people kick me, I kick back. I never lost my faith nor did the guys in here. We knew we were going to win. I knew I had to be a leader to help this team do that, and that's definitely what I took upon myself to make happen."

Jay McNeil echoed Burris's comment, saying, "We showed real character today."

The crucial win was followed by a loss in Montreal and a 45–45 tie with B.C. in Calgary, an exciting game that featured 985 yards combined offense. Trailing by seven with 2:46 left in regulation, Burris led his troops 75 yards to tie the game at 31. They each scored twice in overtime. While the players wanted to go for the two-point convert, Higgins played it safe and settled for the tie.

Was Higgins disappointed his defence had surrendered 45 points? "Yes, but it's a young defence. It's not a lack of effort. They will be good. We just have to be patient."

Heading into Labour Day, the Stamps led the West in total offense and passing. Although they gave up a staggering 31 points per game, they were second in the division against the pass. Their giveaway–takeaway at –10 was the worst in the league. They made big plays and gave up big plays, typical of a team in transition. Higgins was troubled by their penchant for penalties.

Labour Day saw a classic Battle of Alberta, the action going back and forth, the good guys winning 35–24. They continued their roll winning 20–17 in Edmonton and 44–22 over the Riders in Calgary, leaving them two points behind first-place B.C.

Then it all came apart. They lost six of the remaining seven games to finish third at 7–10–1. The worst loss was in Vancouver, 42–9, the most embarrassing in Hamilton,

24–20, only the second win of the season for the Toothless Tabbies. Defensive coordinator Denny Creehan was fired after the loss to B.C.

Burris sat out the losses to B.C. and Saskatchewan with a shoulder injury. He returned against Winnipeg. Higgins' decision? Maybe. "He had to convince me he was okay, that he was one hundred percent healthy," said Momma Burris. "I heard all week that my boy was thinking of playing on Sunday, and I said to my husband, 'I've got to talk to that child.'" When she was satisfied, she gave the green light, although during the game she was heard to yell at the Bombers, "Don't you go hittin' my Henry!" Calgary won 38–25.

Over the course of the season, the Stampeders threw the most interceptions, fumbled the most, allowed the second-most sacks and were the most penalized. On the other hand, they led the league in passing and rushing yardage. Off to Regina for the semi-final.

The Riders had finished nine points ahead of Calgary in the standings. They had won the season series. Their giveaway-takeaway total was +16, Calgary's –20. The Stampeders hadn't won a single game outside of Alberta. Saskatchewan was hosting a playoff game for the first time since 1988. The Riders had won six straight. There was no way they should lose.

But they almost did. Defence being the Stampeders' weak link all year, it was appropriate that on the first play of the game Kerry Joseph combined with D.J. Flick for a 62-yard touchdown. Burris fumbled on Calgary's second play, setting up a field goal. With 2:46 gone, Saskatchewan led by 10. The Riders added another field goal on their next possession.

Late in the second quarter, the Riders drove down to the Calgary 11, where Joseph was picked off by Dwaine Carpenter, who lateraled to Trey Young, who ran the last 39 yards for the score. Saskatchewan replied with two field goals, giving them a 19–7 lead at halftime.

Returning to the field, Burris narrowed the gap with a TD strike to Rambo. Near the end of the quarter, Brandon Browner set up a field goal by blocking a punt. After 45 minutes, the score stood Saskatchewan 22, Calgary 17.

In the final frame, after a single, Kerry Joseph ate up the clock with an 11-play drive resulting in a field goal. The Stamps scored once more, making the final 26–24.

Calgary was 11–7 in Higgins' first year, then 10–8, finally 7–10–1. No playoff wins. Enter John Hufnagel.

Wally Buono's offensive coordinator in the 1990s, Hufnagel was a head coach in the Arena League for two years from which he left to seek fame and fortune in the NFL, first as quarterback coach in Cleveland, Indianapolis, Jacksonville and New England, his prize pupils being Peyton Manning, Mark Brunell and Tom Brady. He was the offensive coordinator for the Giants from 2004–06, playing a leading role in the maturation of Eli Manning. When the Giants didn't meet the owner's expectations in 2006, Hufnagel took the fall. Insiders knew that he deserved a lot of the credit for New York's subsequent Super Bowl victory. Proving you can go home again, Hufnagel returned to Calgary.

"I was very interested in having another opportunity to be a head coach," said Hufnagel, "and when I had my year off, I gave a lot of thought to the direction I wanted to take. I knew the CFL would be looking for head coaches before the NFL would be. I spent a lot of time thinking about it, realized the direction I wanted to go if a possibility came up, and when it did, I jumped at the situation."

Aware of what had gone on in the Stampeders' executive suite and realizing the Stamps hadn't finished 7–10–1 because Tom Higgins was a poor coach, Hufnagel made sure he would control the football operation with no interference before accepting the job. His first priority was fixing a defence that ranked at or near the bottom in most categories. He hired former Alouette Chris Jones to solve the problem.

"When I took the job and watched some film," said Hufnagel, "I wanted to change the style of defence. Chris Jones' name came up, so I watched a lot of Montreal's film. I enjoyed how he played his defence. He'll make the players better, and he'll make his assistant coaches better." The 2008 Stampeder defence was first or second in most categories, including points.

Hufnagel cleaned out the line-backing corps, including Brian Clark, Scott Coe, Trey Young and sack-leader Cornelius Anthony. "He was a free guy. We're not playing that style of defence where you're going to have a lot of loops and stunts. Let the defensive linemen get the sacks. I expect my linebackers to stop the run. I want a physical middle linebacker. I'm not going to stand on the sidelines and just watch the other team run the ball. I mean, I don't know why anybody passed against them last year."

The 2007 team had the most penalties in the league and the worst giveaway–takeaway ratio at –20. "You can do a lot of good things on offense and then just throw the game away because you're not taking care of the football. We need to have more poise on both sides of the ball and play within the rules because you can't be killing yourself each week with penalties," cautioned Hufnagel.

"Some games we were able to overcome it, but that's not the sign of a good football team. If we are to become a good football team, we need to address those areas. I don't think the defence was as big a contributor to penalties as the offense. I did an in-depth study during the off-season about the offensive penalties to try and figure out why they were happening. I met with all the players in town and asked them for their thoughts. I have a pretty good idea what the problem was, and hopefully we'll have good luck in turning it around."

What about the turnovers? "We gave a lot away and created very few. We need to raise some havoc defensively to create turnovers. I want us to be faster, bigger and more physical," Hufnagel concluded.

Soon into the season, Hufnagel found the combination he wanted on the D-line: Mike Labinjo, Charleston Hughes, Eddie Freeman

and Howard Hodges. He had the physical middle linebacker in Saleem Rasheed, but he was injured the first half of the season, his place taken by JoJuan Armour, flanked by Shannon James and Dwaine Carpenter. The secondary he settled on was Brandon Browner and Branson Smith, J.R. Ruffin, Dwight Anderson and Milton Collins.

The 2008 team had the best ratio at +20. They reduced the number of penalties but were still second worst in the league. Despite the fact Calgary won only seven games, Burris led the league in passing efficiency and touchdown passes, maturing under the tutelage of coordinator George Cortez. Hufnagel was impressed with Burris's ability to bounce back.

"Last year Henry didn't play well during the second and third games. To be able to put that behind him and move on and play the brand of football he played for the rest of the year tells you a lot about him. He made mistakes—he put them behind him. That's an attribute you want in a quarterback."

Dave Dickenson was signed to back up Burris and help with his growth.

Although receivers Copeland and Lewis were over 1,000 yards and Rambo was at 983, the coach was unimpressed. "I think the 1,000-yard mark is very average in the CFL. If a guy's a role-player and he gets a 1,000 yards, okay, but I'm not going to say you're Allen Pitts."

Joffrey Reynolds was the best running back in the league, the kicking game superb.

Punter Burke Dales.
COURTESY CALGARY STAMPEDERS

After what happened to Higgins, Hufnagel said his biggest challenge was "Trust between me and the locker room. Them trusting my decisions, and them knowing they were my decisions and no one else's."

With 16 new faces in the line-up, the Stampeders opened at home against the Lions, winning 28–18. When injuries stuck the offensive line, rookie Dimitri Tsoupas started against B.C. Chosen second over-all in the draft by the Eskimos, the Edmonton native was traded to Calgary for centre John Comiskey and receiver Kevin Challenger. His baptism of fire went well, according to Henry Burris. "Dimitri did a heckuva job. He played against two of the best tackles in the league in Aaron Hunt and Tyrone Williams. He was really physical. If there were any mistakes I didn't see them, which is pretty good playing against that all-star defence."

Reynolds, who ran for 125 yards, agreed. "[Tsoupas] did well against arguably the best tackles in he league. He didn't have any real breakdowns. They couldn't take advantage of anything. They couldn't tee off on a pass or sit on a run."

Growing up, Tsoupas had dreamed of playing in Commonwealth Stadium, the site of Calgary's second game of the season. It was a thriller, his family and friends going home happy with 34–31 Eskimo victory. "That was a great experience because I remember sitting in the stadium there and thinking about playing pro football. Obviously that was a dream and a goal of mine. Being at Commonwealth Stadium and playing on that field was great."

Said Jeff Pilon, "He's doing real well. He's wearing a legendary number. Jamie Crysdale was Number 67. I hope he can live up to the iron man who played 210 straight games. If he can do half of what Jamie did, he's going to have a long career."

Next was a 23–19 Stampeder win at Montreal. Burris was brilliant, completing 28 of 37 with one touchdown and no interceptions,

Rookie Dimitri Tsoupas. COURTESY CALGARY STAMPEDERS

followed by another strong performance at home against Hamilton, winning 43–16. Ken-Yon Rambo caught six for 127 yards, and Nik Lewis 9 for 125 yards and two touchdowns.

Hufnagel was happy. "It was a great team effort out there. We were flying around in all three phases. A tremendous play by Brandon Browner on the punt coverage, where he dislodged the ball and recovered it. Nik Lewis has played extremely well for us the first four games, in all areas, not just catching the ball. He's done a great job blocking. Joffrey played well. He was a runaway train sometimes. The more we see that type of play, the better we'll be offensively. Henry is playing great football. George Cortez has done an excellent job with him."

The following week in Winnipeg, Hufnagel was tearing his hair out. Facing a winless team with a quarterback devoid of CFL experience, the Stamps stunk up the place. After falling behind 12–0 early in the second quarter, Calgary woke up and began to battle back, finally taking the lead 28–25 with 41 seconds left. But the defence couldn't hold, giving up a last-second touchdown to lose 32–28.

The Stamps returned home to face the defending champion Saskatchewan Roughriders and to induct Doug Flutie, Frank Andruski and Rocco Romano onto the Wall of Fame. While the Battle of Alberta is big, the team the Stampeders most hate to lose to is the Roughriders because of all the green and white in the McMahon Stadium stands. But old habits came back to haunt them, and they went down 22–21. JoJuan Armour was ejected for running over a referee in the first quarter. Dwight Anderson kept two Rider drives alive with roughing calls.

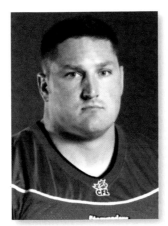

Veteran Jeff Pilon.
COURTESY CALGARY STAMPEDERS

Once again they started slowly, falling behind 21–7 by the half. And once again, the running game got the best of them with the Riders picking up 122 yards in the first half. Late in the fourth quarter, on third and one, Joffrey Reynolds was stuffed. The game ended with DeAngelis missing a 54-yard field goal. Saskatchewan stars were Marcus Crandell and Wes Cates.

Hufnagel was not amused. "We took way too many penalties," he argued. "It's coming to a point where we have to do a lot better with our discipline. We just can't play hard and expect to win. We beat ourselves. Until we correct that, it is going to be a long season.

"There were too many dropped balls and not many yards in the first half. The effort was there, but it takes more than that to win."

After winning the return match in Regina 30–25, the Stampeders went west and beat the Lions 36–29, bringing a record of 5–3 into Labour Day. Reynolds picked up 126 yards rushing against B.C. Burris had 70 in Regina. Whenever Burris ran for over 50 yards, the Stampeders won.

In the Battle of Alberta, Calgary finally moved into a four-point lead against the Eskimos at 4:18 of the third quarter, but that was the last scoring. Edmonton won 37–16. This time the problem wasn't turnovers and penalties—they couldn't move the ball. Burris was 8 of 14 for 81 yards. He was replaced by Dickenson, who wasn't much better.

After the game, Hufnagel was despondent. "I told them all they had accomplished through nine games was lost. We have to go right back to square one and start all over again."

The team responded, winning eight of their last nine games. Burris was in a league of his own down the stretch, moving up the team quarterback record book to second place behind Doug Flutie. "That's huge," said Burris. "It's a complement to the guys I'm working with here. We just want to continue. It's great to have your name up there with the best, but there is one thing they have that I don't have and that's a championship. I won't be satisfied until I get that ring."

Key to their season was responding to the Labour Day loss with a win in Edmonton four days later. The Stamps concluded their schedule by beating B.C. 41–30 with a lot of second stringers, a game the Lions wanted to win to finish second. The Stamps were first at 13–5.

"I'll be back in two weeks," vowed Buono. And so he was, winning the semi-final in Regina 33–12.

The pressure was on Joffrey Reynolds and Smilin' Hank. In the 2005 semi-final, Reynolds had fumbled twice. The following year he fumbled again while rushing for 55 yards. In 2007 he had only 11 yards against Saskatchewan. In the 2005 semi, Burris had four interceptions and a fumble, followed by four turnovers in 2006 and fumbles on the opening drive of the 2007 semi-final. Arguably Tom Higgins would not have lost his job if Burris and Reynolds had played better. At 33 years of age, it was time for the quarterback to produce in November.

On a gorgeous Saturday afternoon it looked like the same old, same old. B.C. jumped into a 12–2 lead, moving the ball at will, Stephan Logan rushing for 94 yards in the first half. But then the much-maligned defence stood tall, especially Mike Labinjo. They bent but didn't break.

B.C. opened with a nine-play, 55-yard drive that ended in the first of six Paul McCallum field goals. The second came late in the quarter. The Lions added two more before the half, while Calgary tallied a safety and a Rambo TD set up by Demetris Summer's 53-yard kickoff return. After 30 minutes, it was 12–9 in favour of B.C.

Early in the third, Labinjo stopped a drive by forcing a Jarious Jackson fumble that was recovered by Charleston Hughes. With the ball on the Calgary 9, Burris threw an interception to Korey Banks. Reynolds knocked him out of bounds on the 1-yard line. First down from the 1, Labinjo threw Ian Smart for a loss. Second down, he did it again, forcing the Lions to go for three. Calgary matched it to tie with 1:24 left in the quarter.

The Stamps went ahead to stay early in the final frame when Burris finished off a 66-yard drive with a one-yard plunge for the touchdown. The Lions added a field goal. After DeAngelis missed, Brandon Browner intercepted Buck Pierce at the Calgary 30. With 1:19 left, the Stamps ran five plays to run out the clock, but they failed, leaving one second left. Pierce tried a Hail Mary to the end zone, which was incomplete. Calgary 22, B.C. 18. It was the fourth straight time, the pupil, John Hufnagel, had defeated his teacher, Wally Buono.

Mike Labinjo.
COURTESY CALGARY STAMPEDERS

Burris was good on 17 of 27 for 236 yards, but had no TDs and one interception. Not a great performance but good enough. Reynolds ran for 43 yards. His major contribution was knocking Banks out of bounds at the 1. Labinjo was the star with three sacks, a forced fumble and two tackles at the goal line.

On to Montreal to face the Alouettes.

Ken-Yon Rambo.
COURTESY CALGARY STAMPEDERS

This would be Burris's first Grey Cup as a starter, having backed up Jeff Garcia and Dave Dickenson earlier. His opposite number was Anthony Calvillo, the quarterback of record when Montreal beat Edmonton in 2002 and lost to them in 2003 and 2005. He and his Als lost Grey Cups to B.C. in 2000 and 2006. To make matters more interesting, Calvillo had been named All-Canadian quarterback over Burris, and the two were contesting the Most Outstanding Player Award.

"We're going to have to score a lot of points to win," said Hufnagel, but they had the weapons to do it. Ken-Yon Rambo and Joffrey Reynolds led the league in receiving and rushing, while Sandro DeAngelis was the leading scorer.

The Grey Cup match would pit the Alouettes' veteran offense against a rookie-laden defence that was fast and tough and played a lot of man to man. Montreal had the great Calvillo, one of the finest passers of all-time. His receivers were Ben Cahoon, Kerry Watkins, Brian Bratton and Jamal Richardson. Avon Cobourne had 950 yards rushing. Their offensive line surrendered the fewest sacks. The Als were first in total offense and points. They took the fewest penalties, none at all in the Eastern Final. Their Achilles' heel, however, was defence, where they ranked sixth or worse in most categories. Calgary had won both regular season games, 23–19 in Montreal, 41–28 at home. On special teams, Calgary had the better kickers, Montreal the edge in returns.

Burris was under pressure to win the big one. So were Lark veterans Calvillo, Cahoon, Bryon Chiu and Scott Flory. Time was running out for them.

Both Hufnagel and Marc Trestman were rookie head coaches in the CFL. Both were exceptionally thorough in their preparation and both created a good feeling in the dressing room. It would be a Grey Cup between two classy organizations with men of exceptional character.

Stampeder determination was heightened by Burris losing the MOP Award to Calvillo, while and De Angelis was bested by return man Dominique Dorsey in the Special Teams category. Neither was a gracious loser.

When the hostilities ended, would they be singing "Dance With Me, Henry" or "Alouette, Gentille Alouette"?

After a rousing pep talk by Hufnagel— "We're playing on the road, we're playing in a dome in front of 65,000 fans, men. We've got them right where we want them!"—the Stampeders took to the field at the Big O before the second largest crowd in Grey Cup history—66,308—most of them loud and proud for the home team.

Nik Lewis leads the charge.
COURTESY CALGARY STAMPEDERS

Montreal opened the scoring on their first possession with a 14-yard David Duval field goal, the key play in the drive a 50-yard Calvillo completion to Richardson and two nine-yard strikes to Cahoon. Shortly after, Burris, starting at his 7, marched 66 yards in 10 plays, completing passes to Copeland, Reynolds and Rambo. With the ball on the enemy 30, Burris threw to Reynolds for 8, but Nik Lewis took a roughing penalty, putting the ball back on the 37. DeAngelis tied the game with a 44-yarder.

After two and out by Montreal, Burris was picked off by Reggie Hunt. Five plays later Cobourne scored, making it Montreal 10, Calgary 3.

The ball on the 35, Burris seemed rattled by the crowd noise and took a time-count violation. Dales punted, and Larry Taylor returned it 44 yards to the Calgary 43. Duval completed the drive with a 19-yard field goal.

Then Burris took control. On first down, he ran for 11 yards. "After Hunt's interception, I saw they were dropping back and not paying any attention to me," he said. It was then 12 to Lewis, incomplete, 18 to Lewis, Reynolds

Sandro DeAngelis.
COURTESY CALGARY STAMPEDERS

JoJuan Armour sacks Anthony Calvillo during second half action at the 2008 Grey Cup.
COURTESY CANADIAN PRESS, PETER MCCABE PHOTO

*Stampeders defensive back
Dwight Anderson intercepts
a Calvillo pass in 96th
Grey Cup action.*
COURTESY CANADIAN PRESS,
RYAN REMOIRZ PHOTO

*Alouette quarterback
Anthony Calvillo is sacked by
the Stampeders' Mike Labinjo
and Charleston Hughes.*
COURTESY CANADIAN PRESS,
NATHAN DENETTE PHOTO

for 3, 12 yards to Reynolds and 20 to Brett Ralph in the end zone. At halftime it was Montreal 13, Calgary 10.

Burris had a great first half, completing 11 straight. He was 15 of 20 for 166 yards, a pick and a touchdown. Calvillo was 16 for 20 and 199 yards.

On Calgary's second possession after the break, Burris began on his 13-yard line with a 30-yard strike to Lewis. Reynolds lost three, and then Burris threw to Lewis for 14. At centre field, Reynolds picked up two, and Henry ran for 14 and 29 yards to the Alouette 10. He then hit Rambo for five before Summers dropped a pass in the end zone.

Calgary's Shannon James intercepts an Anthony Calvillo pass in the end zone in Grey Cup action, 2008.
COURTESY CANADIAN PRESS, DAVID BOILY PHOTO

214

DeAngelis kicked for the tie. After Montreal replied with a single, Burris marched his team 61 yards for another three points. At the end of three quarters, Calgary led for the first time, 16–14.

On the first play of the fourth quarter, Dwight Anderson intercepted. The Stamps moved 35 yards into field goal range to take the lead by five.

The same Anderson took a dumb objectionable conduct call, allowing Calvillo to move into good field position. He got to the Calgary 36 on a 22-yard pass to Cahoon, was sacked by Labinjo for 8, but then struck for 22 to Richardson. With the ball on the 22, Calvillo threw into the end zone to Brian Bratton. Shannon James came up with a game saving interception. DeAngelis iced the cake with a 50-yard field goal. The final score, Calgary 22, Montreal 14. The Stampeders had won their sixth Grey Cup.

Nik Lewis celebrates.
COURTESY CALGARY STAMPEDERS

Left to right:
Markus Howell,
Saleem Rasheed and
Jermiane Copeland
whoop it up at the Big O.
COURTESY CALGARY STAMPEDERS

Burris was named Grey Cup MVP, DeAngelis top Canadian for his five field goals. Not a gracious winner, DeAngelis berated the media after the game for giving the Outstanding Special Teams Award to Dorsey.

Calgary won because of Hufnagel's coaching, a defence that held the Lark's high-flying offense to one point in the second half and a quarterback who proved he could win the big one. Knowing Calvillo's quick release, the Calgary defence decided to distract him by waving their hands in the air to block his vision and knock down or tip passes. "They did a great job getting their hands up and knocking the ball down," said the dejected Montreal quarterback. "They played more zone than we thought they would."

Indeed, the Stamps had trouble with Cahoon and Richardson, who each had five first half receptions. Richardson had 101 yards in 30 minutes. So Chris Jones switched from man to zone, a gutsy move to change your strategy in the middle of the most important game of your career.

After the game, Burris was ecstatic. "It's a huge win," he proclaimed, "and it shows the character of this team and how we bonded together and showed our true colours. It's time to celebrate what we did all year.

"Montreal's a tough team. We knew it wasn't going to be a cakewalk, and they played their hearts out in front of their fans. This team is resilient. We were truly on a mission and it showed.

"It's all about managing the game. That's one thing I've learned from watching Anthony Calvillo over the years. Dave Dickenson, also.

"And Sandro DeAngelis was on fire tonight. The way he was putting it through the uprights showed his true colours. I told him it was much better being named Canadian player of the game and taking the

Grey Cup home. He and I were both crying and saying, 'Yes, it was!'"

What was his thinking on the touchdown drive? "I was able to move around and make things happen and threw the touchdown pass to Brett Ralph. When they were dropping off and leaving that large seam, it was clear to me if I used my feet we could make plays.

"If you were told you could win the Cup and only score one touchdown? Wow. I wouldn't have believed it because of the firepower both teams have. I believed in our defence. As long as we could keep Calvillo off the field and win the battle of possession like we did in the second half, [we had] the

opportunity to just score one touchdown and give DeAngelis the chance to kick the ball through the uprights time and time again."

The heart of the defence was Mike Labingo. Down with the flu, he sacked Calvillo in the second half and knocked down three passes.

Said Hufnagel, "Henry made plays with his legs against Montreal during the regular season, and it was definitely part of the game plan. We struggled offensively in the first half. It wasn't as much not being able to complete passes, we just weren't getting enough yards for first downs. All along we wanted to get the running game going, and Henry was a big part of that."

Randy Chevrier hoists the Grey Cup as teammates Juwan Simpson (left) and Miguel Robede celebrate after their 22 14 victory over the Alouettes.
COURTESY CANADIAN PRESS, RYAN REMIORZ PHOTO

Calgary Stampeders quarterback and game MVP Henry Burris holds the Cup after the win over the hometown Alouettes at Montreal's Olympic Stadium.
COURTESY CANADIAN PRESS, RYAN REMIORZ PHOTO

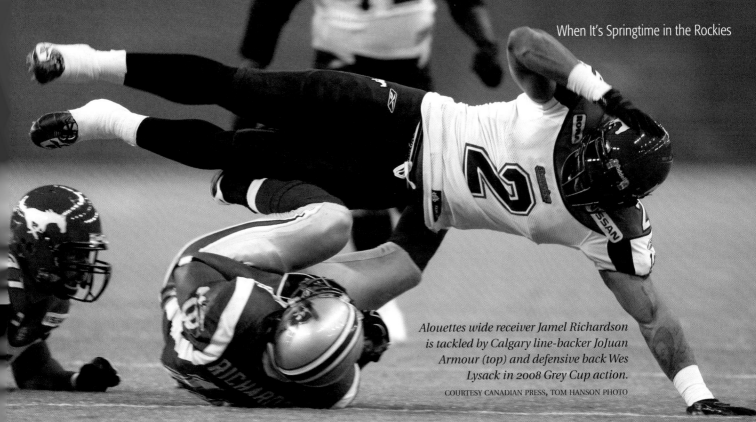

Alouettes wide receiver Jamel Richardson is tackled by Calgary line-backer JoJuan Armour (top) and defensive back Wes Lysack in 2008 Grey Cup action.
COURTESY CANADIAN PRESS, TOM HANSON PHOTO

"Every team has the objective of winning the Grey Cup," said John Forzani. "But for us to win with a brand new head coach who hadn't coached in Canada for a decade was certainly unexpected. But it was extremely gratifying—and a lot of fun."

Sixty years to the day after the Stampeders won their first Grey Cup, the city and team celebrated in front of the City Hall. It was a glorious end to a glorious season.

After winning the Grey Cup in his first year as a CFL head coach, Hufnagel was asked what he would do for an encore. He said, "Go to training camp and start over again."

In the off-season Hufnagel was chosen Coach of the Year. They went to training camp, made the playoffs, but lost to Saskatchewan in the final. Still, it was happy trails again at McMahon Stadium and the city by the Bow.

Go Stamps Go!

John Hufnagel, 2008 Coach of the Year.
COURTESY CALGARY STAMPEDERS

Karen Drake aboard Quick Six, the Stampeders' touchdown horse.

Calgary fans watch as the team is honoured by the City of Calgary following their 2008 Grey Cup victory.
COURTESY CANADIAN PRESS, JEFF MCINTOSH PHOTO